Cambridge Studies in Applied Econometrics

NUMBER 3

PUBLIC POLICY AND THE CORPORATION

WORKS OF THE CAMBRIDGE GROWTH PROJECT PUBLISHED FOR THE DEPARTMENT OF APPLIED ECONOMICS, UNIVERSITY OF CAMBRIDGE, BY CHAPMAN AND HALL

General Editor: RICHARD STONE

A PROGRAMME FOR GROWTH

1. A Computable Model of Economic Growth (July 1962). Richard Stone and Alan Brown.
2. A social Accounting Matrix for 1960 (October 1962). Richard Stone and others.
3. Input-Output Relationships, 1954–1966 (September 1963).* John Bates and Michael Bacharach.
4. Capital, Output and Employment, 1948–1960 (April 1964). Graham Pyatt assisted by Patricia Hutcheson.
5. The Model in its Environment (July 1964). Richard Stone.
6. Exploring 1970 (July 1965).* Alan Brown and others.
7. The Owners of Quoted Ordinary Shares (November 1966). Jack Revell and John Moyle.
8. The Demand for Fuel, 1948- 1975 (November 1968). Kenneth Wigley.
9. Exploring 1972 (May 1970). Terence Barker and Richard Lecomber.
10. The Determinants of Britain's Visible Imports, 1949–1966 (December 1970). Terence Barker.
11. The Financial Interdependence of the Economy. 1957–1966 (October 1971). Alan Roe.
12. Structural Change in the British Economy, 1948–1968 (May 1974). Alan Armstrong.

CAMBRIDGE STUDIES IN APPLIED ECONOMETRICS

1. Models and Projections of Demand in Post-War Britain. Angus Deaton.
2. Economic Structure and Policy. Terence Barker and others.
3. Public Policy and the Corporation. Mervyn King.

* *Out of print*

PUBLIC POLICY AND THE CORPORATION

MERVYN KING

Faculty of Economics and Politics,
University of Cambridge

CHAPMAN AND HALL

LONDON

A Halsted Press Book
John Wiley & Sons, New York

First published 1977
by Chapman and Hall Ltd
11 *New Fetter Lane, London EC4P 4EE*

Photosetting by Thomson Press (India) Ltd., New Delhi
and Printed in Great Britain by
J. W. Arrowsmith Ltd., Bristol 3

ISBN 0 412 15330 0

Distributed in the U.S.A.
by Halsted Press, a Division
of John Wiley & Sons, Inc., New York

Library of Congress Cataloging in Publication Data

King, Mervyn A
Public policy and the corporation.

(Cambridge studies in applied econometrics; no. 3)
Bibliography: p.
Includes index.
1. Corporations—Great Britain – Finance.
2. Industry and state—Great Britain. I. Title.
II. Series.
HG4136.K56 1977 338.7′4′0941 77–2–167
ISBN 0–470–99263–8

FOR MY PARENTS

CONTENTS

FIGURES

TABLES

PREFACE

This book arose out of my work on corporate behaviour as a member of the Growth Project in the Department of Applied Economics at Cambridge. It became clear that to construct an econometric model of the corporate sector which could be used to analyse the effects of government policy, required a reappraisal of the foundations of the theory of corporate behaviour. The contents of this book reflect my thinking on the theoretical and empirical analysis of the impact of public policy on the behaviour of the corporation. In any book there must be omissions, and at various points the reader will find that I have curtailed discussion of those issues which I feel are covered well by the existing literature. References in the text are recorded by the author's name and date of publication, and the full reference may be found in the list of works cited at the end of the book.

I should like to record my intellectual debt to many friends and colleagues who commented on various papers and manuscripts. In particular I should like to express my thanks to my colleagues on the Cambridge Growth Project for continual encouragement and stimulus, and also to Tony Atkinson, Peter Diamond, Martin Feldstein, John Flemming, Oliver Hart, Hayne Leland, Jan Mossin, Steve Nickell, Agnar Sandmo, Michael Sumner, and Adrian Wood. I must also express my gratitude to various members of the Government Economic and Statistical Services who met all my requests for help with the construction and interpretation of data with unfailing courtesy and speed. None of the above should be held responsible for any errors which this book may contain.

I owe Richard Stone a very special debt. Not only did he introduce me to research and offer me my first job, but to me, as to many others in the past, Richard Stone has been the source of both encouragement and intellectual inspiration.

Finally, I should like to thank John Hills and Bernard Jehin for research assistance, and all the members of the assistant staff of the Department of Applied Economics, especially Christine Hudson who typed the manuscript with a speed, precision, and patience which was truly remarkable.

January 1977 M.A. King

Chapter 1

INTRODUCTION

> Did you ever expect a corporation to have a conscience, when it has no soul to be damned, and no body to be kicked? (Edward, First Baron Thurlow 1731–1806).

Despite the modern and rather fanciful conception of the 'soulful' corporation, economists by and large continue to regard corporations, or firms, as operating on behalf of their owners and responding in a somewhat mechanistic fashion to changes in the economic environment. Perhaps economists might be allowed to invoke the decree of Pope Innocent IV who forbad the excommunication of corporations on the grounds that the latter, in contrast to the former, having neither minds nor souls, could not sin. Yet politicians often condemn corporations as being amongst the greatest of sinners, partly no doubt because, in modern capitalist societies, the corporation can lay claim to be the most important economic institution outside government.

The same politicians have been busy devising new policies to encourage firms to move in certain directions, while at the same time trying to restrain their worst excesses. Also the growth in the power and importance of large corporations has attracted a great deal of attention in the professional literature, with the focus of this discussion being mainly concentrated on the alleged separation of ownership and control and the increase in industrial concentration. Only relatively recently, however, have the more advanced and rigorous techniques of economists been brought to bear on the study of corporate behaviour. Within the last twenty years we have witnessed a burgeoning of work on, for example, the investment and financing decisions of firms, but there still remain a great many unresolved questions. This book is an attempt to explore some of the theoretical and empirical issues raised by an analysis of the impact of public policy on the behaviour of corporations, and in particular the responses of companies to changes in the tax system. I hope that this study will be of interest not just to academics and students, but to all those concerned, directly or indirectly, with improving the efficiency of public policy in the future.

Corporations now dominate economic activity in most advanced industrial countries, especially in manufacturing industry, and large corporations, in particular, are growing in importance. In 1970 the largest 100 firms produced 42% of the total manufacturing net output in the U.K., and 33% in the U.S. By 1968 the 12 largest companies accounted for more than a quarter of the assets of all U.K. quoted companies. Of the largest 100 U.K. quoted companies in 1948, no fewer than 27 had been taken-over or involved in mergers by 1968, and a further nine had been nationalized (Whittington (1972)).

The growth and development of the corporate form of enterprise and especially the rise of the large corporation, might suggest that a revolution has occurred in both the position of the corporation and the perception of its role by economists. In fact, concern over the potential power of corporations has been expressed in various ways over a long period of time, as the following opinions show:

> First, I put downe for a Maxime that all Monapolies have bin condemned by all politique men and in all well governed Comonweales ... For where there be fewe sellers and many buiers, there of necessitie must be highnes of price at the will of the seller, wherein the governours ought to have great care. For those kingdomes contynue longest and people best pleased where most men feele plentie and fewe fele want, wherein, whatsoever may be replied to the contrarie, who list to reade Stories of time past may observe respublicas, Comonwelthes, to have continued longer than kingdoms, and kinges longer than Tyrantes. But the mischief of Monapolies can neuer be avoided as longe as there be any Corporacions (pamphlet, 1587 reprinted in Tawney and Power (1924), **III**, p. 266).

> When the modern corporation acquires power over markets, power in the community, power over the state, power over belief, it is a political instrument, different in form and degree but not in kind from the state itself (Galbraith (1973)).

Nevertheless, although the viewpoints are similar, there can be no denying that the two authors of these quotations were observing very different objective circumstances. Giant corporations occupy a dominant position in the economy, especially in manufacturing industry, and the evolution of this strength has increased public scepticism of the virtues of unreined private enterprise and of the simple identification of the interests of the firm and the community as expressed in the words of Charles Wilson in 1952: 'What is good for the country is good for General Motors, and what's good for General Motors is good for the country.'

The classic statement of the position that the power and influence of large corporations has grown enormously is the book by Berle and Means published in 1932. They identified three factors which both they and subsequent writers have stressed as being of importance for an understanding of the modern capitalist system. Firstly, they pointed to increasing industrial concentration. This phenomenon has been documented in much greater detail since. Secondly, they stressed the separation of ownership from control with an accompanying centralization of economic power in the hands of a relatively small group of managers. Thirdly, one of the consequences of this divorce of ownership from control is that major changes have taken place in the pattern of corporate behaviour.

Clearly, institutional developments of this kind will play an important role both in determining the nature of the 'optimal' public policy towards corporations, and in fashioning the response of companies to changes in those policies; for the theoretical models used to analyse the effects of different policies must make some basic assumptions about the institutional framework within which companies operate. Although the idea that the separation of ownership from control has transformed the modern corporation has been widely canvassed, this line of thought has not, unfortunately, produced a satisfactory theoretical successor to the profit-maximizing entrepreneur of Marshall. The more recent managerial theories of the firm have been notably unsuccessful in stimulating new and useful empirical results, and at the theoretical level it is sometimes difficult to distinguish between the qualitative predictions of managerial theories on the one hand, and the more conventional neoclassical theories on the other. (For an elegant demonstration of this see the paper by Solow (1971)). Although the notion that the managers of a firm may have discretionary power to pursue their own objectives is valuable as a basic insight, it does not take us very far in the direction of analysis; nor is the concept of separation of ownership from control a new one. Writing in 1776, Adam Smith was extremely critical of both the efficiency and the responsibility of joint-stock companies, and in discussing the role for the shareholders, or 'proprietors', he foreshadowed a good deal of later comment:

> But the greater part of those proprietors seldom pretend to understand any thing of the business of the company; and when the spirit of faction happens not to prevail among them, give themselves no trouble about it, but receive contentedly such half yearly or yearly dividend, as the directors think proper to make to them (Smith (1776), **II** p. 232).

The traditional neoclassical theory of the firm has a great deal to say of value about the financing of the firm, and offers a rich analysis of the influence of taxation on company behaviour. In particular, as we shall see in Chapter 4, some of the commonly accepted assertions about the determinants of corporate financing, such as the claim that the observation that retained earnings are the predominant source of finance for corporations implies that the capital market is an inefficient allocator of investment funds, can be refuted by straightforward application of the neoclassical theory to the field of taxation.

It is when we come to look at the effects of uncertainty, however, that the weaknesses of the neoclassical theory become apparent. The assumption that the goal of the firm is to maximize its profits becomes less convincing when profits are uncertain, and we are forced to examine more closely the structure of ownership and control. The theory of the firm under uncertainty is a branch of economics which has seen some important recent theoretical contributions, and we shall see in Chapter 5 that it is possible, by building on the traditional foundations, to extend the theory to encompass a world of uncertainty in a way which opens up the possibility of introducing certain institutional features of modern capitalist society into the theoretical models. This development affords fruitful insights into corporate behaviour which in turn suggest ideas for empirical testing, and it also offers a way in which the apparently inconsistent approaches of the neoclassical and managerial theories may be reconciled and integrated into a model concerned explicitly with uncertainty.

The institutional framework and the 'rules of the game' according to which firms operate are themselves susceptible to controls imposed by public policy. The system of private property encourages competition of one sort, channelled into organized markets, while limiting competition in other directions, by prohibiting violence and theft, for example. Corporations are subject also to more specific legal controls on their behaviour covering such matters as monopoly and competition, providing published information on their activities, trading in the stock market, and at times there have been laws governing pricing policy.

The idea that public officials should intervene in the setting of prices goes back a long way. The Schoolmen of the Middle Ages insisted that: 'to leave the prices of goods at the discretion of the sellers is to give rein to the cupidity which goads almost all of them to seek excessive gain.'

Prices must be set to enable each man to 'have the necessaries of life suitable for his station'. (Henry of Langenstein, quoted by Tawney (1926; p. 41)). Such a view is reminiscent of the arguments for differential commodity taxation revived recently by some economists who, in the debate on 'optimal taxation', have analysed the properties of the structure of a system of taxation designed to minimize the efficiency loss for any given level of revenue, or to maximize some chosen social welfare function. Although our concern with problems of optimal taxation will be limited to the effects of corporate taxation, the discussion of public policy will focus on the effects of the tax system, and in particular the impact of fiscal policy in Britain.

The reasons for this choice of emphasis are not hard to discern. Fiscal policy is a major and flexible tool of government policy, and the U.K. experience in the use of taxation to influence corporate behaviour is unique. Four major reforms of the corporate tax system have taken place since the war, the most recent being in 1973, and tax rates have been altered at frequent intervals. Most conceivable kinds of investment incentives have been tried, and there have been important changes in personal taxation of income from property. In terms of willingness to change the tax system we have discovered one league table where the U.K. comes out top.

Because of this experience of different tax systems, Britain is an ideal place in which to study the effects of company taxation, providing the economist with a unique opportunity of observing sufficient variation in the variables in which he is interested, to offer hope that it might prove possible to identify the effects of changing from one tax system to another. Questions of this sort are important not just for economic theory but also for future policy because recent trends have increasingly highlighted the need for a complete reappraisal of company taxation.

It can be argued that the excessive frequency with which the tax system was changed imposed substantial economic costs because of the uncertainty created, which in turn diminished the response of companies to the very changes which were supposed to induce a favourable response. Clearly, there is some force in this argument, but it should not be forgotten that there is some potential advantage in changing tax rates in terms of what we can learn about the effects of taxes. Maintenance of the existing order and existing rates produces no information, whereas more information can be obtained by making changes. In this respect the U.S., with a relatively stable fiscal treatment of companies, is at a disadvantage in comparison with the U.K. A good illustration of this is afforded by the excitement generated amongst American economists in the 1960s by the investment tax credit and the attempts to assess its effects. A British economist would have shrugged this off as a mere trifle compared to the changes he had witnessed over the years. Thus, if we have suffered costs from past changes in our tax system, it would be foolish not to take advantage of the benefits which are held out by this opportunity to increase our stock of knowledge.

Public policy is of course not restricted to fiscal policy, and we shall examine some of the implications of the legal system within which companies operate. Legal restrictions on corporate behaviour affect the financial and investment decisions of the firm, the influence of taxation on those decisions, and also the way in which we choose to model the behaviour of the firm in a world of uncertainty. Other areas of policy, however, such as monopoly and competition control, will be ignored, and succeeding chapters will be concerned principally with the economic theory of the firm and the effects of taxation on corporate behaviour. Some readers will no doubt he surprised by the omission of certain subjects; no treatment will be found, for example, of multinational corporations. This is not because they are unimportant, but because the issues in this book do not always require a separate treatment of multinational corporations: nor is the problem as recent as has been claimed. Tawney's description of the changes which took place in the sixteenth century, 'the rise of commercial companies, no longer local but international and based, not merely on exclusive privileges, but on the power of massed capital to drive from the field all feebler competitors', should remind us that the multinational corporation is not a new phenomenon. (Tawney, (1926; p. 70)).

One major weakness in much popular discussion on taxation is the failure to consider the interaction between the different taxes involved. The effect of a tax may depend quite critically on the constellation of other taxes with which it is employed, and we shall see examples of this in terms of the interaction between personal and corporate taxation. The response of investment to a change in the corporate tax rate will depend upon a whole range of other taxes. One theme of this book will, therefore, be the need to take a look at the tax system as a whole, if useful statements are to be made about the choices facing those charged with deciding public policy.

The theoretical and conceptual issues mentioned above are fundamental to the analysis of the behaviour of the firm and are of far-reaching practical significance. Our reaction to them will have an important influence on our choice of economic institutions for the future, for choice we do have. A complete study of the potential and desirability of institutional change (for example, sharing the responsibility for decision-making within the corporation between employees and shareholders in proportion to the degree of risk incurred by each group) is beyond the scope of this book. Nevertheless, there is, perhaps, room for an assessment of the current state of knowledge of the effects of public policy on corporations as they exist today, in the hope that this will suggest possible avenues along which to direct future policy. In more specific terms, the kinds of questions we shall attempt to answer are:

(1) What is the effect of taxing corporations separately from individuals and unincorporated businesses?

(2) What are the determinants of the financial structure of the firm, and how far can changes in the pattern of financing be accounted for by changes in taxation?

(3) To what extent have tax allowances and subsidies been successful in stimulating the level of investment expenditure?

(4) Are there good reasons for believing that company taxes are reflected in the level of prices?

(5) Is there any empirical evidence in support of the proposition that the power in large corporations resides with the managers and not with the shareholders, and that this discretionary power is used to further the managers' own goals and objectives?

(6) Does the identity of the owners of ordinary shares affect corporate policy, and have recent changes in the composition of share ownership had a detectable effect on the policies chosen?

(7) What influence do the legal restrictions imposed on corporate behaviour have on the choice of policy, and what role should insti-

tutional factors such as the legal system play in economic analysis?

(8) What is the appropriate way to construct a theory of the firm when we wish to explicitly model a world of uncertainty?

(9) Can we obtain quantitative estimates of the likely responses of the company sector to changes in policy variables which might be used for economic forecasting?

These, and other questions, will be dealt with at length in subsequent chapters. As a background to this discussion, however, Chapter 2 provides a survey of the role of the corporation in advanced capitalist economies. It looks at the historical development of the corporate form of business organization and the impact of this on the theory of the firm. It then continues with an examination of the legal framework within which the corporation operates, and concludes with a look at the evidence of the pattern of share ownership and its implications for company behaviour.

The main theme of this book is the effect of taxation on companies, and Chapter 3 attempts to describe the different taxes and tax systems, both personal and corporate, which are relevant to our study and to embed them into a general conceptual framework. This provides a basis for the analysis of the effect of taxation on corporate financial policy given in Chapter 4. Two factors are of special importance in influencing financial policy, taxation and uncertainty. Chapter 4 concentrates on the former and looks at how far the available evidence bears out the theoretical expectation about the influence of taxation on the method of financing. It also contains an examination of the effect of uncertainty although a deeper discussion of this topic is postponed until Chapter 5 because the introduction of uncertainty into the model raises some fundamental issues about the motivation of the firm, and the relationship between the objectives of the firm and those of its shareholders.

Unlike a physical commodity which provides satisfaction or utility in its own right, equity shares are desired for their property rights. They confer upon their owners a right to a future and uncertain stream of monetary rewards with a limited liability, so that the potential loss is limited to the initial investment. In a world of perfect certainty knowledge of the appropriate values of all prices, rates of output, taxes and the state of technology would enable us to say exactly what value should be placed upon this financial asset. This value would be unambiguous and all transactions in the equity shares of a given company would take place at this price.

The assumption of perfect certainty is useful in that it provides a helpful starting point for the discussion of certain issues, such as, for example, the effect of different taxes on the method used by companies to finance their investment, a subject which is analysed in Chapter 4. However it disregards some interesting problems and we shall attempt to explore two of these; namely the heterogeneity of shareholders and the scope for managerial discretion. Conventional models assume shareholders to be a homogeneous group of investors endowed with perfect knowledge so that the management has little scope for pursuing its own goals because to do so would invite a take-over bid. Once uncertainty is allowed into the picture, the differences between shareholders in terms of their information and expectations, and the tax rates which they face, become important. The growth of institutional investors with their expertise, and special tax position, emphasizes the potential conflict of interest between different shareholders, and raises the question of who determines the firm's objective function.

One aspect of financial behaviour, namely corporate dividend policy, is singled out for special attention in Chapter 6. In this chapter we examine a model which attributes to dividends a special role as a signalling mechanism by which management may convey information to shareholders in an uncertain world, and we discuss the results of an econometric study of dividend behaviour in the U.K. over the period 1949–71. The U.K. experience is of particular value because of the numerous changes in taxation imposed by successive governments in various attempts to encourage either dividends or retentions. The econometric evidence provides quantitative estimates of the impact of these policies which are necessary to any assessment of the relative merits of different systems of company taxation. Some of the empirical results of Chapter 6 provide a link between the simple theoretical models of Chapter 4, and the more complex, but correspondingly less precise, formulations of company behaviour suggested by the study of uncertainty in Chapter 5. Indeed, much of the motivation in developing the discussion contained in Chapter 5 sprang from a desire to 'explain' the empirical results contained in Chapters 6 and 7. Chapter 7 contains an econometric analysis of other aspects of corporate financial behaviour, the choice of financial policy and the determinants of the debt–equity ratio.

In Chapter 8 we move on to discuss the effects of taxation and investment incentives on investment behaviour and pricing policy. Again the U.K. affords a unique opportunity to evaluate the effectiveness of different policy instruments because the low rate of economic growth and poor investment performance of the British economy since the war has prompted governments to use a bewildering variety of different fiscal incentives to investment. A related issue is the incidence of the corporate profits tax which depends critically on the magnitude of the incentives given in the form of tax allowances.

The subject matter of this book, then, is the theoretical and empirical study of the behaviour of corporations; its theme is the role of public policy in changing this behaviour, and in particular the impact of the tax system; and its methodology encompasses both mathematical and econometric analysis of the response of corporate behaviour to changes in policy. No reader need, however, be discouraged by the level of technical expertise demanded of him. I have tried to structure the argument in such a way that the degree of technical difficulty starts at a low level and increases as the book proceeds. However, it has not proved possible to make this progression monotonic, and some of the most important propositions are contained in later chapters although the discussion required is not mathematical.

In this there is, of course, a danger of falling between two stools. Some readers will feel that there is too much mathematics, others too little. Some might prefer to see more econometric analysis, others may doubt the value of such an approach. Nevertheless, I have tried to call on whatever method of analysis seemed appropriate for the task at hand, regardless of the degree of its mathematical and statistical content. In defence of the resulting mixture of both verbal and mathematical theorizing, and of both econometric and noneconometric empiricism, I can only plead that the subject matter itself dictates the necessity for these various approaches, and appeal to the authority of Keynes who, in a tribute to the qualities of Alfred Marshall, described the need for versatility in the study of economic problems in these words:

> The study of economics does not seem to require any specialised gifts of an unusually high order. Is it not, intellectually regarded, a very easy subject compared with the higher branches of philosophy and pure science? Yet good, or even competent, economists are the rarest of birds. An easy subject, at which very few excel! The paradox finds its explanation, perhaps, in that the master-economist must possess a rare *combination* of gifts. He must reach a high standard in several different directions and must combine talents not often found together. He must be mathematician, historian, statesman, philosopher—in some degree.

> He must understand symbols and speak in words. He must contemplate the particular in terms of the general and touch abstract and concrete in the same flight of thought. He must study the present in the light of the past for the purposes of the future (Keynes (1933; p. 173)).

Such lofty sentiments are to be seen more by way of inspiration than as practical advice to the economist; nevertheless they provide an appropriate starting point for this study.

Chapter 2

THE CORPORATION IN THE ECONOMY: AN OVERVIEW

> Science is built up of facts as a house is built of stones; but an accumulation of facts is no more a science than a heap of stones is a house (J.H. Poincaré, 1905).

In one sense this chapter could be said to represent an attempt to present some of the 'stylized facts' about companies and the company sector in advanced capitalist economies. In fact, its aim is rather different. The first reason for this is that the constructed stylized facts could be extremely misleading because of the temptation to generalize from what may be inadequate evidence. Econometric estimation is to be preferred in general to casual empiricism.

More importantly, however, I want to draw attention to a number of factors which are sometimes overlooked in studies of the response of companies to changes in public policy, and these can best be illustrated by the preliminary discussion of this chapter which will form a background to the subsequent formal analysis. Firstly, the close relationship between the development of the theory of the firm and the historical rise of the corporate economy, which we briefly examine in Section 2.1, demonstrates the potential contribution which an appreciation of institutional factors can make to our theoretical models. Secondly, the legal constraints and environment within which corporations operate are often ignored in economic theory, and yet they can be an important influence on corporate behaviour. Section 2.2 looks at those aspects of law which are relevant to our enquiry. Thirdly, the structure of ownership of companies has implications for the determination of control which thus becomes a function of the distribution of income and wealth in society, and in Section 2.3 we examine the empirical evidence on the pattern of share ownership.

2.1 *The evolution of the corporation*

As in other branches of economics, changes in current theoretical thinking about the economic behaviour of corporations were inspired by developments in the historical evolution of joint-stock companies. Although this book is concerned with the theoretical and econometric analysis of the company in an advanced capitalist society, some insight into the importance of institutional factors may be gleaned from a brief discussion of the historical development of the company as an economic force and the theoretical ideas which accompanied it.

We may certainly go back to the Italian city states of the fifteenth century, if not earlier, to find institutions which contained the seeds of the concept of a joint-stock corporation. The *Commenda* was a form of partnership in which the liability of the investor, who himself had no direct control over the operations of the enterprise, was limited to his initial investment. A more direct forerunner of the modern joint-stock company was the *Societas*, which was an association endowed with legal rights and duties independent of its members. In Britain the Crown had the right to grant charters of incorporation but these became common only with the expansion of foreign trade in the sixteenth and early seventeenth centuries. Companies such as the Russia Company, the East India Company, the Hudson's Bay Company and the South Sea Company were created in this period, and parallel developments took place in Holland and Germany. Although Tawney (1926; p. 176) has claimed that: 'The age of Elizabeth saw a steady growth of capitalism in textiles and mining, a great increase of foreign trade and an outburst of joint-stock enterprise in connexion with it', the companies created at this time bore little resemblance to what we now think of as corporations. Each member of these companies traded on his own account quite separately from the other members, and in most cases the charters were granted either for the purpose of creating a monopoly, or for reasons of foreign policy. For example, some of the charters granted to corporations in the American colonies included the right to exercise powers on behalf of the Crown, such as the coinage of money and the maintenance of law and order. It was not until the end of the seventeenth century that a form of company emerged which traded as a single person with a stock contributed jointly by its members. These companies could be formed only by a special Act of Parliament, or by charter, but the form of organization was ideally suited to the needs of growing business.

The beginning of the eighteenth century was marked by a boom in the flotations of new companies, often accompanied by grossly inflated claims by the promoters of these companies, culminating in the infamous South Sea Bubble in 1720. Many company promoters had purchased the charters of nearly defunct companies as a way of obtaining incorporation. Such companies were outlawed by the Bubble Act of 1720, but this first attempt at company legislation could hardly be described as successful, for it made it very difficult for firms to legally adopt a corporate form and yet imposed few rules on those joint-stock companies that continued. The speculative boom of 1720, which was based on inflated expectations, collapsed in August and September of that year. In a few months the stock of the South Sea Company fell in value from 1000 to 125. The bursting of the bubble did little to enhance the confidence of the public in the activities of company promoters, and the effect of this, together with rigorous enforcement of the Bubble Act, made it difficult for a firm to obtain the legal authority to raise capital on a large scale. The progress of the joint-stock company was impeded for more than a century, and Adam Smith writing in 1776 showed little confidence in the efficiency and desirability of joint-stock companies:

> The directors of such [joint-stock] companies, however, being the managers rather of other people's money than of their own, it cannot well be expected, that they should watch over it with the same anxious vigilance with which the partners in a private copartnery frequently watch over their own. . . . Negligence and profusion, therefore, must always prevail, more or less, in the management of the affairs of such a company (Smith (1776, **II,** p. 233)).

Adam Smith was even less confident of the entrepreneurial ability and innovative quality of companies:

> To buy in one market, in order to sell, with profit, in another, when there are many competitors in both; to watch over, not only the occasional variations in the demand, but the much greater and more frequent variations in the competition, or in the supply which that demand is likely to get from other people, and to suit with dexterity and judgment both the quantity and quality of each assortment of goods to all these circumstances, is a species of warfare of which the operations are continually changing, and which can scarce ever be conducted successfully, without such an unremitting exertion of vigilance and attention, as cannot long be expected from the directors of a joint stock company. . . . The only trades which it seems possible for a joint stock company to carry on

> successfully, without an exclusive privilege, are those, of which all the operations are capable of being reduced to what is called a routine, or to such a uniformity of method as admits of little or no variation (Smith (1776, **II,** pp. 245–6)).

Changes in technology, however, created a continuing and increasing demand for some form of joint-stock enterprise, and this pressure was translated into legislative action in the nineteenth century. From the late eighteenth century onwards the introduction of new machine technologies and the application of steam power to manufacturing transformed the nature of capitalist organization. Nevertheless, it was not until the middle of the nineteenth century that joint-stock limited liability companies could be formed legally and easily by the simple process of registration.

The inhibiting Bubble Act was repealed in 1825 when it appeared that the legality of several large unincorporated enterprises was in question, and even the Attorney-General of the day admitted of the Act, that 'it appears to be agreed on all hands that its meaning and effect are altogether unintelligible' (*Hansard* (1825), XIII, 1019). A Committee on Joint Stock Companies was set up in 1841 and reported in 1844 under the chairmanship of Gladstone. The result was the passage in the same year of the Registration Act which allowed, indeed compelled, joint-stock companies to come into existence through registration, rather than go through the extremely difficult and expensive process of applying for a charter. Limited liability, however, was not yet available to incorporated enterprises. The Italian form of *Commenda* in which some investors were granted limited liability in return for foregoing any control over the company, found no favour in England. However, in 1855 general limited liability was introduced by the Limited Liability Bill, and from then on the joint-stock company grew in popularity so that today this form of organization dominates manufacturing industry.

Similar developments were taking place in the U.S. Originally incorporation was a privilege granted by charter but general incorporation was first allowed by North Carolina in 1795, Massachusetts in 1799 and New York in 1811. There were still problems in inter-state transactions though, and it was 1866 when New Jersey took the lead in allowing its corporations to own property in other states.

In the U.K. the year 1862 saw the first of the Companies Acts, and, although other Acts have followed, subsequent legislation has tended to move away from the *laissez-faire* attitude of the mid-nineteenth century towards increasing the legal requirements demanded of corporations. The legal structure of the modern corporation is examined in Section 2.2, where some of its implications for economic theory which are taken up in later chapters, are discussed.

From the latter half of the nineteenth century joint-stock companies flourished, and public opinion shifted from a desire to free companies from artificial restraints on their actions, to apprehension about the effects of allowing corporations to pursue their goals uninhibited by considerations of public policy. Recognition of the possibilities open to managers of large corporations was not confined to the more recent exponents of managerial theories of the firm, as is well illustrated by the writings of Marshall. Alfred Marshall shared many of Adam Smith's doubts about the competence of joint-stock companies, and he thought that they worked only because of a growth of business morality:

> ... the great body of the shareholders of a joint-stock company are, save in a few exceptional instances, almost powerless; though a few of the larger shareholders often exert themselves to find out what is going on; and are thus able to exercise an effective and wise control over the general management of the business. It is a strong proof of the marvellous growth in recent times of a spirit of honesty and uprightness in commercial matters, that the leading officers of great public companies yield as little as they do to the vast temptations to fraud which lie in their way. If they showed an eagerness to avail themselves of opportunities for wrong-doing at all approaching that of which we read in the commercial history of earlier civilization, their wrong uses of the trusts imposed in them would have been on so great a scale as to prevent the development of this democratic form of business (Marshall, (1980; p. 253)).

In the last eighty years increasing concern has been expressed about three tendencies in capitalist organization; the growth in business concentration, the increase in separation of ownership and control, and the importance of mergers and the role of the capital market in general. These developments have occurred in several countries, though at differing rates and in a discontinuous fashion.

A sharp increase in the degree of industrial concentration occurred in both the U.K. and the U.S. in the last decade of the nineteenth century, induced largely by a merger boom which reached a peak in both countries in 1899. The wave of mergers seems to have been larger

Table 2.1 The share of the largest 100 firms in manufacturing net output, U.K. and U.S. 1909–70, (per cent).

Year	U.K.	U.S.
1909	15	21
1919	17	23
1930	26	25
1948	21	23
1958	32	30
1963	37	32
1970	42	33

Sources: Prais (1976), Bain (1970), Hannah (1976b; Chart 1).

in the U.S. resulting in higher levels of concentration there, which the U.K. caught up with in later years. There is little evidence about the degree of concentration in individual industries in the U.K. before the 1935 Census of Production but it does not seem unreasonable to conclude that in 1935 concentration in the U.K. was at roughly the same level as that in the U.S. (see, for example, Prais (1976)). This suggests a very rapid increase in industrial concentration in the U.K. in the inter-war years which is confirmed by the figures on the degree of overall concentration given in Table 2.1. This shows estimates of the share of manufacturing output produced by the largest 100 firms in selected years from 1909 to 1970. A substantial increase in the share of the top 100 firms took place between 1919 and 1930, and the 1920s witnessed also a wave of mergers of an unprecedented magnitude surpassed only by the merger boom of the 1960s. The importance of mergers in increasing industrial concentration, and the emphasis in the 1920s on 'rationalization', has led one economic historian to date the rise of the corporate economy from this period:

> Many of the features which distinguish the modern corporate economy from the Victorian economy of small family firms were, then, firmly established in Britain by the early nineteen thirties. Over large sectors of manufacturing industry the position of large integrated firms had been strengthened by vigorous internal growth and by the unprecedented merger waves of the dozen years following the First World War. These firms were also diversifying their product ranges through the acquisition of businesses in related fields and some of them had laid the basis for continued growth by investment in new technologies and well equipped research laboratories. The possibilities of expansion through vertical

> integration at home and abroad, and through overseas manufacturing subsidiaries, were also being more fully explored than they had been in earlier decades. Typically the large corporations were quoted companies and their shareholdings were widely dispersed beyond the entrepreneurial families to which most of them owed their Victorian origins (Hannah (1976a; Chapter 9)).

Between 1930 and 1950 the degree of concentration in U.K. industry probably declined or at least remained stationary. Table 2.1 shows that the share of the largest 100 manufacturing firms in total manufacturing net output fell from 26% in 1930 to 21% in 1948. A similar pattern in the trend of concentration was obtained in the U.S., as can be seen from Table 2.1, although here the changes were less dramatic than in the U.K. In the postwar period, however, industrial concentration has resumed its upward trend and by 1970 the largest 100 firms accounted for no less than 42% of manufacturing net output in the U.K., and 33% in the U.S.

These figures relate to the aggregate concentration of manufacturing industry, and not to the degree of concentration within each individual market. Nevertheless, there is little doubt that market concentration too has been increasing, although this tendency is much less evident in the U.S. than in the U.K. (see Adelman (1964), Bain (1972)), and levels of market concentration appear to be slightly higher in the U.K. than in either the U.S. or the other EEC countries, (Hughes (1976)). Aggregate concentration measures the extent to which production decisions in the economy are concentrated in the hands of a small number of firms, whereas market concentration is concerned with the degree of competition in the product market, although it must be stressed that concentration cannot be equated with monopoly, especially in a period when international trade, and hence competition from imports, was expanding rapidly. These developments led a number of economists to doubt the effectiveness of the market in disciplining corporate behaviour, and this attitude is summed up by Galbraith:

> In place of the market system, we must now assume that for approximately half of all economic output there is a planning system. . . . The planning system consists in the United States of, at the most, 2000 large corporations (Galbraith (1973)).

This viewpoint does, however, overlook the existence of one important market in which all firms, large and small, compete, the capital market.

And as we shall see throughout this book, the relationship between the individual firm and the capital market plays an extremely important role. The influence, or lack of it, of the capital market has been emphasized by some of the 'new theories' of the firm (e.g. the work of Marris (1964)), and, in particular, these theories have stressed the importance of take-overs and mergers.

Until recently little was known about the historical pattern of merger activity, but Table 2.2 contains some estimates which enable a very crude comparison of the rate of merger activity to be made for the U.K. and the U.S. There are numerous difficulties involved in using these numbers to draw inferences about the historical experience, and any conclusions based on them must be tentative. Nevertheless the numbers do demonstrate clearly the merger booms of the 1920s and the 1960s. Two series of data on mergers in the U.K. are shown in Table 2.2. The first column simply gives the number of firms dis-

Table 2.2 Merger and take-over activity, U.K. and U.S. 1880–1969

Year	U.K.		U.S.	
	Number of firms disappearing	Value of firms deflacted	Number of firms disappearing	
1880–9	207	136	n.a.	
1890–9	769	401	1649[1]	
1900–9	659	483	1903	
1910–9	750	1031	1076	
1920–9	1884	1770	2194	6818
1930–9	1414	833		2264
1940–9	778	n.a.		2411
1950–9	1867	1507		4789
1960–9	5635	4906		12579

Source: Columns 1 and 2, derived from Hannah (1976a; Appendix 1).
Column 3, Nelson (1968) and Eis (1969)
Column 4, Thorp (1931), and *Statistical Report on Mergers and Acquisitions* (annual), Federal Trade Commission, Washington DC.

Notes: [1]For 1895–9 only
n.a. not available
(a) In the second column the figures for 1910–39 are averages of the upper and lower bounds given by Hannah.
(b) The second column is deflated by the share price index 1961 = 1.0
(c) The third column was calculated by linking the figures given by Eis for 1920–9 to the earlier series from Nelson using overlapping data.

appearing by take-over or merger. Ideally this should be deflated by a variable such as the total number of firms in the economy to obtain a normalized series. However, the absence of data on the number of firms in the economy (and indeed the rather nebulous nature of the concept which this represents) precludes such calculations. The second series, shown in the next column, gives the value of the assets of those firms taken-over or merged, deflated by the share price index to give a normalized series. It should be stressed that these figures are at best no more than rough estimates, but that they constitute the only source of information at our disposal.

Both series show clearly the merger waves of the 1920s and 1960s, although the spate of mergers in the late 1890s is less apparent. The peak year for take-over activity in the whole period was 1968. Unfortunately, there is no single time series for merger activity in the U.S. available for a continuous period throughout the century, but some figures on the number of firms taken-over are given in columns (3) and (4) of Table 2.2. The two series have rather different coverage, the first excluding small mergers, and so no attempt was made to link the two series. These show that in the U.S. the merger waves occurred in the periods 1898–1902, 1926–31, and in the 1960s; very much at the same time as the merger waves in the U.K. It is interesting that in both countries the peak year was 1968.

There is a close relationship between the pattern of take-over and merger activity, and the growth in industrial concentration. In a fascinating study of the problems involved in measuring concentration, Hannah and Kay (1977) have shown that both in the interwar period and in the 1960s, take-over and merger activity was the major force leading to the observed increase in concentration in the U.K. Indeed, it seems quite possible that merger activity accounted for the whole of the increase in concentration. Similar conclusions about the role of mergers in promoting industrial concentration have been drawn from the U.S. experience (Nelson (1968)).

The coincidence of the timing of the two sets of merger waves in the U.K. and the U.S. is a matter for further research, but it is possible to see on both sides of the Atlantic concomitant developments in theoretical thinking; the evolution of the theory of the firm in market situations of monopolistic or imperfect competition in the 1930s (Chamberlin (1933), Robinson (1933)), and the exploration of new assumptions about the behaviour and motivation of firms in the 1960s (Baumol (1959), Marris (1964), Williamson (1964)).

Despite the dominant role which the corporate form of enterprise occupies in productive activity in all the major industrial countries, the overall picture conceals enormous differences between industries. Agriculture, for example, is dominated by non-corporate forms of organization, and the aggregate figures include income from professional services which are almost exclusively performed by individuals or partnerships. So, to appreciate the role of the corporate sector, it is necessary to disaggregate the profits statistics and examine the importance of companies in individual industries. For this purpose the primary sources of information are the tax returns filed by individuals and companies. The results of analysing these data for the U.K. are contained in Table 2.3 which shows the proportion of gross trading profits of various industries earned by companies, in selected years between 1909 and 1968. The profits of corporations are expressed as a percentage of all profits earned by private enterprises. Thus the activities of nationalized industries have been excluded. In the U.K. nationalized industries embrace mining, the public utilities (gas, electricity, water), most transport, and iron and steel production.

It is clear from Table 2.3 that whereas companies play only a small role in agriculture, in manufacturing they dominate the scene to the extent that in 1968, 96% of manufacturing profits were earned by corporations. This figure has been steadily increasing throughout the century and, in view of the attractions of limited liability in a sector where large organizations are necessary in order to exploit economies of scale, this picture is hardly surprising. Even in distribution, however, where companies are much less important than unincorporated business, the role of the company has been steadily increasing. In 1909 only one quarter of profits in distribution were earned by companies, by 1968 the corporate share had risen to two-thirds. If we define an 'all industries' group, which excludes agriculture and banking, insurance, and finance (to avoid the well-known problem of how one measures the profits of the financial sector), then three-quarters of the profits of these economic activities were earned by corporations in 1968. Thus, the increase in the dominance of corporations is not due simply to a changing industrial structure; it is a factor common to different industries and different countries.

We may conclude from this brief survey that the main empirical observations, or 'stylized facts', which emerge are the dominant role of joint-stock companies in manufacturing production, the growth of industrial concentration, the importance of the capital market, and

Table 2.3 Share of gross trading profits in various sectors earned by corporate business, U.K. 1909–68, (per cent).

Industry	Year					
	1909	1927	1937	1948	1958	1968
Agriculture[1]	n.a.	n.a.	n.a.	18	6	6
Manufacturing	76	84	92	90	95	96
Construction	n.a.	n.a.	n.a.	36	47	42
Distribution	25	26	39	53	54	67
All Industries[2]	59	55	67	71	74	76

Source: 1909–1937, Worswick and Tipping (1967): Table III.12.
1948, 92nd *Report of HM Commissioners of Inland Revenue*: Tables 40–76.
1958 and 1968, *Inland Revenue Statistics 1972*: Tables 29, 49 and 54; *National Income and Expenditure 1961*: Table 30; *National Income and Expenditure 1973*: Table 31.

Notes: (a) The importance of unincorporated businesses is overstated because their profits include the remuneration of proprietors.
(b) For 1948 figures for company profits are available only for profits net of profits tax. So the published figures for company profits have been multiplied by the ratio of published profits plus profits tax charged in 1948 to published profits. The figures for profits tax were taken from Table 124 of 92*nd Report of HM Commissioners of Inland Revenue.*
(c) In 1958 and 1968 the published profits figures exclude capital allowances. These were added back in using data from *National Income and Expenditure*, making an estimate for agriculture. In addition the published figures for 1968 exclude interest payments out of profits. These were added back in from Table 54 of *Inland Revenue Statistics* 1972.

[1] Agriculture includes forestry and fishing.
[2] 'All industries' group excludes agriculture and banking, insurance and finance.

the magnitude of take-over activity. The legal constraints on companies and the changing pattern of share ownership will be discussed in the next two sections. However it is already clear that major changes in the position of the corporation in the economy have taken place, and it is not surprising, therefore, to find that new theories of corporate behaviour have been proposed to challenge the traditional view of mechanistic profit-maximizing firms. In general, these alternative theories fall into two groups. On the one hand there are the 'managerial' theories which propose a new objective function in which profits are replaced by other variables such as growth or sales. On the other hand, there are 'behavioural' theories which see the firm not as a unitary economic agent, but as an organization of competing interest groups whose collective behaviour cannot be represented by the outcome of the maximization of a well-defined objective function; rather, the norm is taken to be 'satisficing' behaviour, the existence of which is justified by induction from empirical evidence.

It would be quite wrong, however, to suppose that the nineteenth century economists were unaware of these arguments as is evident from the following remarks of Marshall:

> ... joint-stock companies are hampered by internal frictions, and conflicts of interest between shareholders and debenture holders, between ordinary and preferred shareholders, and between all these and the directors; and by the need for an elaborate system of checks and counter-checks. They seldom have the enterprise, the energy, the unity of purpose and the quickness of action of a private business. ... When powerful joint-stock companies are working in harmony, and are not directly or indirectly involved in speculative ventures on the stock exchange, or in campaigns for the crushing or for the compulsory fusion of rivals, they generally look forward to a distant future, and pursue a far-seeing if a sluggish policy. They are seldom willing to sacrifice their reputation for the sake of a temporary gain; they are not inclined to drive such extremely hard bargains with their employees as will make their service unpopular (Marshall (1890; p. 502)).

In such a mood Marshall is reminiscent more of the behavioural school of thought than of the neoclassical school he is often alleged to represent. Yet to pose these viewpoints in such a stark contrast is to misunderstand the nature of the firm in neoclassical economics. In mathematical general equilibrium theory, as, for example, in the work of Debreu (1959), firms have no independent existence or role. They are no more than theoretical constructions for carrying out production plans, and profit maximization is taken as an axiom. The neoclassical theory of the firm is not a description of an economic institution, nor is it intended to be so, but it is a powerful analytical device for exploring the implications of various assumptions about the workings of a competitive market economy. We shall be able to make great use of this device in later chapters, but we cannot rest content with it as an adequate theoretical model of the modern corporation, and we shall return to these matters in Chapter 5.

2.2 *The company as a legal institution*

One of the contentions of this book is that to understand the economic behaviour of the firm we must view it as an institution operating in a particular social and legal environment. Whatever economic theory may assume about the motives and behaviour of the firm, the company itself has to operate within the framework laid down by law. Thus, some knowledge of the 'rules of the game' by which companies must play is indispensable for an appreciation of the likely effect of changes in public policy. Moreover, one important aspect of public policy is the set of rules, regulations, and institutions which comprise the legal system. In this section, therefore, we shall briefly describe the legal structure of the corporation, emphasizing those aspects which are necessary for an understanding of the firm as an economic institution.

What, then, is a company, and what is the role of the legal system in regulating its behaviour? Put very simply a company is an association of a number of individuals for the pursuit of economic gain. This immediately differentiates a company from the classical concept of an owner-managed firm, and suggests that a corporation is not best visualized as an individual with a given utility function representing innate preferences; rather as a coalition of individuals, the membership of which will be an important determinant of the behaviour of the firm. One role of the law is to act as a system of checks and balances between different groups within the company. The need for this system of checks and balances stems from the conflict of interests created by the existence of uncertainty about the effects of different policies, and by unequal access to information. The economic consequences of these conflicts are discussed in later chapters. In part, they will depend upon the particular legal framework within which they are resolved, and also upon the organizational form of the company.

In most countries on the continent of Europe, firms, whether they be sole traders or incorporated enterprises, are subject to a different set of laws from that governing the conduct of private individuals. English and American law, however, has rejected the idea of a separate commercial law as such, and instead makes a legal distinction between three different categories of firms. These are:

(1) the individual trader,
(2) the partnership,
(3) the limited liability, or 'incorporated', company which may be private or public.

In the Anglo-Saxon world there is no special law relating to the operation of individual traders. Individuals in the pursuit of their business interests are subject to the same tax and other laws as relate to the conduct of any private citizen. When a number of individuals combine, however, to form a joint business it is no longer sensible to regard them as individual traders. For tax purposes it is natural to consider the profits and losses of the firm as belonging to a single account. However, once the concept of the unity of the firm is accepted, the rights, duties, and liabilities of the partners can be determined only by specifying some rule which attributes a portion of the total responsibility to each partner. This rule is the law of partnership. It is a statement of how the benefits and costs of the enterprise are to be divided between the partners, and of the relationship between the enterprise and third parties. The contractual nature of partnership, and the need for some externally imposed rules governing the behaviour of this coalition, is reminiscent of the kind of interaction between economic agents studied by mathematical economists in their analysis of market economies. The study of the interaction between agents has been prominent in economic writing from the work of Cournot and Edgeworth down to the modern studies of game theory and equilibrium in exchange economies. The relationship between the legal and institutional framework surrounding companies, and their economic behaviour, is a subject to which we shall return in later chapters.

The basis of a partnership is a 'partnership deed' which is drawn up to regulate the rights and liabilities of each partner. This specifies the relationship between the various partners. Death or bankruptcy of any one partner terminates the partnership. Creditors usually sue the partnership as a whole, although it is perfectly open to them to sue any individual partner for the full amount of a debt owed to them by the firm, leaving it to the partner concerned to recover any contribution which may be due from the other partners. A partnership has no genuine legal personality of its own, although tax is charged on the profits of the firm viewed as a unit.

In England there is a limit on the size of partnerships. No partnership of more than 20 members is permitted, although recent changes in the law allow larger associations of professional partnerships such as accountants, lawyers, and stockbrokers. (Companies Act 1967, Section 120.) This restriction on size together with unlimited liability means that a different institution is required to satisfy the requirements of modern industry.

This institution is the limited liability company. Its name derives from the fact that in the event of failure the liability of any member, or shareholder, is limited to the amount of his contribution. The limited liability company has a legal personality of its own, distinct from that of its members. It can sue and be sued in its own name, and also own property. It can continue for ever independent of the fate of its members. 'During the war all the members of one private company, while in general meeting, were killed by a bomb. Still, the company survived; not even a hydrogen bomb could have destroyed it' (Gower (1957; p. 71, footnote 58.)). In fact, the idea of a company as a legal person goes beyond the simple notion of separating the liability of the company from that of the shareholders. Companies have been prosecuted for criminal offences (even manslaughter) and corporate personality is an important legal reality. The assumption of lawyers is that 'this conception of a company as a person separate and distinct from the other persons who are its shareholders and directors is the fundamental principle of Company Law', (Cain (1972; p. 7)). Or 'the veil of incorporation ... is as opaque and impassable as an Iron Curtain' (Gower (1957; p. 66)).

Limited liability provides the incentive for individuals to combine their resources to form a joint enterprise on a scale which would be too large for the firm to be based on the essentially personal nature of a partnership. The problems facing the individual member, or shareholder, of a large corporation are twofold. On the one hand, he may have insufficient information to judge the profitability of current operations and the likelihood of bankruptcy, and on the other hand he can change the policy of the company only by persuading a sufficient number of his fellow shareholders to dismiss the directors. With limited liability, individuals are more willing to invest their money in an enterprise which, because of its size, they have little hope of controlling. Since the risk of investing in such companies is, then, strictly limited, this both encourages individual investors to put their money into risky ventures, and also makes it easier for the company to raise capital to finance its expansion. Thus, one view of the development of the corporation would emphasize the separation of ownership from control; another would stress the bringing together of two distinct groups, managers and investors. As an eminent company lawyer puts it:

The modern public company meets the need for a new type of property

> in which the relationships between the owner and the property plays little part, so that the owner can recover his wealth when he needs it without removing it from the enterprise which requires it indefinitely. The modern public company is therefore one further piece of machinery . . . whereby the property of individuals is managed by other individuals (Gower 1957; p. 10)).

In return for these privileges companies are obliged to follow certain rules laid down by company law. These are designed to protect both creditors and shareholders. The company is seen as a coalition, or club, of individual shareholders governed by a constitution. The two aims of company law are, firstly, to protect individual members of the coalition by ensuring that the firm adheres to its constitution, and secondly, to regulate the behaviour of the firm in its conduct with individuals outside the coalition. This is to prevent the interests of creditors and customers being unfairly sacrificed to the interests of members of the coalition, (that is, the shareholders) who themselves are protected by limited liability. An example of this is the law which prevents the capital of the company from being distributed to shareholders. This stops shareholders withdrawing their contribution to the company thus depriving the creditors in the event of a possible bankruptcy.

The constitution of a company is known as its Memorandum and Articles of Association. These lay down the rules under which the company is to be run and describe the voting rights of the shareholders, the way in which profits are to be distributed, and the relationship between the directors and shareholders. Although the company is free to choose its own constitution, with the role of the legal system being simply to prevent the company from violating its own constitution, certain matters are compulsory for all firms. For example, among the general requirements are the holding of an annual general meeting, the preparation of properly audited accounts, and the disclosure of certain information about the company, the amount of which varies from country to country. Decisions of shareholders are usually reached by majority rule, although the law does contain provisions for the protection of small groups of shareholders to prevent 'oppression of minorities'. The effects of some of these laws will be analysed later when we come to look more closely at the structure of the company in economic terms in Chapter 5. Meanwhile we may note some of the broad outlines which the legal system imposes on company structure.

The law on the organization of the company varies between countries. American law provides for a company president and French law for a *chef d'entreprise*, each being ascribed certain statutory functions. German law divides responsibility between various groups within the company, and gives the work force a special place in the constitution of the company as of right. English law places very few requirements on the internal management structure of the company. As the company has no physical, only a legal, existence, the management of its affairs must be placed in the hands of 'human instruments' who are called directors. Their exact relation to the company is hard to define. They are partly trustees of the company's property, and partly agents of its business which they must manage 'for the benefit of the company as a whole'. The policy of the company is the responsibility of the directors, and the shareholders do not have the power to change this policy but may only remove the directors from office. The directors may appoint and dismiss employees but not each other. That right is reserved to the shareholders. However, the managing director is held to be an employee, and thus responsible to his colleagues. This was decided in a case in which a managing director was dismissed by his fellow directors for misconduct, which consisted of 'assaulting a co-director by the firing of a revolver at a directors' meeting'. (Anderson v. James Sutherland (Peterhead) Ltd., 1941, S.C. 203.) The essential point is that the directors are not the servants of the shareholders; rather the directors and shareholders are both organs of the company between whom the company's powers are divided. The law lays down the division of powers. Neither the management, as opposed to the directors, nor the employees are given any role in the company by the present state of the law.

On the financial side the total capital of the company consists of share capital and loan capital. Share capital comprises ordinary, or equity, shares which are given full voting rights and a share in the profits of the company, and preference shares, which usually give the holders a fixed dividend which has priority over dividends on ordinary shares, but in return they often have only limited voting rights. Loan capital is raised by the issue of debentures. The holders of debentures receive a fixed rate of interest on their loans and receive no voting rights. The essential difference between share and loan capital is that whereas loan capital may be repaid at any time, share capital may not be returned to the shareholder without following the formal procedure laid down by law for the reduction of the company's capital. Thus in the event of bankruptcy the holders of debentures are on equal terms with the company's creditors.

These legal provisions apply to all limited liability companies, but there are, in fact, two types of limited liability company, namely private and public companies. Private companies are those where the directors can control the transfer of shares between individuals, thus allowing a family firm, for example, to retain control within the family. They are not exposed to the risk of take-over. However, in England the number of shareholders in such firms is limited to a maximum of fifty, and this severely restricts the ability of these firms to raise finance. They are prohibited from offering shares or debentures to the public. In consequence most private firms are very small and the main focus of this study will be on the behaviour of public companies. A public company is defined as any company which is not private. As we shall see in the next section these companies are the dominant force in the economy and their behaviour is crucial to an analysis of the effects of public policy.

The distinction between public and private companies is a legal one. More meaningful to the economist is the difference between quoted and unquoted companies. The essential characteristic of a quoted company is that there is a public market where its shares may be freely traded. This market, the stock market, has an important role in the economic theory of the corporation as we shall see later. Unquoted companies, though, are not directly influenced by the stock market and so are less exposed to the risk of take-over. A quoted company must, therefore, be a public company but not all public companies are quoted on a stock exchange. At the end of 1973 there were about 600 000 registered companies in the U.K. but a substantial proportion of these, perhaps up to one half, must have been dormant because the number of assessments to corporation tax is rather stable at around 300 000. Of these only 15 000 were public companies of which 3200 were quoted companies.

Since the distinction between quoted and unquoted companies is an institutional, not a legal, distinction, there is no separate body of law relating to the two groups. There are, however, important sets of controls on the behaviour of quoted companies imposed by the authorities responsible for controlling the stock market, whether they be committees of the Stock Exchange in England or the Securities and Exchange Commission (SEC) in the U.S. The SEC was set up in 1934 in the aftermath of the Wall Street crash and is a regulatory agency with substantial powers backed by law. In contrast the Stock Exchange has no legal sanctions at its disposal, but the fact that it may deprive a company of its quotation is a powerful weapon in itself. This act of suspending a company's quotation has been used in situations when, for example, the market was unable to place a 'realistic' value on a company's shares, as happened with Rolls Royce in 1971 when the company declared that it was unable to meet its obligations, or when there was a dispute about the accuracy of published accounts, as in the case of Pergamon Press in 1969.

For quoted companies the influence of these regulatory agencies is at least as important as the Companies Acts. The Stock Exchange demands greater disclosure of information from companies seeking a quotation than the law requires from public companies; and both it and the SEC outlaw various practices such as manipulation of the share price for speculative purposes, and 'insider trading', where an individual makes use of confidential information to enable himself, or others, to profit from trading in a company's shares.

In later chapters we shall explore in more detail how the law affects company financial policy, and the way in which it regulates the influence of the shareholders on company policy. The kinds of questions we shall try to answer are:

(1) What effect does the legal framework within which a company operates have on its economic behaviour?

(2) Can an empirical study of the behaviour of firms throw any light on the interaction between the various groups which form the coalition which is the basis of the modern corporation?

(3) Is the relationship between shareholders and managers simply a matter of the 'separation of ownership from control', or can we be more specific about the role of managers and the influence of shareholders?

2.3 *Share ownership*

In this section we introduce the main issues and summarize the empirical evidence on the pattern of ownership of ordinary shares.

Ownership of equity shares is one of the few ways in which investors may purchase the right to share in the future profits of industry, and as such is a way in which the scale of ownership may be separated from the scale of management. As we have seen in Section 2.2 the shareholders have at least the nominal power to exercise control over the company, and although there has been growing scepticism about the ability of shareholders to exercise *direct* control over the company's affairs either through the annual general meeting or by the power to elect the board of directors, they still have an *indirect* influence through their activities in the stock market, where decisions to buy or sell shares reveal the preferences of shareholders. Thus the composition of share ownership can be an important factor in determining company policy, as we shall see in Chapter 5.

Yet, despite the potential role of the structure of share ownership, we know remarkably little about the owners of ordinary shares, and so it is perhaps not surprising that when the British government set up a Royal Commission on the Distribution of Income and Wealth in 1974 one of the first items to be included in the terms of reference was 'to prepare a report showing the pattern of distribution of ownership of equity capital, and of income arising from it'. (HMSO (1975, *Cmnd.* 6172, p. v.)).

We may distinguish three characteristics of share ownership, each of which deserves separate analysis. First, there are different categories of shareholders, such as individuals, trusts, insurance companies, pension funds, unit trusts, charities, the public sector, and overseas holders of shares. The relevance of this distinction is that the different types of shareholders might be expected to display different kinds of behavioural motivation. For example, the models which economists are accustomed to use when analysing the behaviour of individual investors might be quite unsuited to an analysis of the response of the institutional investors such as pension funds. An individual will be concerned with maximizing his expected utility of current and future consumption, whereas an institution might be more concerned with maintaining a steady growth of income over a very long time horizon. Their attitudes towards risk may be very different. At times the interests of these two groups of shareholders will coincide, but there may be other times when their interests clash.

The second characteristic to be examined is the wealth of shareholders. This is a question not only of the average wealth of shareholders taken as a group, but also of the disparity in wealth between different groups of shareholders. Shareholders in different income or wealth ranges may differ from each other in at least two relevant respects. Firstly, they face different tax rates which may lead them to want conflicting financial and dividend policies to be adopted by the firm. Secondly, the desired structure of an investor's portfolio will be a function of his wealth because only in special cases will his aversion to risk be independent of his wealth, and in general the proportion of a portfolio invested in highly risky assets will be related to the wealth of the shareholder.

The third phenomenon to be distinguished is the extent of dispersion of share ownership. In their work on the changing nature of American capitalism Berle and Means (1932) placed great emphasis on the role of increasing dispersion of share ownership in permitting the development of the separation of ownership and control. Presumably the implicit hypothesis here is that the greater the dispersion of shares among the owners of a company, the easier it is for the management to ignore the shareholders' wishes and pursue instead motives and goals of their own. This need not necessarily be the case, however, and we shall argue in Chapter 5 that a more fundamental cause for the existence of discretionary managerial power is the differences of opinion between shareholders, which suggests that in addition to looking at the relationship between management and shareholders we should also examine differences between shareholders. Some shareholders may exert more influence than others, (the institutions, for example), but clearly the scope for differences of opinion is larger, the wider the dispersion of share ownership.

If matters such as these are of any importance then a change in the composition of share ownership with respect to any of the above three characteristics will have an effect on company behaviour. What changes, therefore, appear to have taken place?

Evidence on the pattern of share ownership is difficult to obtain because companies' share registers contain little information useful to economists and very often shares are listed not under the name of the real owners but are registered as nominee holdings. In Britain the most authoritative surveys of share ownership are the two Cambridge surveys by Stone, Revell and Moyle (1966) and by Moyle (1971), which give estimates of the relative importance of different categories of shareholders, and these have been up-dated by the work of the Royal Commission on the Distribution of Income and Wealth (HMSO (1975)). In addition, there are the results of a detailed sample survey of the personal shareholders of a large industrial corporation by Vernon, Middleton and Harper (1973), which attempted to discover information about the motives, investment behaviour, personal characteristics and wealth of the shareholders of this particular company.

In the United States information on share ownership can be obtained from the various publications of the New York Stock Exchange, and from a major study on holdings of corporate stock with special reference to institutional investors carried out by the National Bureau of Economic Research for the Securities and Exchange Commission. (Goldsmith (1973.)).

The Cambridge surveys on share ownership in Britain were based on a stratified sample survey of all companies quoted on the London Stock Exchange; about 300 companies in all were included in the surveys out of the 2765 companies which had a quotation in 1969. A further sample was then taken of the shareholders listed in the registers of shareholders of those companies. One of the most useful features of the surveys was that they attempted to allocate nominee holdings to their beneficial owners. This is certainly necessary if we are to obtain a true picture of the pattern of share ownership because nearly 20% of shares are accounted for by nominee holdings. Very often these exist for reasons of convenience rather than concealment: many of them are held by bank nominee companies as collateral for bank lending to customers, and the same explanation can be advanced for holdings by other financial institutions, such as the holdings of members of the Stock Exchange. In addition, banks place shares in nominee holdings to facilitate the management of their clients' portfolios with which they have been entrusted.

The main findings of these surveys are shown in Table 2.4. The first three columns show the proportions of shares belonging to each category of beneficial owner on the three dates, 1 July 1957; 31 December 1963; and 31 December 1969. The Royal Commission carried out what they described as a 'mini-survey' of the owners of 30 companies chosen from the largest 100 U.K. quoted companies on 20 March 1975, and the results are shown in the fourth column of Table 2.4. For this survey the Clearing Banks agreed to analyse the beneficial ownership of all shares registered in the names of their nominee companies, which account for about 70% of all nominee holdings. The small size of the sample makes it difficult to compare the fourth column with the earlier columns, although the main trends are evident.

It is clear from the table that the major shift in the composition of share ownership has been the decline in the proportion held directly by the personal sector and the growth in the holdings of institutions. Two-thirds of corporate equity were owned by persons in 1957, but by 1969 the personal sector share had fallen below one half, and

Table 2.4 Share ownership in postwar Britain (per cent).

Category of owner	Date			
	1957	1963	1969	1975[3]
Persons[1]	65.8	54.0	47.4	43.7
Insurance companies	8.8	10.0	12.2	14.9
Pension Funds	3.4	6.4	9.0	15.2
Unit and investment Trusts	5.7	8.7	10.5	7.8
Charities and non-profit Bodies	1.9	2.1	2.1	4.2
Overseas	4.4	7.0	6.6	7.3
Others[2]	10.0	11.8	12.2	6.9
Total	100.0	100.0	100.0	100.0

Source: Moyle (1971; Table 4.2).
HMSO (1975; Table 6).

Notes: [1]Includes executors and trustees.
[2]Banks and other financial institutions, corporations, and the public sector (which is largely accounted for by the 49 per cent public holding in British Petroleum).
[3]The figures for nominee holdings were allocated as follows, 50% to overseas, 20% to persons, 15% to unit and investment trusts, 15% to 'others', (based on Table 5 of HMSO (1975)).

this trend has continued since then. The holdings of non-profit organizations, overseas residents, and others, have remained roughly constant, and the fall in personal holdings has been matched by a corresponding increase in institutional holdings. 'Institutions' comprise insurance companies, pension funds, unit trusts and investment trusts. Table 2.4 shows that the relative importance of all these types of institutional investor has increased, in some cases quite dramatically. The proportion of equity owned by pension funds, for example, more than quadrupled in the eighteen years between 1957 and 1975. Although the table does not give the holdings of unit trusts and investment trusts separately, Moyle's figures on which it is based show that the share of the market accounted for by unit trusts increased six-fold between 1957 and 1969 from 0.5–2.9%. Whether this change might be expected to alter company behaviour, and whether there is any evidence of this, are two of the questions to which later chapters are addressed.

Similar developments have been taking place in the stock markets of the United States. Using some of the figures from Goldsmith's study of institutional shareholders in the U.S., it is possible to construct estimates of the proportion of equity owned by different categories of shareholder on a basis which is reasonably comparable with the U.K. figures derived from the Cambridge surveys. These estimates are shown in Table 2.5. One striking feature of these figures is the much higher proportion of equity directly owned by the personal sector in the United States than in Britain. Over 80% of shares are owned by persons in the United States whereas in Britain the proportion is less than one half. The institutions in Britain are correspondingly much more important than in the United States with unit trusts, pension funds, and especially insurance companies, all owning considerably larger shares of the equity market. The figures for the share of the personal sector given in Table 2.5 are higher than estimates based on data provided by the New York Stock Exchange, which accounts for about two thirds of the total market valuation of U.S. companies. This is probably because these data do not deal with the problem of nominee holdings which we saw was an important feature of share ownership in the U.K. and which accounts for almost 20% of the market in the U.S. also. Data are published in the New York Stock Exchange *Fact Books*; (see also Stone, Revell and Moyle (1966;

Table 2.5 Share ownership in the U.S. (per cent).

Category of owner	Date (end of year)			
	1952	1957	1963	1968
Persons[1]	85.7	82.0	81.6	81.0
Insurance companies	3.8	3.8	3.4	3.1
Pension funds	1.0	2.9	4.8	6.0
Investment companies[2]	4.1	5.2	5.4	5.7
Non-profit bodies	3.4	3.8	2.7	2.4
Overseas	2.0	2.3	2.1	1.8
Total	100.0	100.0	100.0	100.0

Source: Own calculations, based on Goldsmith (1973), pp. 326–8.

Notes: [1]Households and personal trusts.
[2]Includes mutual savings banks (and also brokers and dealers but whose holdings are in fact negligible).

p. 8.), Lorie and Hamilton (1973; p. 5.)). These sources put personal holdings at around 70% of the market and the discrepancy between this figure and our estimate could be explained by the non-allocation of nominee holdings. It may also be that the institutions are more likely to invest on the New York Stock Exchange than on the other exchanges.

Nevertheless, as in the U.K., there has been a tendency for the share of the personal sector to fall over time, although in the U.S. this appears to have been much less marked than in the U.K. The increase in the holdings of the institutions has been largely due to the dramatic rise in the proportion of the market held by pension funds from a mere 1.0% in 1952 to 6.0% in 1968. Investment companies also increased their share of the market, although the importance of insurance companies actually declined over the period 1952–68.

The growth in the holdings of institutions in the market has resulted not only from an increase in the total funds which were made available to them, but also from a switch in their portfolio policy in favour of investment in corporate equity. Institutional investors are an increasingly important factor to be considered in any evaluation of stock market behaviour. Table 2.6 summarizes the data on the relative size of personal and institutional shareholders in Britain and the United States. In both countries the institutional sector has been growing in importance, but this process has been much more rapid,

Table 2.6 Personal and institutional shareholdings in the U.K. and the U.S. (per cent).

Shareholder	U.K.				U.S.		
	1957	1963	1969	1975	1957	1963	1968
Persons	65.8	54.0	47.4	43.7	82.0	81.6	81.0
Institutions	17.9	25.1	31.7	37.9	11.9	13.6	14.8
Others	16.3	20.9	20.9	18.4	6.1	4.8	4.2
Total	100.0	100.0	100.0	100.0	100.0	100.0	100.0

Source: Tables 2.4 and 2.5

Notes: 'Institutions' are defined as insurance companies, pension funds and, in the U.K., unit and investment trusts and, in the U.S., investment companies and mutual savings banks.

and has gone much further, in Britain where more than one third of corporate equity was owned by the institutions in 1975. This trend constitutes a major shift in the pattern of share ownership. In the U.S. around 15% of corporate equity was held by institutions in 1968 but this figure too is likely to have risen, and in both countries the largest source of this growth is the steady expansion of pension funds.

It would be quite wrong, however, to dismiss personal shareholders from consideration altogether. It has been estimated that in 1965, 2.5 million people in Britain, or 7% of the adult population, owned shares directly in one corporation or another (Vernon, Middleton, and Harper (1973, p. 21)). In the same year the proportion of the adult population in the U.S. owning shares directly was 17%, but in most other European countries the figure was only of the order of 2–3%, reflecting the much greater role played by the banks in financing corporate investment in those countries. Although the number of people owning shares directly is not large, a majority of the population owns shares indirectly through the medium of life assurance companies and pension funds.

Since the number of direct personal shareholders is small, it would be interesting to know what their distinguishing personal characteristics are, other than the well-known fact that on average shareholders are considerably wealthier than the population at large, as we shall discuss later. Some evidence on this is provided by a survey of the personal shareholders of a large British industrial company in 1968 (whose shares were in the 'blue-chip' class, but whose identity was not revealed) carried out by Vernon, Middleton, and Harper (1973). The VMH survey consisted of sending a postal questionnaire to a random sample of 5000 personal shareholders and supplementing this with 55 interviews designed to check the results of the questionnaire and to elicit further information. It appears that quite a large number of shareholders refused to co-operate at the interviewing stage and, although the response rate to the questionnaire was a respectable 35%, both the evident unwillingness to disclose information about personal financial matters and the size of the sample should make us cautious in drawing conclusions from the statistical findings. Even so, the following picture of the characteristics of shareholders emerges from the VMH survey:

(1) they tend to be older than the rest of the population.

(2) they are more likely to be male, although not predominantly so and there is an important minority of shareholders (VMH suggest

1 in 10) which consists of women on their own with no income other than that coming from their ownership of shares.

(3) they are of a higher socio-economic status than the average person. In fact 1 in 40 of the shareholders in the VMH survey were peers, although to balance this one of the respondents was a bus conductor with more than £10 000 invested in shares.

(4) About one third of the sample became shareholders by inheritance, this proportion being almost twice as high for women as for men.

Whether this picture gives an accurate representation of the body of shareholders or not, there is no denying that personal shareholders have higher incomes and greater wealth than the rest of the population. The VMH survey found that shareholders received an average income of more than twice the national average, and even this figure was felt to be an underestimate. Estimates of the marginal tax rates paid on dividend income which will be discussed in Chapter 3, suggest that the average income of shareholders weighted by the fractions of corporate equity which they own is rather large and places the 'average' shareholder in a high tax bracket. This fact, together with the change in the relative sizes of personal and institutional shareholdings has implications for the optimal pattern of company financing and its path over time.

Moreover, almost all shares owned *directly* by persons belong to the wealthy. In a study of wealth distribution in Britain, Lydall and Tipping (1961) found that in 1954 no less than 81% of corporate stock owned directly by the personal sector was held by the top 1% of the wealth distribution, and the richest 5% owned 96%. The situation appears to be similar in the United States. Lampman (1959) found that in 1953 the 'top wealth-holders' (defined as those with estates in excess of $60 000 who comprised 1.6% of the adult population and about 1% of the total population) owned 82% of corporate equity. Since then, however, the proportion of shares owned by the wealthy seems to have declined quite sharply. Table 2.7 shows some alternative estimates of the share of corporate equity owned by the richest 1% in the United States.

Although the table shows a substantial reduction over the last twenty years in the proportion of stock accounted for by the very wealthy, the distribution of corporate shares is more unequal than the distribution of wealth as a whole. Whereas the top 1% owned 50.8% of the corporate stock owned by the personal sector in 1969,

Table 2.7 Proportion of privately held corporate stock owned by the wealthiest 1% in the U.S. (per cent).

Year	Percentage
1953	86.3
1962	79.7
1969	50.8

Source: Rows 1 and 3, Smith and Franklin (1974; Table 1).
Row 2, calculated from Bossons (1973; Table V-6).

they accounted for only 24.9% of personal net worth. This reflects the fact that the portfolios of the rich contain a much higher proportion of corporate stock than do the portfolios of the less wealthy. Bossons (1973) found that in 1962 23.7% of total personal assets were held in the form of corporate stock. Some calculations I have made based on his data indicate that for the top 1% of wealth-holders corporate stock accounted for 52.8% of their total assets.

Recent data for Britain are hard to come by, but calculations based on Inland Revenue data suggest that by 1974 the proportion of corporate equity owned by the richest 1% had fallen to 58.2% compared to Lydall and Tipping's estimate for 1954 of 81%. (*Inland Revenue Statistics*, 1976). As in the United States, company shares are a more important part of the portfolios of the rich, with ordinary shares accounting for 56.3% of the wealth of the richest 1% but only 14% of personal wealth as a whole.

The final aspect of share ownership to be considered is the extent to which share ownership is dispersed. We have seen that a large, although declining, proportion of shares held by the personal sector is owned by the very wealthy. This does not, however, imply that these wealthy investors exercise effective control over the companies which they own, and the more widely dispersed is share ownership the more difficult it is to organize the owners into a coherent body of opinion. Berle and Means were under no doubt that the dispersion of share ownership could lead to the separation of ownership and control and, writing in 1932, they could already see evidence of this having occurred:

> It is clear that the dispersion of ownership has gone to tremendous lengths among the largest companies and has progressed to a considerable extent among the medium sized. Further, it may be said that in

general the larger the company, the more likely is its ownership to be diffused among a multitude of individuals (Berle and Means (1932; p. 53)).

This phenomenon was investigated in Britain by Florence (1961). Unfortunately, his study related to 1951 and significant changes must be expected to have occurred since then. Despite this shortcoming three of his findings are of interest. Firstly, the median percentage of votes held by the largest 20 shareholders in large companies was in 1951 only 19%. (Florence (1961; p. 72)). Secondly, the directors owned a majority, or even a substantial fraction, of the shares in their company in only a very few of the large companies. The median percentage of the shares owned by the Board of large companies was 1.5%. (Florence (1961; p. 90)). Thirdly, even in 1951, institutions were often found to be among the largest of all shareholders, and of course as we have seen, this has been reinforced by the growth in institutional shareholding.

The observation that management usually owns a small proportion of the equity and that the ownership of shares is widely dispersed, provides the basis for the Berle and Means argument that the composition of share ownership is irrelevant to the determination of corporate policy because control rests with managers. The weakness in this line of argument is, on the one hand, that there is no immediate theoretical link between the dispersion of share ownership and the divorce of ownership from control, and on the other hand, that it ignores the enormous growth in institutional shareholding that we have witnessed. We shall suggest later that it is the failure to examine the composition of share ownership which can account for some of the inadequacies of the received theory of the firm.

Despite these shortcomings, empirical work in this area has tended to associate the concept of management control with statistics on the size of the largest shareholdings. For example, Larner (1966) in his study of the largest 200 U.S. non-financial corporations in 1963, defined a company as 'management-controlled' if no individual, family, corporation, or group of business associates, owned more than 10% of the voting stock. Comparing his results with those of Berle and Means (1932), he found that the proportion of companies which were management-controlled had risen from 44% in 1929 to 84.5% in 1963. Some additional evidence is provided for the U.K. by Radice's (1971) study for 1963. He looked at 89 large firms in three industries, food, electrical engineering, and textiles. Companies in which the largest 'definable interest group' held less than 5% of the voting shares were classified as management-controlled. With this definition it turns out that 60.7% of the total assets of the companies in 1963 were in firms described as management-controlled.

None of this, however, demonstrates that the body of shareholders have lost control, but simply that no individual or tightly knit group of shareholders retains control. The proportion of ownership used to define management control in these studies is arbitrary, and in criticizing this approach Yarrow (1974) advocated classifying companies according to the size of one of the parameters of a Pareto distribution fitted to the biggest shareholdings. Even this method, though, does not go to the heart of the matter, for, if all the shareholders agree on what policy the firm should be pursuing, no management could safely adopt a different policy without inviting a take-over raider to make a bid which he should have little difficulty in getting accepted. It follows from this that it is important to know the theoretical conditions under which shareholders are unanimous in their choice of policy and this problem will be investigated in Chapter 5, where we shall see that the commonly held belief that different shareholders would like the same policy is mistaken.

Although the evidence on all three of the aspects of share ownership which we have considered is surprisingly small given the nature of the subject, it is sufficient to suggest that changes in the composition of share ownership play an important role in the models to be developed in subsequent chapters.

Chapter 3

THE TOOLS OF PUBLIC POLICY

In this world nothing can be said to be certain, except death and taxes (Benjamin Franklin, 1789).

The famous words of Benjamin Franklin would bring an ironic smile to the face of an English businessman in the 1970s for one of the most uncertain features of postwar British life has been the taxation of companies. Four major reforms of the corporate tax system have taken place, and the tax rates have rarely remained constant from one year to the next. One of the few changes which have not been made to corporation tax is its abolition. In other countries, too, corporate taxation has been the subject of both academic debate and political experimentation. Within the European Economic Community there has been considerable discussion about harmonizing corporate tax systems, and several draft Directives have been issued. Even in the United States, where both the structure and rates of corporation tax have been relatively stable, use was made of the investment tax credit to stimulate investment, and, more recently, there has emerged a growing interest in the integration of personal and corporate taxation.

Taxation, however, is only one of the various policy tools open to government for controlling the activities of corporations. We might classify these tools into three broad categories:

(1) Direct administrative control of individual firms' activities.

(2) The provision of a general legal framework within which individual agents are free to operate.

(3) Fiscal policy.

Under the first heading come control by edict, planning of the interventionist type concerned with the activities of specific firms, and other patterns of *dirigisme*. A more common example of administrative control, at least in the Anglo-Saxon world, is direct price and profit control which has been practised by governments for centuries. Control of prices in the seventeenth century evoked the sort of criticism that can be heard today in discussions of prices and incomes policies.

In contrast, monopoly and merger policy has consisted both of direct control and also of changes in the legal rules of the game by which companies must abide. An example of the latter type of policy is the U.S. legislation on competition embodied in the Sherman Antitrust Act of 1890 and the Clayton Act of 1914. Active government policies towards monopoly developed much later in the U.K. and have more often taken the form of *ad hoc* administrative decisions, (for a discussion of the reasons for the late development of monopoly policy in the U.K. see Hannah (1976a; Chapter 4)). However, the most recent innovation in public policy towards corporations has been the extensive use of fiscal policy to influence their behaviour. The increasing dominance of the corporate form of enterprise has led to the separate taxation of companies, and fiscal policy is seen as a major element in any co-ordinated government policy to stimulate investment and raise the rate of economic growth.

An analysis of the development and effectiveness of all these types of policy is beyond the scope of this book. Inevitably we must be selective, and we shall take as our theme the role of the tax system. There are several reasons for choosing to focus on taxation. Firstly, there is a great deal of intellectual dispute and disagreement about the effects of company taxes, and certainly a total lack of concensus amongst economists about the incidence and incentive effects of company taxation. Despite this, or perhaps because of it, there are repeated and various suggestions for reforming the system of company taxation.

Secondly, these issues are of more than purely academic interest, for the level and incidence of company taxation are politically sensitive subjects with opinions ranging from those who believe company taxes are an unfair burden on the owners of corporate capital, to those who agree with Ralph Nader, the American consumers' champion, that 'the tax system has become, to a disgraceful degree, an indirect subsidy to corporations and other privileged groups', (Nader (1973; p. 10)).

Thirdly, the U.K. provides an excellent case study for examining the effects of different taxes because of the frequent changes of system which provide the economist with an opportunity of observing a situation in which there is sufficient variation in the policies used to enable him to discern the effects of changes in those policies. In this respect the U.K. experience is unique and may afford lessons for the future both for the U.K. and other countries.

Finally, the study of fiscal policy is amenable to the use of econometric techniques which inject a desirable degree of rigour into the formulation and testing of hypotheses about the effects of different taxes.

3.1 *Company taxation*

The idea of a separate tax on corporations, rather than on the owners of corporations, is a comparatively recent innovation in fiscal policy. The corporate income tax in the U.S. was introduced in 1909 and separate taxation of corporate profits appeared in the U.K. only in 1947, before which time companies were integrated into the personal income tax structure. Yet, the industrialized countries have developed a number of quite different systems of company taxation which it is the task of this section to explain.

Two of the principal aims of company taxation are, firstly, to raise revenue, and, secondly, to provide additional tools for the policy-maker to guide the allocation of resources and influence financial flows. We shall be primarily concerned with the incentive effects of taxing companies, but it may be helpful as a background to this to look at the relative importance of corporate tax revenues in different countries.

Table 3.1 shows the percentage of total current revenue provided by direct taxes on companies in various OECD countries. There are problems in making comparisons of this kind, not least because of the different proportions of economic activity carried out by corporations as opposed to individuals and partnerships in the various countries. For example, the Richardson Committee (Cmnd. 2300) found in 1960 that whereas 70% of trading profits in the private sector in the U.K. were earned by companies, the available information suggested that only some 30–40% of trading profits in France and Germany were earned by companies.

Nevertheless, certain features can be discerned. Firstly, there is a wide disparity in the importance of corporate tax revenues in the different countries, this source being relatively more important in Japan and North America. Secondly, the contribution of taxes on

Table 3.1 Direct taxes on companies as a percentage of total current tax revenues, OECD countries.

Country	1955–57 (average)	1972–74 (average)
Canada	19.0	12.0
U.S.	19.8	11.2
Japan	17.9	20.8
France	6.4	6.9
Germany	9.3	4.8
Italy	5.9	6.5
U.K.	15.5	7.6
Total above[1]	16.5	11.1
Austria	6.9	4.0
Belgium	6.7	7.7
Denmark	5.6	2.9
Finland	12.6	4.6
Ireland	8.8	5.4
Luxembourg	17.9	17.4
Netherlands	13.5	6.7
Norway	9.9	2.7
Sweden	12.2	3.9
Switzerland	8.9	7.8
Total above[1]	10.0	5.6
OECD Total	16.0	10.5

Source: OECD (1972; Table A 10), OECD (1976; Table 15).

[1]Weighted by GNP at current market prices and current exchange rates.

companies to total revenue has been declining in importance in most countries. The ratio of company taxes to total revenue fell in 13 of the 17 countries shown in the table.

Since this phenomenon has occurred at a time when, in most countries, the ratio of overall taxation to GNP was rising, the decline in the contribution of corporate tax revenues reflects either a fall in the share of profits or a fall in the tax burden on companies, or a combination of both. Comparable international data are notoriously

Table 3.2 Corporate tax burden in major OECD countries (per cent).

Country	1955–57	1967–69
U.K.	30.5	23.0[1]
U.S.	39.7	36.4
Canada	30.4	31.6
Japan	26.5	21.2
France	18.1	14.7
Germany	22.5	15.5
Italy	12.8	14.4

Source: from data kindly provided by OECD.

Note: The tax burden is defined as the ratio of corporate taxes to the sum of corporate taxes and gross corporate savings. The figures are approximate and give an idea only of the broad trends.

[1]not allowing for investment grants.

hard to come by but there is clear evidence that whatever may have happened to the share of profits the corporate tax burden has been falling in many countries. Moreover the sharpest reduction has been in the U.K. Table 3.2 shows the trend in the tax burden on companies in the major OECD countries over a twelve-year period. The definition of the tax burden in this table is unsatisfactory in that the 'profits' used as the tax base exclude all distributions by companies, and so not only is the tax rate overstated, but also any comparisons will be affected by differences in the proportions of profits which are distributed in different countries or different time periods. However, the lack of suitable national accounting data on a consistent basis precludes the construction of a better series, and it is unlikely that the direction of the trend in the tax burden is mis-stated. In five of the seven countries the tax burden declined over the period from 1955–7 to 1967–9, in some cases quite sharply, and the increases in Canada and Italy were very small. Both Germany and the U.K. show major declines in the tax burden, and, if we take account of the fact that cash grants for investment replaced tax allowances in 1966, the decline in the effective tax rate in the U.K. was even more striking, falling from 30.9% in 1955–57 to 17.2% in 1967–69 as a proportion of gross trading profits; and from 41.5% to 25.4% as a proportion of profits less stock appreciation and capital consumption, (King (1975a)). By and large, the universal reduction of company taxes has been due to policies of encouraging investment by granting higher tax allowances or giving cash subsidies to firms.

Clearly then, the corporate tax system has been used less as a means of raising revenue than as a tool to stimulate investment and influence the working of the capital market. In fact, we may identify five main roles for the corporation tax in terms of its effects on:

(1) The division of economic activity between corporate and unincorporated forms of business enterprise; we return to this topic in Chapter 4.

(2) The financial policy of firms; this is discussed in Chapters 4 and 5.

(3) The investment decision of firms, which forms the subject matter of Chapter 8.

(4) Risk-taking and entrepreneurship; Chapter 5 deals with the difficult subject of corporate behaviour in a world of uncertainty.

(5) International capital flows; we shall not examine the impact of the tax system in this area because it depends upon the technicalities of the tax treatment of the foreign income of residents and the domestic income of non-residents, and involves policies such as double taxation treaties.

It is to these issues that we shall turn in subsequent chapters. First, however, we shall set out a general framework for describing the different systems of company taxation that are in use in different countries, and this is the aim of the following section. The remaining sections of this chapter discuss those aspects of the personal tax system which are relevant for understanding the economic impact of the corporate tax system, (in particular capital gains taxation), and some important differences in the tax treatment of various categories of shareholders.

3.2 *Alternative systems of company taxation*

There are several ways of classifying company tax systems. The most common sees alternative systems as differing principally in their treatment of the taxation of distributed profits (dividends) *vis-à-vis* the taxation of undistributed profits (retentions). This is a useful distinction which we shall follow here, although, as we shall see in the next chapter, it is important also to take into account the personal tax system which is superimposed on the corporate tax structure. Other approaches classify systems in terms of their effects on the incentive to invest, often interpreted as the minimum pre-tax rate of return necessary to induce the owners of a firm to invest, or in terms of horizontal equity between domestic and foreign shareholders and between domestic and foreign companies. In subsequent chapters we shall examine the former question but not the latter, which, although of great importance in the formulation of a policy of tax harmonization between countries, is largely a matter of rather technical international tax considerations.

Before discussing the operation of the different systems we shall introduce a method of representing the systems within a common framework. In fact, we shall define two tax variables the values of which are sufficient to enable us to classify tax systems in terms of their domestic economic effects. The first variable is concerned with measuring the degree of discrimination between retentions and distributions imposed by different tax regimes. We may give a formal definition of the extent to which the tax system discriminates against dividends in terms of a 'tax discrimination variable', (denoted by θ), which we shall define as the opportunity cost of retained earnings in terms of *net* dividends foregone. Net dividends are dividends after payment of all taxes, both corporate and personal, and so θ equals the additional potential disposable income which shareholders could receive if one unit of retained earnings were distributed. If cash in the hands of the company and cash in the hands of the shareholder can be interchanged without attracting an additional tax liability (or credit), then there is no discrimination, and the value of θ is unity. If θ is less than unity, dividends are taxed more highly than retentions, whereas retentions bear the heavier tax burden when θ exceeds unity. Defined in this way the value of θ depends upon the personal tax rates of the shareholders. For some purposes it is useful to define the degree of discrimination in terms of a variable whose value is independent of the identity of the shareholders and depends only upon the system of company taxation. An appropriate definition is the opportunity cost of retained earnings in terms of *gross* dividends foregone and this measure is denoted by θ. Gross dividends are dividends before deduction of personal income tax. If m denotes the marginal rate of income tax, then the relationship between the two measures of the degree of discrimination is given by the simple formula

$$\theta = (1 - m)\hat{\theta}. \tag{3.1}$$

Both measures will be used when we come to analyse corporate financial policy and dividend behaviour in Chapters 4 and 6.

The second company tax variable is what might be termed the basic rate of corporate income tax. It is defined as the rate of tax which would be paid if no profits were distributed and is denoted by τ; the value of τ is the rate of corporation tax or rate of tax on undistributed profits.

Given these definitions it is easy to see that the total tax liability of the company and its shareholders together, is equal to the basic rate on taxable profits plus any additional tax, (or minus any credit), which arises because dividends are taxed at a different rate from that levied on retentions. From the definition of θ we know that if one unit of retentions is distributed, the shareholders receive θ and the remaining $1 - \theta$ goes in tax. Hence the additional tax liability per unit of net dividends is $(1 - \theta)/\theta$. If the total tax liability is denoted by T, taxable profits by Y, and net dividends by D, then we have

$$T = \tau Y + \left(\frac{1 - \theta}{\theta}\right)D. \tag{3.2}$$

This definition includes in the tax liability, taxes paid both by the company and by the shareholders, with the exception of any capital gains tax liability arising out of an increase in share values. Capital gains taxation is discussed in the next section but its omission from the definition of corporate tax liability should not be taken to imply that it is to be ignored altogether, and its effect on financing behaviour will be analysed in Chapter 4. The case for leaving capital gains tax liability out of equation (3.2) rests on the argument that this liability cannot be expressed as a function of company income and its division between dividends and retentions. There are two reasons for this. Firstly, capital gains tax is normally charged only when the gains are realized, not when they accrue, and so the charge in any year is related to the accrued gains of previous years. Secondly, even accrued gains in a given year cannot be identified with the value of retained profits in that year except under a set of very restrictive assumptions which are unlikely to hold in practice (we return to this later). Moreover, since we shall be using equation (3.2) principally to identify the values of τ and θ under different company tax systems, the omission of capital gains tax in this context is unimportant.

Using the fact that gross dividends, G, are related to net dividends by the relationship $D = (1 - m)G$, we may rewrite equation (3.2) as

$$T = \tau Y + \frac{(1 - \theta)(1 - m)}{\theta} G. \tag{3.3}$$

We may now use the variables θ and τ to classify the different systems of company taxation, of which there are four basic types:

The classical system When the corporate income tax was first introduced in the U.S. in 1909, it was defended as a tax on the privilege of having corporate status. From this idea follows naturally the concept of separate taxation of the company and its shareholders, with the tax liability of the company to corporation tax being independent of the tax liability of the shareholders to personal taxes. This concept is embodied in the classical system of company taxation, under which the company pays a flat rate of corporation tax (which we shall denote by c) on all taxable profits, and then the shareholders in their turn are liable to personal income tax on their receipts of dividends. No attempt is made to allow the shareholders credit for tax paid by the company. The total tax liability as we defined it above is therefore given by

$$T = cY + mG. \tag{3.4}$$

Since equations (3.4) and (3.3) are effectively the same equation, we may identify coefficients which imply that $\tau = c$, and $(1 - \theta)(1 - m)/\theta = m$. The classical system, therefore, is characterized by

$$\begin{aligned} \tau &= c, \\ \theta &= 1 - m. \end{aligned} \tag{3.5}$$

The classical system is used in a number of countries, notably the U.S. (although here the first $100 of dividends are exempt from income tax), Australia, Denmark, Holland, Luxembourg, Spain and Switzerland. It was employed in the U.K. in the period 1965–73, and also tried and subsequently abandoned in both France and West Germany.

The two-rate system One of the major objections to the classical system which has been raised, is that it involves the 'double taxation of dividends', since dividends are subject both to corporation tax and to income tax whereas retentions bear only the former. In this way, it is argued, the tax system encourages inefficient firms to retain profits and discourages the growth of the capital market. The reasoning behind this argument and the economic effects of different systems will be scrutinized in Chapter 4. At this point we shall simply note that it is not the number of times which a quantity is taxed that is important, rather it is the ultimate rate of tax which is relevant, and so the different company tax systems should be evaluated in terms of their implications for the values of τ and θ.

The two-rate system aims to alleviate at least some of the double taxation of dividends by taxing distributed profits at a lower rate than undistributed profits. For this system the total tax liability is composed of a rate of corporation tax on undistributed profits (denoted by c_u), *plus* a different rate of corporation tax on distributed profits (denoted by c_d), *plus* the shareholders' rate of income tax on dividends.

$$\begin{aligned} \therefore T &= c_u(Y - G) + c_d G + mG \\ &= c_u Y + (m + c_d - c_u)G. \end{aligned} \tag{3.6}$$

Comparing this with equation (3.3) we have

$$\begin{aligned} \tau &= c_u, \\ \theta &= \frac{1 - m}{1 + c_d - c_u}. \end{aligned} \tag{3.7}$$

Variants of the two-rate system have been tried in West Germany, Australia, Finland, Norway, Japan, and between 1948 and 1958 the system was used in the U.K.

The imputation system As with the two-rate system, the imputation system attempts to give shareholders credit for tax paid by the company which may be used to offset their personal tax liability on dividends. Unlike the two-rate system, however, there is only a single rate of corporate profits tax. Part of the corporate tax liability on distributed profits is 'imputed' to the shareholders and regarded as a pre-payment of their personal income tax on dividends, which the shareholders receive in the form of a tax credit.

The operation of the system is as follows. First, the company pays a rate of corporation tax (denoted by c) on all profits. After this any profits which are distributed are regarded as already having borne personal tax at a certain rate, which we shall call the 'rate of imputation' and denote by the symbol s, and so shareholders have to account directly for tax on dividends only at the difference between their personal marginal rates of income tax and the rate of imputation. If their marginal rates exceed the rate of imputation shareholders pay a positive extra sum to the tax authorities, but if their marginal rates are less than the rate of imputation they receive a refund. In the U.K., where the imputation system has been in force since 1973, the rate of imputation is set equal to the standard rate of income tax, so that for a large number of dividend recipients no net payment or refund is required.

Under the imputation system the total tax liability comprises the single rate of corporation tax on all profits, *plus* the difference between the shareholders' personal rate and the rate of imputation on distributed profits.

$$\therefore\ T = cY + (m - s)G. \tag{3.8}$$

Using equations (3.3) and (3.8) we have for this system that

$$\tau = c,$$
$$\theta = \frac{1 - m}{1 - s}. \tag{3.9}$$

In some countries the system is defined not in terms of the rate of imputation as such, but in terms of the rate of tax credit, as, for example, in France. When profits are distributed shareholders receive an amount in cash (say C) which, because it is regarded as having paid personal tax at a rate s, is equivalent to a gross dividend of $C/(1 - s)$, i.e. the cash receipt is 'grossed up' at the rate s. Since this gross dividend is deemed to have paid tax at the rate s, the tax credit received by shareholders against their personal tax liability on dividends (known in France as the *avoir fiscal*) is equal to $s\,C/(1 - s)$. The rate of credit as a proportion of the cash dividend received by the shareholders from the company is $s/(1 - s)$, and this ratio is sometimes used to define the operation of the system. In France the rate of credit is one half which is equivalent to a rate of imputation of one third, almost identical to that in the U.K. where the rate of imputation has fluctuated between 0.3 and 0.35 since the system was introduced. Other countries which employ the imputation system are Belgium, Canada, Italy, Ireland, and between 1958 and 1964 the U.K. employed a variant of the system, switching to the classical system in 1965 only to revert to the imputation system in 1973.

The integrated system Neither the two-rate nor the imputation system succeeds in completely eliminating the tax discrimination between dividends and retentions, which, given our definition of discrimination, would require the value of θ to be identically equal to unity for all shareholders. In addition, the very idea of a corporate profits tax implies that the tax rate on retained profits will differ from the shareholders' rate of income tax. These features have led to the suggestion that the corporate tax system should be completely integrated with the personal tax system. Profits would be imputed to shareholders in proportion to their shareholdings, and this imputed income would be subject to personal income tax. Under such a system we have

$$T = mY, \tag{3.10}$$

which implies that

$$\begin{aligned} \tau &= m, \\ \theta &= 1. \end{aligned} \tag{3.11}$$

A fully integrated system was recommended for Canada by the Royal Commission on Taxation in Canada (the Carter Commission) in 1966, and was seriously considered by West Germany in 1971. In neither country, however, was the system adopted. Since companies are rather efficient tax collectors, a company tax could be retained and used as a withholding tax. In the Carter Commission proposals the rate of tax would be equal to the highest rate of personal income tax, and shareholders with personal tax rates lower than this would apply for a refund. In other countries where the highest tax rate exceeds the maximum feasible value for a withholding tax rate, (in the U.K., for example, the highest rate has been 98%), and where it might be undesirable for almost all shareholders to be involved in applications for refunds, a more appropriate rate of withholding tax might be the 'standard' or modal tax rate on unearned income.

We have described above four different systems of company taxation, and represented them in terms of the tax variables θ and τ. Before looking at the use of these systems in practice we shall note the existence of two constraints on the range of values which θ and τ may take. The two constraints are: (a) that the tax system is not confiscatory so that it is possible for a company to pay a positive dividend, and (b) that the system does not allow a company to distribute income to its shareholders on terms more favourable than would be the case for an unincorporated business, which implies that the tax burden on distributions must be no less than the shareholder's rate of income

Table 3.3 Company tax systems in various countries.

Classical	Two-Rate	Imputation
Australia	Austria	Belgium
Denmark	Finland	Canada
Iceland	Greece	France
Italy	Japan	Ireland
Luxembourg	Norway	Turkey
Netherlands	West Germany	U.K.
Portugal		
Spain		
Sweden		
Switzerland		
U.S.		

Note: The systems are those in force in 1975.

tax. If a company earns an extra unit of taxable profits the amount that shareholders can receive in dividends after payment of all taxes is $\theta(1 - \tau)$. Hence the two constraints may be written as

$$0 \leqslant \tau \leqslant 1,$$
$$0 \leqslant \theta \leqslant \frac{1 - m}{1 - \tau}. \tag{3.12}$$

These conditions will always be satisfied provided the rates of income and corporation tax lie between zero and unity, and that under the imputation system the rate of imputation is less than or equal to the rate of corporation tax.

With the exception of the integrated system, all of the above systems can be found in use in different countries and Table 3.3 shows the main countries employing each of the systems. In itself, however, this conveys little information about the quantitative impact of the different country tax systems, and Table 3.4 attempts to rectify this by giving values for effective corporate tax rates in 1975. The construction of these rates ignores the fact that in many countries the first slices of company income are taxed at rates lower than those shown in the table. The first two columns show the values of the tax variables τ and θ, with the latter, since it is a function of the rate of income tax, calculated on the assumption of a marginal rate of personal income tax of 35%. With the exceptions of Spain and Switzerland, most countries have rather similar values for τ, but the value of θ varies widely, those countries with the classical system having the lowest

Table 3.4 Corporate tax variables, selected countries 1975.

Country	τ	θ	$\theta(1-\tau)$	ACID Test Statistic
1. Norway	0.465	1.215	0.650	1.000
2. Belgium	0.42	0.884	0.513	0.789
3. Ireland	0.4995	1.000	0.501	0.770
4. Japan[1]	0.40	0.833	0.500	0.769
5. West Germany[2]	0.51	1.016	0.498	0.766
6. France	0.50	0.975	0.488	0.750
7. U.K.	0.52	1.000	0.480	0.738
8. Finland[3]	0.43	0.828	0.472	0.726
9. Switzerland[4]	0.275	0.650	0.471	0.725
10. Italy[5]	0.35	0.700	0.455	0.700
11. Spain	0.30	0.650	0.455	0.700
12. Canada	0.49	0.867	0.442	0.680
13. Denmark[6]	0.37	0.650	0.410	0.630
14. Luxembourg	0.40	0.650	0.390	0.600
15. Austria	0.5764	0.913	0.387	0.595
16. Australia	0.475	0.650	0.341	0.525
17. Netherlands	0.48	0.650	0.338	0.520
18. U.S.	0.48	0.650	0.338	0.520
19. Sweden[7]	0.52	0.650	0.312	0.480

Source: own calculations.

Notes: Column 1 is the basic rate of corporate profits tax.

Column 2 is the tax discrimination variable, assuming a marginal personal income tax rate of 0.35.

Column 3 is the maximun net dividend per unit of pre-tax profits, assuming a personal tax rate of 0.35.

Column 4 is the ACID Test Statistic. This *does* depend on the value of the personal tax rate in Italy and Japan where there are upper limits to the tax rate on dividend income, but not on the income of unincorporated businesses.

Columns 2, 3 and 4 are shown to three significant figures.

[1]There is a maximum personal tax rate on dividends of 25%.

[2]Excluding the temporary surcharge.

[3]In Finland the effective rate of corporation tax on distributed profits is normally 0.6 τ, but equals zero for dividends on new capital subscribed between 1969 and 1978. It is assumed that on average $c_d = 0.5\ \tau$.

[4]In Switzerland the Federal, Cantonal, and Communal taxes on total average between 25 and 30% of profits; it is assumed that $\tau = 0.275$.

[5]There is a maximum personal tax rate on dividends of 30%.

[6]Since the Table refers to marginal tax rates, the exemption for the lesser of 50% of income or 2.5% of paid up capital has been ignored.

[7]This ignores a slight alleviation of dividend taxation in Sweden, where there is a deduction against tax of part of the dividends paid on newly issued shares in 10 of the first 15 years after the issue. Since the deduction is limited to 5% of the capital issue the alleviation is likely to be small.

values and the country with the highest value being Norway which imposes a zero rate of corporation tax on distributed profits. Several countries employing either the imputation or the two-rate systems achieve values of θ close to unity, and both the U.K. and Ireland have θ equal to unity because their rates of imputation in 1975 were 35%, the value of the personal income tax rate used in the calculation of the second column. Variations in personal tax rates between shareholders are considered in Section 3.5 below.

The characteristics of a tax system are defined by the values of θ and τ, although a different light can be cast on the effect of a system on distributed income by combining the two variables in some way. Two such calculations are shown in the third and fourth columns. The third column shows the maximum additional disposable income shareholders can receive if the company earns an extra unit of taxable profits, and given our definitions this is equal to $\theta(1 - \tau)$. This column also is calculated on the assumption of a marginal personal income tax rate of 35%. We can see that for 100 units of pre-tax profits the amounts which could reach the pockets of shareholders with a marginal tax rate of 35%, vary from 31.2 units in Sweden to 65 units in neighbouring Norway. In the U.K. and West Germany the figure is just under 50 units, whereas in the U.S. the amount is only 33.8 units. It was this statistic expressed in the third column which was used in France to justify the introduction of the imputation system in 1965. Before the change the figure was 32.5 units, and it has subsequently increased to 48.75 units.

Another way of looking at the tax system is to ask how far the existence of separate taxation of companies imposes a higher tax burden on distributed profits, than would be the case if profits were taxed simply at the shareholders' personal tax rates, as, for example, in a partnership. In the latter situation an extra unit of profits would yield a post-tax dividend of $1 - m$, whereas with separate company taxation we have seen that the shareholders could receive $\theta(1 - \tau)$ of an extra unit of profits, as shown in the third column of Table 3.4. A test of the additional tax burden on distributed profits imposed by corporate taxation is the ratio of the maximum net dividend with company taxation to the maximum net dividend with only personal taxation. This ratio is equal to $\theta(1 - \tau)/(1 - m)$, which equals $\hat{\theta}(1 - \tau)$, and is independent of the value of the marginal tax rates of the shareholders, which is not true for either the second or third columns. It measures the extent to which the corporate tax system allows for, or adds to, the personal taxation of dividends, and because it tests the Attempted Corporate Integration of Dividend taxation, we shall describe the ratio as the ACID Test Statistic for company tax systems. Clearly, the ACID Test Statistic lies between zero and unity. A value of zero implies complete confiscation of dividend income by company taxation, and a value of unity means that the system imposes no tax on dividends over and above the level of personal taxation. Although important, the ACID Test Statistic does not measure the degree of complete integration of personal and corporate taxation, because it is concerned only with the integration of the taxation of distributed profits, and takes no account of differences between personal tax rates and the basic rate of corporation tax.

The values of the ACID Test Statistic for various countries are shown in the fourth column of Table 3.4, and the countries are ranked in descending order of the statistic. Only Norway achieves a value of unity because it imposes no corporation tax on distributed profits, and the lowest values of the statistic are to be found in the U.S., the Netherlands, and Sweden. Of the EEC countries, we may identify two distinct groups. The first group, comprising Belgium, France, Ireland, U.K. and West Germany, is characterized by very similar values of the ACID Test Statistic lying in the band between 0.74 and 0.79. In contrast, the second group of Denmark, Italy, Luxembourg and the Netherlands exhibit much lower values in the range 0.52 to 0.70, with only Italy attaining a value close to that of the first group. Harmonization of the taxation of distributed profits, which is a stated aim of the EEC, should involve harmonization of the values of the ACID Test Statistic in member countries. This appears to be the logical approach, although the EEC has not as yet adopted a policy based on the use of the ACID Test Statistic.

In fact the EEC proposals for harmonization of member countries' corporate tax systems are concerned more with the form of the tax system than with the underlying reality. For example, it does not seem that depreciation allowances have been discussed seriously in the context of harmonization, despite the fact that, as we shall see in later chapters, changes in these allowances can change the whole nature of the corporation tax. The harmonization proposals are concerned solely with the taxation of distributed profits, and consist of two basic recommendations (EEC, 1975). The first is that harmonization should be under the imputation system with the basic rate of corporation tax lying within the range 45–55%. We saw above that the imputation system could be defined in terms of the rate of credit instead of the rate of imputation, and that the credit as a proportion of the dividend received is equal to $s/(1-s)$. The second of the EEC Commission's proposals is that 'the tax credit shall be neither lower than 45% nor higher than 55% of the amount of corporation tax at the normal rate on a sum representing the distributed dividend increased by such tax' (Article 8, EEC (1975)). The effect of this proposal is that if the harmonized rate of credit is denoted by H, the amount of credit given on a unit dividend is $Hc/(1-c)$, where c is the basic corporate tax rate. Hence $H = s(1-c)/c(1-s)$. The ACID Test Statistic under the imputation system is $(1-c)/(1-s)$, and so

$$H = \frac{s}{c}\,(\text{ACID}).$$

Thus if the corporate tax rate is 50% and the rate of imputation is one-third, an ACID Test Statistic of 0.75 corresponds to a value for H of 0.5. There are, however, a number of objections to defining harmonization in terms of H. Firstly, there is no economic principle behind the use of H, whereas the economic meaning of the ACID Test Statistic is clear. Secondly, a given change in H does not correspond to an equal absolute or proportionate change in the ACID Test Statistic, the relationship between them depending on the values of c and s in the country in question. Finally, the proposed range of allowable variation in H implies very little flexibility in the rate of imputation. For example, suppose the corporate tax rate were 50%; then for H to lie between 0.45 and 0.55, the rate of imputation must fall in the range 31.03% to 35.48%, which allows little scope for variation especially when it is remembered that in the U.K. the rate of imputation is the standard rate of income tax. In contrast, using the same example, if the ACID Test Statistic had to lie between 0.7 and 0.8, the rate of imputation could vary between 28.57% and 37.5%.

This completes our exposition of the different systems available for taxing companies. At this stage we shall not attempt to evaluate the merits of particular systems or of particular concepts, such as those of a nondiscriminatory tax system. These will be discussed in due course when we come to analyse the implications of different systems for corporate financial policy and for investment behaviour.

3.3. *Personal taxation*

The taxation of dividends by corporate and personal taxes was discussed in the previous section. Of the remaining elements of the personal tax system which need to be taken into account, by far and away the most important is the taxation of capital gains. As we shall see in the next chapter a discussion of the economic effects of company taxation which ignored the provisions for taxing capital gains would be seriously incomplete.

A separate discussion of capital gains taxation in this chapter is warranted because of the existence of one special feature of such a tax, namely that on practical grounds it has been found impossible to tax capital gains when they *accrue*, and instead they are taxed only on *realization*. The objection to taxing accrued gains rests primarily on the difficulties which would be entailed in the regular (e.g. annual) valuation of an individual's assets. Since many countries already operate an annual wealth tax it might be thought that the problems of valuation had been overcome, but, in practice, these taxes are restricted in coverage in terms of both assets and individuals who are liable to the tax, and, more importantly, do not involve annual revaluation of all assets. This process may produce a suitable approximation to the *level* of an individual's wealth, but it leaves a great deal to be desired as a method of calculating *changes* in the value of his net worth. This, in a nutshell, is the practical case against the implementation of a comprehensive income tax.

The implication of taxing capital gains on a realizations basis is that the effective tax rate differs from the nominal rate of tax for the following three reasons. Firstly, the tax is paid at the date when the gain is realized, and if this occurs sometime after the gain accrues then the taxpayer benefits from deferral of the tax payment. Deferral is equivalent to an interest free loan from the revenue authorities to the taxpayer of an amount equal to the tax liability on the accrued gain, and hence is also equivalent to a reduction in the effective rate of tax. The extent to which realization will be deferred will depend upon the investor's desired holding period for securities, which in turn will reflect the balance between his current income and his desired level of consumption, and the expected gains to be derived from reshuffling his portfolio of investments. It is clear that the longer the holding period the larger will be the benefit of deferral, but it is also true that the greater the benefit of deferral the greater is the incentive to hold the asset and hence the longer will be the holding period. The latter phenomenon is the 'lock-in' effect which arises from taxing realized instead of accrued gains.

Secondly, defining the tax base as realized gains introduces an additional possibility for deferral over and above that which results from the two factors just cited. If an individual with a diversified portfolio makes a capital gain on one stock which he wishes to realize, then he has the possibility of realizing a loss on another security by selling it and immediately repurchasing the same security, thus eliminating the tax liability in the current period and postponing it until the second security is sold at some future date. Transactions to establish losses for tax purposes by selling securities at the end of one trading day and buying the same securities back at the beginning of the next day, are described in the U.K. as 'bed and breakfast' deals. The effect of this sort of deal is that for a given mean rate of return on a portfolio, the greater is the variance of its constituent component capital gains, the greater are the opportunities for postponing payment of tax.

Thirdly, the rate of tax which the investor will pay will be the rate prevailing in the period when the gains are realized. This may differ from the rate prevailing when the gains accrue either because the tax rate changes over time, or because in a progressive tax system without adequate averaging provisions, it is possible that the cumulative gain will place the investor in a higher tax bracket thus increasing his marginal rate of tax on the gain.

By adopting a very simple model of investors' behaviour it is possible to compute an effective tax rate on capital gains from the value of the actual nominal rate. Leaving aside the third consideration mentioned above, we can see from the other two factors that the ability to defer the tax charge depends on the desired time profile of realizations and the variability of changes in the prices of assets in an investor's portfolio. For a given overall net capital gain on his total portfolio, the more divergent the price movements of the individual assets the more gains he will be able to realize for the purposes of consumption or reinvestment without incurring a current tax liability. Moreover, the bigger the variability in the price changes of the constituent components of the portfolio, the more likely it is that the investor will wish to re-allocate his holdings. Hence, *ceteris paribus*, the bigger the dispersion of the changes in the prices of various assets, the shorter will be the average holding period.

The desired pattern of realizations will vary from individual to individual, reflecting both the balance between desired consumption and current income receipts, and the expected gains from switching from one asset to another. The average holding period of an asset will depend upon the age of an investor because this will influence his optimal savings plan. We might expect younger investors to assume fairly long holding periods if they are saving to provide for consumption in retirement, whereas older investors might be drawing upon their savings and realizing gains as they accrue. In any one year some investors will be realizing their gains while others will continue to hold the same securities. In aggregate let the proportion of accrued gains which are realized by investors facing a particular tax rate in a given period be π. Suppose for the moment that π is constant; the determinants of π will be discussed below. Then, if a gain of one unit accrues in period one, there will be a realized gain of π in the first period and an unrealized gain of $1-\pi$. In the second period a proportion π of the unrealized gain will be realized, and so realizations will be equal to $\pi(1-\pi)$. Given the assumption that π is constant this process will continue indefinitely. If a rate of capital gains tax equal to z is imposed on realized gains, the present discounted value of the stream of tax payments resulting from a unit accrued gain is given by the sum

$$S = z\pi + \frac{z\pi(1-\pi)}{1+i} + \frac{z\pi(1-\pi)^2}{(1+i)^2} + \dots \tag{3.13}$$

$$= z\pi \sum_{t=0}^{\infty} \left(\frac{1-\pi}{1+i}\right)^t$$

$$= \frac{z\pi(1+i)}{\pi+i}, \tag{3.14}$$

where i is the typical investor's rate of discount.

This expression may be interpreted as the Effective Accrued Tax Rate, or EAT Rate, since it denotes the effective tax payments on a unit accrued gain given the assumption that the pattern of realizations may be represented by the process described above. The ratio of the EAT Rate to the actual nominal rate of capital gains tax may be described as the Effective to Actual Tax Ratio, or as the EAT Ratio. Hence we have

$$\text{EAT Rate} = \text{Nominal Rate} \times \text{EAT Ratio}$$

and

$$\text{EAT Ratio} = \frac{\pi(1+i)}{\pi+i}. \tag{3.15}$$

Table 3.5 EAT Ratios.

π \ i	0.02	0.04	0.06	0.08	0.10	0.20
0.05	0.729	0.578	0.482	0.415	0.367	0.240
0.10	0.850	0.743	0.663	0.600	0.550	0.400
0.20	0.927	0.867	0.815	0.771	0.733	0.600
0.50	0.981	0.963	0.946	0.931	0.917	0.857
1.00	1.0	1.0	1.0	1.0	1.0	1.0

Note: The EAT Ratio is the Effective to Actual Tax Ratio, and is defined by equation (3.15).

The value of the EAT Ratio depends upon both the proportion of gains which are realized in a given period, and the investor's rate of discount. The effective tax rate increases with the proportion of gains which are realized, and decreases with the discount rate. Table 3.5 shows the value of the EAT Ratio for different values of π and i. For example, if the discount rate is 10% and 10% of gains are realized each year, then the effective tax rate on capital gains is only 0.55 times the nominal rate.

The expression for the EAT Ratio which is given by equation (3.15) was derived on the assumption that realizations follow a deterministic process with a constant proportion π of gains being realized each year. However, the same model may be given a probabilistic interpretation. Suppose that the probability that an investor will realize a given gain is equal to π in each period. Realizations will then follow a binomial process and the probability of the gain being realized in period t will be equal to $\pi(1-\pi)^{t-1}$. This process generates a probability distribution of tax payments whose expected present discounted value is exactly equal to the sum given in equation (3.14), and so the EAT Ratio is again given by equation (3.15).

It is clear that the benefit received from deferral of payment of capital gains tax until realization is a reduction in the effective rate of tax. The value of this benefit therefore is equal to the difference between the nominal rate of capital gains tax and the effective tax rate. If we denote the reduction in the effective tax rate by R then we have

$$R = z - \frac{z\pi(1+i)}{\pi + i}$$

$$= \frac{zi(1-\pi)}{\pi + i}. \tag{3.16}$$

We know that for a given value of z, the effective tax rate is positively related to π and inversely related to i. At first sight it might appear that the value of the benefit from deferral increases with the value of the tax rate. In other words, it seems natural to suppose that the higher the investor's tax rate, the bigger the gap between the effective tax rate which he pays and the nominal rate of tax. This proposition, however, is false. To demonstrate this we need to make some assumption about the relationship between capital gains tax rates and income-tax rates, and we shall suppose that the rate of capital gains tax is equal to a constant multiple of the income tax rate. Let $z = \lambda m$, where λ is any constant not equal to zero. In most countries which tax capital gains a certain fraction of the taxable gain is added to income, and λ is the value of this inclusion rate. Of the 19 countries listed in Table 3.4, six tax capital gains arising on corporate shares held for more than one year (Ireland, U.K., Canada, Denmark, U.S., and Sweden), and, with the exception of Denmark, each tax system can be described by the relationship $z = \lambda m$ (subject to an upper bound on z in Ireland and the U.K.). A particularly common form is where one half of gains are taxed as income so that $\lambda = 0.5$. Taxation of capital gains as income would imply that $\lambda = 1.0$.

The investor's rate of discount is the rate at which he is prepared to exchange money today for money tomorrow, and so is equal to the net of tax interest rate, which implies that $i = (1 - m)r$, where r is the market rate of interest. Equation (3.16) therefore becomes

$$R = \frac{\lambda rm(1-m)(1-\pi)}{\pi + r(1-m)}, \tag{3.17}$$

$$\frac{\mathrm{d}R}{\mathrm{d}m} = \frac{\lambda r(1-\pi)\left[\pi + r(1-m)^2 - 2m\pi\right]}{\left[\pi + r(1-m)\right]^2}. \tag{3.18}$$

Assuming that $r > 0$ and $\pi < 1$, the value of m which maximizes R is given by the solution to the equation

$$\pi + r(1-m)^2 - 2m\pi = 0, \tag{3.19}$$

which may be rewritten as

$$r(1-m)^2 + 2\pi(1-m) - \pi = 0. \tag{3.20}$$

This is a quadratic equation in $1 - m$ which may be solved to yield

$$1 - m = -\frac{\pi}{r} \pm \frac{\pi}{r}\sqrt{\left(1 + \frac{r}{\pi}\right)}. \tag{3.21}$$

The reader may easily verify that the second order condition shows that for a maximum of R the value of $(1 - m + \pi/r)$ must be positive, and so the value of m which maximizes R is given by the solution which uses the positive sign in equation (3.21). Denoting this value of the income tax rate by m^* and π/r by x, we have

$$m^* = 1 + x - x\sqrt{(1 + 1/x)}. \tag{3.22}$$

Since x is strictly positive it is easy to see that $0 < m^* < 1$, and hence we are assured of a unique interior maximum with the value of m^* given by equation (3.22). The explanation for the existence of an optimal value of m is that the reduction in the effective tax rate on capital gains is the product of two terms: the first is the nominal tax rate on capital gains which obviously increases as the income tax rate rises, and the second is unity minus the EAT Ratio which falls as the income tax rate increases because a higher rate of income tax leads to a lower investor's discount rate, and a lower discount rate results in a higher EAT Ratio. It is clear from this argument, and from equation (3.17), that when $m = 0$, $R = 0$, and that when $m = 1$, $R = 0$ again. At some intermediate value of m the value of the benefit conferred by taxing gains only on realization is maximized (a similar result has been derived by Diamond (1975)). Evidence supporting this result is provided by some figures on realized capital gains in the U.S. produced by Bailey (1969; p. 36) which show that realizations are most important for shareholders

Figure 3.1 Plot of m^* against x

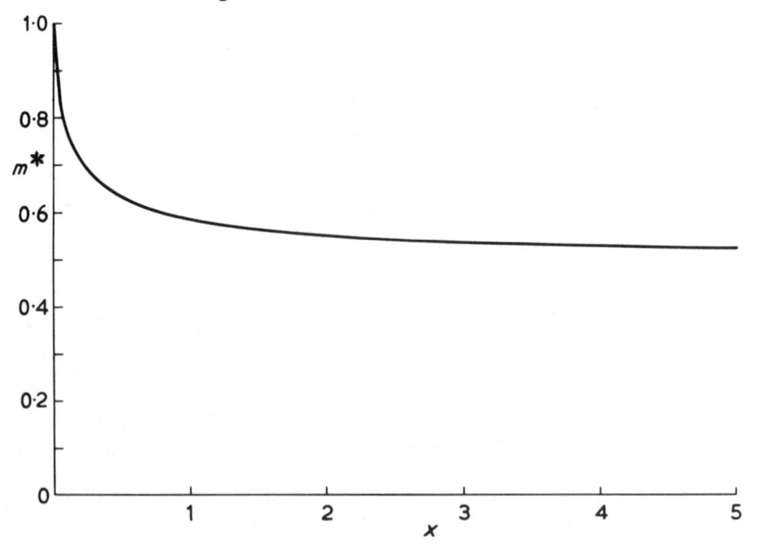

with low incomes or high incomes, but for those in the middle income groups, where the advantage of deferral is greatest, realizations are much less important.

What determines the value of the optimal income tax rate? Firstly, we may note that it does *not* depend upon the value of the inclusion rate λ, so that the value of the tax rate which maximizes the benefit of deferral is the same when capital gains are taxed as income as it is when capital gains are taxed at concessionary rates. Secondly, the value of m^* depends only on the ratio of π to r, and not on their absolute values. The relationship between m^* and x (the ratio of π to r) is illustrated in Figure 3.1. This shows that as x increases the value of m^* falls rapidly from unity towards the range between 0.5 and 0.7, approaching 0.5 asymptotically. The maximum benefit of deferral must accrue to shareholders whose income tax rates are greater than 50%, and some illustrative values for this optimal rate are given in Table 3.6 for various combinations of π and r. For example, if the proportion of accrued gains which is realized is 10%, and the rate of interest is also 10%, then the value of the income tax rate at which the maximum benefit from deferral occurs is 58.6%.

The size of the benefit conferred by deferral is given by the expression for the effective reduction in the tax rate on capital gains shown in equation (3.17). This is a function of m, π, r, and λ. In fact, the reduction in the effective tax rate is proportional to λ, the inclusion rate of capital gains in the income tax base. We know that the value of the reduction is zero both when m is equal to zero and when m is equal to unity, and that it reaches a peak at some value of m greater than one half. The exact shape of the function relating the reduction in the tax

Table 3.6 Deferral benefit maximizing tax rate.

π \ r	0.04	0.06	0.08	0.10	0.15	0.20
0.01	0.691	0.726	0.750	0.768	0.800	0.821
0.02	0.634	0.667	0.691	0.710	0.745	0.768
0.05	0.573	0.597	0.617	0.634	0.667	0.691
0.10	0.542	0.559	0.573	0.586	0.613	0.634
0.20	0.523	0.533	0.542	0.551	0.570	0.586
0.50	0.510	0.514	0.519	0.523	0.533	0.542

Note: The entries in the table are the values of m^* given by equation (3.22) corresponding to different values of π and r where $\pi/r = x$.

Figure 3.2 Reduction in the effective tax rate on capital gains (for $\lambda = 0.5$ and $r = 0.1$)

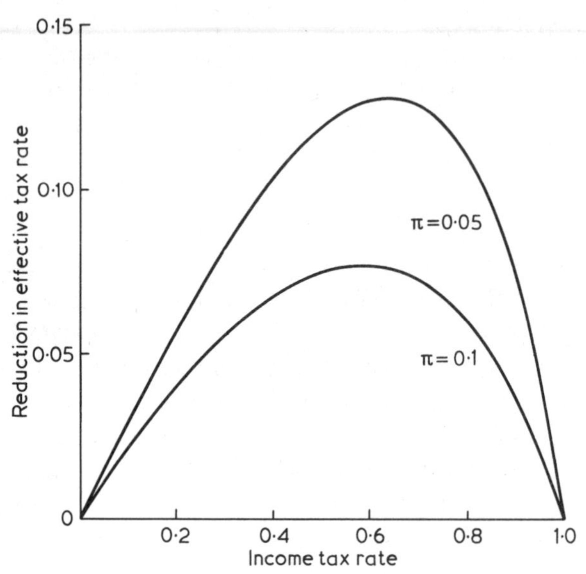

rate to the value of the income tax rate depends upon the values of λ, π and r. Figure 3.2 shows the relationship between R and m for the values $\lambda = 0.5$ (one half of capital gains taxed as income), a rate of interest of 10%, and for the two cases $\pi = 0.05$ and $\pi = 0.1$.

Suppose the tax system were indexed so that tax was charged only on real capital gains and real interest receipts. Then, in the above analysis, π would be the proportion of real gains realized, and r the real rate of interest. It can easily be seen that the benefit from deferral would be much reduced because in real terms we would expect π to be higher and r to be lower. This is a further argument for indexation of the tax system in addition to the obvious claims of such a reform.

So far we have taken the value of π to be constant over time so that we might convert a given nominal tax rate into an effective rate of tax; but is this assumption reasonable? For any particular individual the extent to which he will wish to realize his current and past accrued capital gains will depend upon the relationship between his desired consumption expenditure and his current receipts of both wage and dividend income. We would expect that the instantaneous value of π for an individual would be a complicated function of his wealth, current earnings and dividend receipts, life-time earnings profile, and attitudes towards consumption later in life and bequests for his heirs. In other words, the value of π will reflect his entire life-cycle consumption plan. To simplify matters we shall assume that all of these many factors can be represented by the *age* of the individual, which implies that

(1) His earnings profile is taken as given.

(2) The payout ratios of companies in which he invests are taken as given. *Ceteris paribus*, the higher the payout ratio, the less need he will have for realized gains, and hence the lower will be the value of π.

(3) A doubling of his life-time earnings would not alter the *proportion* of gains which he realized at any particular age.

Given these assumptions the value of π will depend on his age, and the post-tax rate of interest at which he can lend, which is a function of his income tax rate and the market rate of interest.

There is one further factor which we must take into account, namely the 'lock-in' effect of taxing capital gains on a realizations basis. This will tend to reduce the value of π, and the magnitude of the effect will be a function of the reduction in the effective rate of tax, R, the expression for which is given by equation (3.17). If an individual i is y_i years old, then we have

$$\pi_i = \pi_i(y_i, m_i, R_i, r), \tag{3.23}$$

and equation (3.17) may be written as

$$R_i = R(m_i, \pi_i, r). \tag{3.24}$$

For a given rate of interest these equations yield

$$\pi_i = \pi(y_i, m_i), \tag{3.25}$$

where the form of the function π is assumed to be the same for all individuals. This means that we have a distribution of realization propensities across individuals which is a joint distribution over age and income tax rates. We can define another joint distribution over age and income tax rate which describes the distribution of accrued capital gains over the population. Let the proportion of total capital gains accruing to those individuals of age y and with an income tax rate m be $a(y, m)$. The realization propensity for the economy as a whole (which is equivalent to the weighted average of the individual π_i) is therefore given by

$$\pi = \int_y \int_m a(y, m)\, \pi(y, m)\, \mathrm{d}y\, \mathrm{d}m. \tag{3.26}$$

One reason for looking at the aggregate value of π is that no data are available for both realized and accrued capital gains of individuals classified by either age or income range, whereas a few data, albeit very approximate, exist for aggregate gains. Before examining this evidence we might ask whether anything further can be said at this stage about the likely behaviour of π. Suppose that we make the strong assumption that the distribution of accrued capital gains over age groups is independent of the distribution of accrued gains over income tax rates. This means that we can write the joint distribution as the product of two independent distributions.

$$a(y, m) = a_1(y)\, a_2(m). \tag{3.27}$$

Suppose also that we make the same independence assumption about the distribution of realization propensities.

$$\pi(y, m) = \pi_1(y)\, \pi_2(m). \tag{3.28}$$

The aggregate realization propensity becomes

$$\pi = \int_y a_1(y)\, \pi_1(y)\, \mathrm{d}y \int a_2(m)\, \pi_2(m)\, \mathrm{d}m \tag{3.29}$$

$$= \pi_1 \pi_2. \tag{3.30}$$

The convenience of the independence assumption is that the aggregate value of π can then be expressed as the product of two terms, π_1 and π_2, which reflect different aspects of economic behaviour. The first term is the weighted average of the values of the realization propensity over the life cycle, which, at least in steady-state growth, will reflect the underlying growth rates of population and real income. The second term is the mean realization propensity for individuals in different tax brackets which will be a function of the distribution of income and the pattern of share ownership on the one hand, and the structure of the tax system on the other. The determinants of the values of π_1 and π_2 are thus seen to be long-run structural factors rather than short-run changes in economic variables. Consequently, it is quite possible for the aggregate value of π to remain constant, even though that for an individual will change over time as he moves through the life cycle and, depending on his earnings profile, through different tax brackets.

Direct evidence on the validity of the independence assumption is hard to come by in the absence of microeconomic data on realized and accrued gains of individuals classified by both age and income. There is, however, some indirect evidence on the independence of the distribution of accrued gains over age and income. Atkinson (1971) found that the distribution of wealth between individuals of the same age in the U.K. was pretty well independent of age, and, if the distribution of capital gains is similar to that of wealth, the independence assumption of equation (3.27) appears to be a reasonable approximation. We have no evidence on the distribution of the realization propensities.

We shall now try to test the hypothesis that the aggregate realization propensity is stable over time. This is not a test of the independence assumption for which microeconomic data would be required. Rather, the independence assumption should be regarded as a convenient expositional device for interpreting the results in terms of the underlying behaviour.

Using data for both realized and accrued capital gains it is possible to test the model we have used above. In any given year, say year t, there is a certain value of accrued gains which we may denote by A_t. Of these a fraction π is realized and the other $1 - \pi$ is unrealized. In the following year a fraction π of the previously unrealized gains is realized in addition to the same fraction of currently accruing gains. Consequently, in year t realized gains are equal to a fraction π of the sum of accruals in year t and the stock of unrealized gains carried over from previous periods. We have

$$B_t = \pi(A_t + S_{t-1}) + u_t \tag{3.31}$$

$$S_t = S_{t-1} + A_t - B_t \tag{3.32}$$

where B_t is the realized gains in year t, A_t the accrued gains in year t, S_t the stock of unrealized gains at the end of year t and u_t the error term in year t.

To estimate this model we can transform these equations to give

$$B_t - B_{t-1} = \pi(A_t - B_{t-1}) + u_t - u_{t-1}. \tag{3.33}$$

In order to estimate the value of π we require data for realized capital gains. These are available from tax returns for the U.S. over a fairly long time period, and for the U.K. only for the period after 1965 when capital gains tax was introduced. Unfortunately, for the U.S. there is no time series for realizations classified by type of asset, so that it is impossible to produce a time series for realized capital gains on corporate securities. Such data are available for the U.K. from 1965–6 onwards providing us with eight observations, and there are two bench-mark estimates for the U.S. for 1959 and 1962. It is clear, therefore, that we shall want to test the model using data for realized capital gains on all assets. This immediately presents one difficulty in that the limited data which are available for accrued capital gains are for gains on corporate securities only. In fact, we may identify three sources of data which could be used to test the model, two for the U.S. and one for the U.K.

(1) From Bailey's (1969) study of capital gains in the U.S. it is possible to construct a series of (i) accrued gains on corporate stock and (ii) realized gains on all assets, to estimate the model (3.33) over the period 1927–60.

(2) Bhatia (1970) has produced a similar series for realized gains in the U.S. for the period 1948–64, but in addition to a series for accrued gains on corporate stock, Bhatia provides estimates for accrued gains on a wider range of assets, including not only corporate securities but also real estate and livestock. We shall describe these gains as gains on 'all assets'.

(3) Inland Revenue statistics on realized capital gains in the U.K. exist for the period after 1965, and it is possible to construct an estimate of accrued gains on corporate securities as follows. The data for realized gains refer to gains by individuals in a particular fiscal year, and so the estimates for accrued gains must be on the same basis. Estimates of total personal wealth held in the form of shares and debentures in U.K. companies can be derived from the tax returns for estate duty by using mortality multipliers. Accrued gains on these holdings may be estimated by assuming that they increased in value at the same rate as the FT Actuaries All Share Index. The resulting estimates of accrued capital gains for the period 1965/6 to 1972/3 are shown in the first column of Table 3.7.

The available data for realized gains are shown in the second column of the table. As one would expect the volume of taxable realized gains increased steadily from 1965 when the capital gains tax was introduced. When estimating the model (3.33) we take the first observation to be for the fiscal year 1965/6, which, since it was the first year of the tax, had a value for B_{t-1} of zero.

In the estimation of equation (3.33) on the three sets of data described above, a constant term was included whose coefficient we might expect to be zero. The model was also estimated with A_t and B_{t-1} introduced as separate independent variables. This was to allow

Table 3.7 Accrued and realized capital gains in the U.K. (£ million).

Year	Accrued gains on corporate securities	Realized gains: corporate securities
1965/6	1302.71	65.44 n.a.
1966/7	− 1375.09	91.61 n.a.
1967/8	5791.64	360.05 n.a.
1968/9	4850.62	798.28 n.a.
1969/70	− 2492.56	488.02
1970/1	− 1032.91	358.22
1971/2	11908.30	834.38
1972/3	− 3279.69	1153.40

Sources: Column 1; based on calculations derived from *Inland Revenue Statistics* 1970 Table 121, and 1975 Table 105; *Financial Statistics*, various issues (details available from the author).
Column 2; *Inland Revenue.*

for the fact that in the U.S. regressions the variable B measures realized gains on all assets whereas the variable A, with one exception, measures accrued gains on corporate securities only. Suppose that accrued gains on corporate securities, A^c, are equal to a fraction α of total accrued gains plus a random error term.

$$A_t^c = \alpha A_t + \eta_t. \tag{3.34}$$

If we interpret the behavioural model in equation (3.31) as referring to total gains then, in terms of variables for which we have data, the equation to be estimated becomes

$$B_t - B_{t-1} = \alpha\pi A_t^c - \pi B_{t-1} + (\pi\eta_t + u_t - u_{t-1}). \tag{3.35}$$

The results of estimating equations (3.33) and (3.35) are shown in Table 3.8.

Given the inadequate nature of the data the results are surprisingly uniform. There are four pairs of results. In all but one the constant term is insignificant, which accords with our prior expectations. The estimates of π obtained by fitting equation (3.33) are all highly significant and rather small, of the order of 0.05, and there seems to be little difference between the U.S. and the U.K. in this respect. In the results for the alternative model (3.35) the point estimate of π is

Table 3.8 Econometric models of capital gains realization (standard errors in brackets).

Sample	No. of observations	Regression coefficients				$\bar{R}^2$	DW
		Constant	$(A_t - B_{t-1})$	A_t	B_{t-1}		
Bailey (1969), U.S. 1927–60	34	0.011 (0.233)	0.028 (0.005)	—	—	0.472	2.52
A_t = accruals on corporate stock (billion dollars)		0.204 (0.290)		0.029 (0.005)	−0.090 (0.056)	0.476	2.54
Bhatia (1970), U.S. 1949–64	16	−0.264 (0.392)	0.056 (0.009)			0.705	2.86
(a) A_t = accruals on corporate stock (billion dollars)		−0.152 (1.033)		0.055 (0.010)	−0.068 (0.108)	0.682	2.85
(b) A_t = accruals on 'all assets' (billion dollars)		−0.972 (0.402)	0.051 (0.007)			0.758	2.88
		−1.256 (0.540)		0.039 (0.026)	0.014 (0.030)	0.720	2.85
U.K. 1965/6–1972/3	8	8.799 (52.866)	0.052 (0.010)			0.815	2.63
A_t = accruals on corporate securities (£ million)		37.565 (157.478)		0.039 (0.019)	0.081 (0.305)	0.482	1.70

given by the regression coefficient of B_{t-1}, but in no case is this term significant. This model was designed to allow for the fact that the data for accrued gains and for realized gains may refer to different categories of assets. Consequently, it is relevant to only two of the four sets of data, and indeed in the remaining cases of samples drawn from the U.K. and from Bhatia (1970), with the coefficient of B_{t-1} having the wrong sign. In the two relevant cases the coefficient has the correct sign and the estimates of π are less than 0.1, although larger than those obtained from the estimation of the model (3.32). Bossons (1971) reports the results of estimating a model similar to (3.35) on U.S. data and suggests a value for π of 0.1 although no standard errors are given.

The use of first differences of realizations as the dependent variable appears to have induced a degree of negative serial correlation in the error structure of equation (3.33), as might be expected if the error term in equation (3.31) exhibited positive serial correlation. Given the approximate nature of the data and the small size of some of the samples, there is probably little to be gained from further estimation, and the goodness of fit of the estimated equations is reasonable.

Although the models which we have estimated are highly simplified and aggregate relationships, the results do show that it is important to distinguish between accruals and realizations of capital gains. We cannot reject the hypothesis that the average aggregate realizations propensity is stable over time, and the estimates suggest that its value is quite small. This implies that it would be quite wrong to suppose that the effective taxation of capital gains is accurately described by the nominal rates of tax on capital gains. Nominal rates are likely to overstate effective rates by a substantial margin, and in Section 3.4 below we present some estimates of the average difference between nominal and effective rates for shareholders in the U.K. It is clear that further data would be required to investigate the determinants of the individual realizations propensities, and their dependance on such factors as age, income, life-cycle earnings profile, and interest rates.

We might conclude that both in the U.K. and in the U.S. the value of the aggregate realization propensity appears to lie between 0.05 and 0.10. Since the mean lag between accrual and realization is equal to $(1 - \pi)/\pi$, a value for π of 0.05 would imply a delay of on average 19 years between the time when capital gains accrued and the time when they were realized. If π were 0.1 the mean lag would be

9 years. The estimates of π given above are based on the behaviour of individuals and not institutions such as pension funds which are not liable to tax, (see the next section), and which might be expected to realize gains more quickly.

The value of the realization propensity should not be confused with the value of the ratio of realizations to accruals in any one year. This will reflect the rate at which accruals are growing. For example, it is clear from equation (3.32) that if the value of accrued capital gains is stationary then, whatever the value of π, current realizations will equal current accruals. If accrued gains are growing at a constant growth rate of g it is easy to show that

$$\frac{B}{A} = \frac{\pi(1+g)}{\pi + g} \tag{3.36}$$

from which it is evident that there is no unique relationship between π and the ratio of B to A.

What light does this evidence throw on the likely values of the effective tax rate on capital gains? Suppose that the independence assumption of equation (3.29) holds. Then, over the life cycle the average value of the realization propensity can be expressed as a function of the tax rate, say $\pi = \pi(m)$. If the nominal capital gains tax rate can be written as $z = \lambda m$, the average effective capital gains tax rate on individuals with a tax rate of m is given by

$$e(m) = \frac{\lambda m\, \pi(m)\, [1 + r(1-m)]}{\pi(m) + r(1-m)} \tag{3.37}$$

where $e(m)$ is the EAT Rate corresponding to a nominal rate of z. The average effective tax rate on capital gains in the aggregate is

$$\bar{e} = \int_m e(m)\, a_2(m)\, dm. \tag{3.38}$$

If we could obtain information on the distribution function $a_2(m)$ which measures the distribution of capital gains between individuals in different tax brackets, we could derive the distribution of effective tax rates, of which one aspect would be the average effective tax rate. Suppose that we discovered the average value of m, $\bar{m}$ say, then we might be interested in knowing when we could use this value in equation (3.36) to compute the average effective tax rate $\bar{e}$. In other words, under what circumstances will $\bar{e}$ be equal to $e(\bar{m})$? In general, the mean value of a function of a variable is equal to the function value of the mean of the variable only when that function is linear. Since the function $e(m)$ is nonlinear the *average* effective tax rate on capital gains is extremely difficult to calculate. The error involved by taking the mean to be $e(\bar{m})$ will depend upon the degree of nonlinearity. In contrast, the *median* effective tax rate is easier to calculate. After some manipulation it is possible to show that $e(m)$ is a monotonically increasing function of m, which implies that the median effective tax rate is given by $e(\tilde{m})$ where $\tilde{m}$ is the median value of m.

Clearly, the effective tax rate on capital gains depends in a rather special way upon the distribution of capital gains between shareholders facing different tax rates. Similarly, the average tax rate on dividends will be a function of the distribution of dividends between shareholders in different income ranges. We have also seen that the maximum benefit from deferral of capital gains tax until realization goes to shareholders whose income tax rates are greater than 50%. It is important, therefore, that we should have some idea of the distribution of income, and hence tax rates, among shareholders, both between individuals in different tax brackets and between individual shareholders and institutional shareholders.

3.4 *Corporate and personal tax rates in the U.K.*

In this section we examine the U.K. experience in more detail in order to illustrate two basic points. The first is to show how marked the changes in corporate tax rates in the U.K. since the war have been in terms of the changes in the two fundamental tax variables described above, τ and θ. The second is that, as we have seen in Section 3.2, the value of θ depends on the personal tax rates of the shareholders, and we shall see below that the differences between shareholders are just as important, if not more so, as the changes that have occurred over time. A similar remark applies to the effective tax rate on capital gains. To this end we shall examine the distribution of tax rates between shareholders.

In 1947 the system of taxing profits in the U.K. was reshaped. The rate of profits tax was raised from 5% to 25%, and individuals and partnerships, who were previously liable to the tax, were exempted. The era of the taxation of corporations as such had arrived. From 1 January, 1947 companies were required to pay the standard rate of income tax on all profits (around 45%), plus a differential rate of profits tax which was higher on that portion of profits distributed than on that retained. When a shareholder received his dividends they were deemed to have already borne income tax at the standard rate, and so only if the shareholder were a surtax payer would additional tax be payable and for those paying rates of income tax below the standard rate the difference was refunded.

The impact of this, and the other tax systems which followed it, can be analysed by expressing the total tax liability of the company and shareholders together, in terms of the statutory tax rates imposed, and then comparing this expression with those derived for general tax systems in Section 3.2.

1947–51; *differential profits tax (with profits tax payments deductible for income tax purposes)*. Between January 1947 and December 1951 payments of profits tax were an allowable deduction for income tax purposes. With this system, the tax liability T is given by (with the same notation as that of Section 3.2)

$$T = m_s[Y - p_u(Y - G) - p_d G] + p_u(Y - G) + p_d G + (m - m_s)G \tag{3.39}$$

where m_s is the standard rate of income tax, p_u the rate of profits tax on undistributed profits and p_d the rate of profits tax on distributed profits.

$$\therefore\ T = [m_s + p_u(1 - m_s)]\,Y + [m - m_s + (p_d - p_u)(1 - m_s)]\,G. \tag{3.40}$$

This system is clearly a version of the two-rate system and by comparing this equation with equations (3.6) and (3.7) above, we have, by inspection

$$\tau = m_s + p_u(1 - m_s)$$

$$\theta = \frac{1 - m}{(1 - m_s)(1 + p_d - p_u)}. \tag{3.41}$$

1952–1958; *differential profits tax (with profits tax payments not deductible for income tax purposes)*

In this case we have

$$T = m_s Y + p_u(Y - G) + p_d G + (m - m_s)G$$

$$= (m_s + p_u)Y + (m + p_d - p_u - m_s)G. \tag{3.42}$$

Again by comparing this expression with equations (3.6) and (3.7) we have

$$\tau = m_s + p_u,$$

$$\theta = \frac{1 - m}{1 + p_d - p_u - m_s}. \tag{3.43}$$

1958–64; *flat-rate profits tax* In 1958 the differential element of profits taxation was abolished, and companies paid a single rate of profits tax in addition to the standard rate of income tax. Shareholders whose marginal rate of tax was equal to the standard rate continued to pay no additional tax on their dividends, and those with personal tax rates different from the standard rate either paid an additional amount of income tax on dividends, or received a refund. Under this system the value of T was given by

$$T = (m_s + p)Y + (m - m_s)G \tag{3.44}$$

where p is the single rate of profits tax.

By referring to equation (3.8) it is easy to see that this system was a form of imputation system, and by looking at equation (3.9) we see that in this case

$$\tau = m_s + p,$$

$$\theta = \frac{1 - m}{1 - m_s}. \tag{3.45}$$

1965–73; *corporation tax* In 1965 corporation tax was introduced, and the U.K. adopted a straightforward classical system of corporate taxation. Hence from equation (3.5) we see that

$$\tau = c,$$

$$\theta = 1 - m, \tag{3.46}$$

where c is the rate of corporation tax.

1973– ; *imputation system* In April 1973 the U.K. switched to the imputation system with a rate of imputation equal to the standard rate of income tax. From equation (3.9) we obtain

$$\tau = c,$$

$$\theta = \frac{1 - m}{1 - m_s}. \tag{3.47}$$

The advantage of these expressions is that they set out the different tax systems in terms of variables which allow comparisons to be made over time. For example, the similarities of the imputation system and the flat-rate profits tax system are evident.

The changes that have taken place in corporate taxation can be

Table 3.9 Corporate tax variables, U.K. 1947–75.

Year	τ	$\hat{\theta}$	ACID Test Statistic
1947	0.505	1.581	0.783
1948	0.505	1.581	0.783
1949	0.505	1.570	0.777
1950	0.5275	1.550	0.732
1951	0.5275	1.361	0.643
1952	0.510	1.356	0.664
1953	0.515	1.333	0.647
1954	0.45	1.311	0.721
1955	0.45	1.277	0.702
1956	0.45375	1.190	0.650
1957	0.455	1.183	0.645
1958	0.470	1.521	0.806
1959	0.4875	1.633	0.837
1960	0.50625	1.633	0.806
1961	0.53125	1.633	0.765
1962	0.5375	1.633	0.755
1963	0.5375	1.633	0.755
1964	0.5625	1.667	0.729
1965	0.40	1.527	0.916
1966	0.40	1.0	0.600
1967	0.41875	1.0	0.581
1968	0.44375	1.0	0.556
1969	0.43125	1.0	0.569
1970	0.40625	1.0	0.594
1971	0.40	1.0	0.600
1972	0.40	1.257	0.754
1973	0.49	1.460	0.745
1974	0.52	1.515	0.727
1975	0.52	1.538	0.738

Source: Tables A.1 and A.2 of Appendix A.

seen by examining the behaviour of the basic tax variables, τ and θ. Since θ is a function of the shareholders' personal tax rates, we shall first compare changes over time in the corporate tax system by the variable $\hat{\theta}$ which, it will be recalled, is defined by $\theta = (1 - m)\hat{\theta}$. In this way we may for the moment abstract from changes in the composition of share ownership. Table 3.9 gives the values of the variables τ and $\hat{\theta}$ in the U.K. over the period 1947–75, and they are also shown in Figures 3.3 and 3.4. The tax rates for any given year are those relating to profits earned in, or dividends paid out of profits earned in, the particular year in question. Details of their construction are given in Appendix A.

There have been significant and frequent changes in both variables over time. The value of τ, the tax rate on retained profits, has fluctuated between 40 and 56.25%, and it remained constant in only 8 years with changes occurring in the other 20 years. Changes in the tax discrimination variable $\hat{\theta}$ have been even more marked; they were made in 17 years, with only 11 years witnessing a no-change situation. Moreover, these changes have not occurred in a simple manner. Neither variable followed a time trend for example, and so we might hope that the U.K. experience would enable us to disentangle the effects of changes in tax rates from the effects of changes in other economic variables.

Figure 3.3 Values of τ, U.K. 1947–75

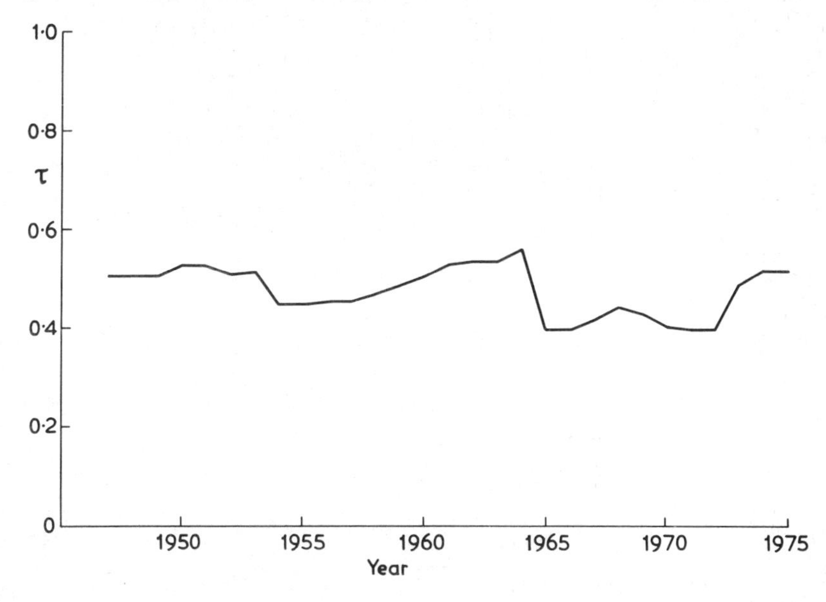

Figure 3.4 Values of $\hat{\theta}$, U.K. 1947–75

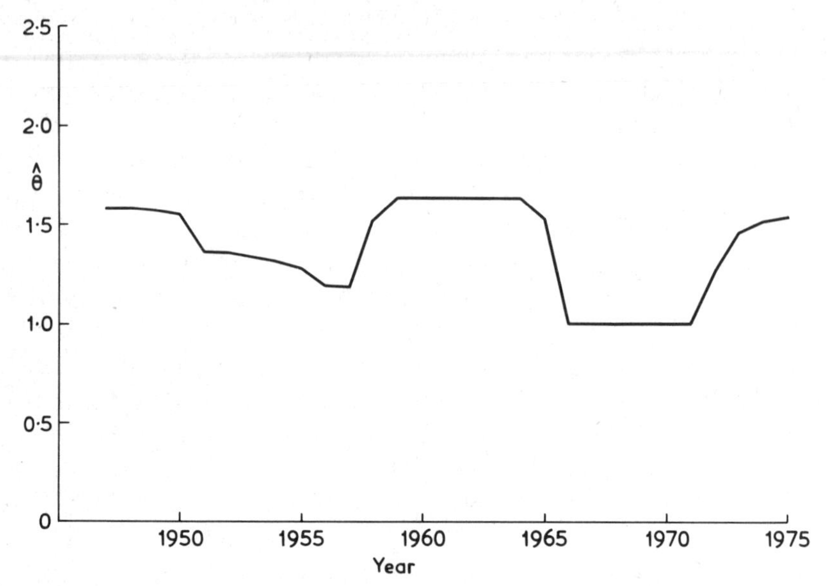

Figure 3.5 shows the behaviour of the ACID Test Statistic in the U.K. also over the period 1947–75. The ACID Test Statistic is the ratio of the maximum net dividend which could be paid after the combined weight of corporate and personal taxation, to the maximum

Figure 3.5 ACID Test Statistic values, U.K. 1947–75

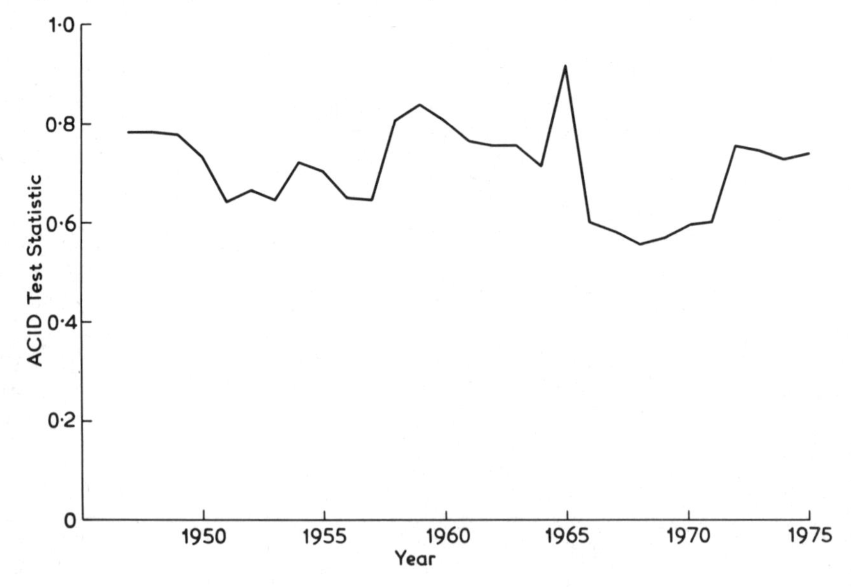

net dividend which could be paid if there were no separate corporate tax system. It measures the additional tax burden on distributed profits resulting from the existence of separate taxation of companies. The ACID Test Statistic too has fluctuated over time, although in a less marked manner than either τ or $\hat{\theta}$. There was a continuous fall in the additional burden of corporate taxation from the early 1950s until 1965 when corporation tax was introduced. Although the value of the ACID Test Statistic rose sharply in 1965 itself, this was the result of generous transitional arrangements which reduced corporate tax liabilities in that year, and the values of the ACID Test Statistic remained low until the tax burden on distributed profits was reduced by the introduction of the imputation system.

Before using these data to test hypotheses about corporate behaviour, we need to know more about the distribution of personal tax rates with which the corporate tax rates interact. The distribution of shareholders' tax rates is a function of two characteristics of the pattern of shareholding. The first is the distinction between different categories of shareholder (persons, pension funds, insurance companies etc.) and the second is the distribution of dividends and capital gains within the personal sector. Appendix A describes the construction of weighted averages of income tax rates and capital gains tax rates for both the personal sector and for shareholders as a class, and the reader is referred to this for details of the calculations.

Our main interest will lie in the incentive effects of the corporate and personal tax system, and so the relevant distribution is the distribution of shareholders' marginal rather than average tax rates. We shall characterize the distribution by its principal summary statistics, the mean, median and mode. The mean marginal tax rate is the weighted average of each shareholders' marginal tax rate where the weights are described in Appendix A. The median and the modal income tax rates on dividends turn out to be equal to the standard rate of income tax in each year for which data were available, 1947–71. The choice of mean or median tax rate will depend on the hypothesis to be tested. In some circumstances a weighted average of shareholders' marginal tax rates will seem appropriate, in others the median may be the relevant concept. Unfortunately little attention is usually paid to the differences *between* shareholders when analysing the behaviour of the firm which they jointly own, and without a theory of how the potentially conflicting desires of shareholders are translated into a collective decision by the firm it is difficult to produce *a priori* arguments for preferring either the mean or the median. The former represents the market's weighting of different shareholders' positions whereas the latter corresponds to decision-taking by majority rule among the shareholders. The issues raised by the existence of differences between shareholders will be discussed further in Chapters 4 and 5. Meanwhile we may note that changes in the pattern of share ownership may affect company behaviour through either the mean or the median tax rate. In the absence of a well-defined theory to focus attention on a particular variable, we should be concerned with the distribution of tax rates in its entirety, but for the purpose of empirical work it is necessary to restrict attention to one or two summary statistics, and we have chosen the mean and median tax rates for this role.

The values of the mean marginal tax rate on personal shareholders, the mean marginal tax rate on shareholders as a whole, and the median marginal tax rate on shareholders are shown in Table A.5 in Appendix A. They are illustrated in Figure 3.6 for the period 1947–71. This shows that for the distribution of tax rates on all shareholders together,

Figure 3.6 Marginal income tax rates on dividends, U.K. 1947–71

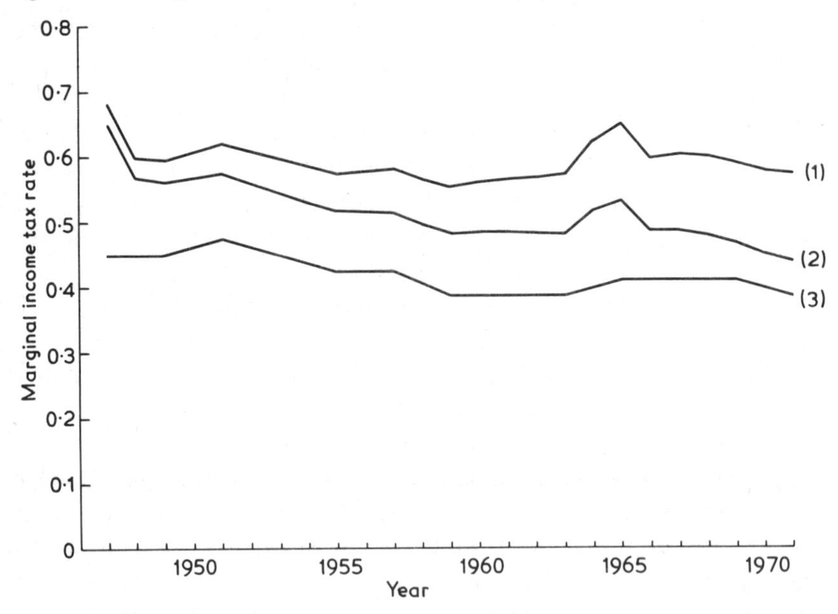

Notes: (1) mean tax rate on persons
(2) mean tax rate on all shareholders
(3) median tax rate on all shareholders

the average marginal tax rate has been falling over time from about 57% at the begining of the period to 45% at the end. This is mainly due to the growth of institutional shareholders who pay either no tax (pension funds) or reduced tax rates (insurance companies). The median tax rate also fell over the period but much less sharply, and we can observe a difference in the trend behaviour of the mean and the median tax rates. This is also reflected in the values of the fundamental tax discrimination variable θ which can now be calculated from the values of $\hat{\theta}$ in Table 3.9 and the values of the income tax rates in Table A.5. Two series for θ may be constructed corresponding to, on the one hand, the average marginal income tax rate on dividends, and on the other hand to the median marginal rates of income tax. We may denote these by θ_a and θ_m respectively. Their values are given in Table A.6 and are plotted in Figure 3.7. The difference between θ_a and θ_m narrowed over the period, which suggests that we might be able to discriminate between hypotheses proposing that either the mean or the median tax rates best measure the influence of shareholders on corporate behaviour.

It is clear that there are quite substantial differences between even the mean and the median values of θ, and that there are much larger differences between the extremes of the distribution, share-

Figure 3.7 Tax discrimination variables, U.K. 1947–71

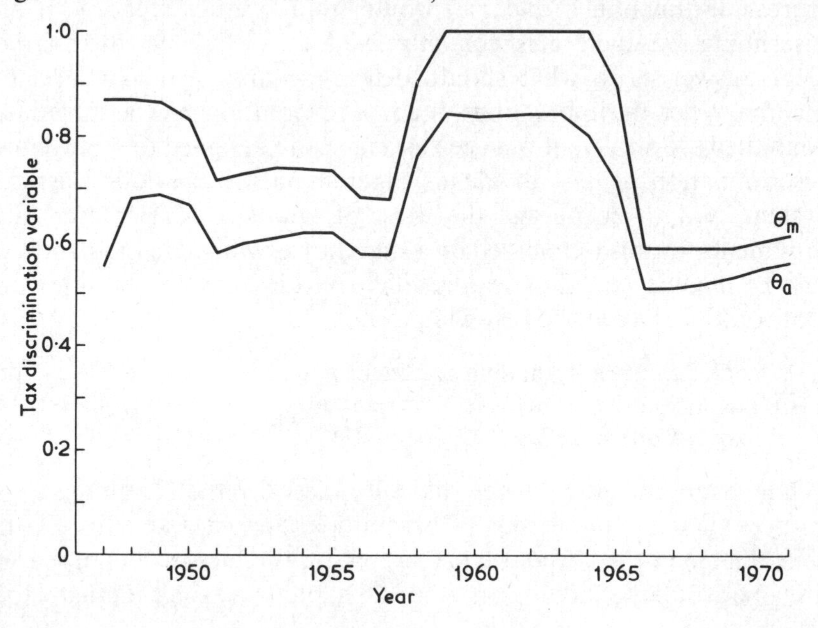

holders such as pension funds who pay no tax having high values of θ, and those paying high rates of tax having low values. In fact it is easy to see that the differences in θ for different types of shareholder are much larger than the changes in θ over time for any one shareholder. This has two important implications.

Firstly, when using a tax discrimination variable in time-series analysis, it is necessary to specify the assumptions being made about the income tax position of the shareholders. A number of econometric studies, (e.g., Feldstein (1970), King (1971)), have used the standard rate of income tax in their specifications without any real justification for so doing. In fact, as we have seen, it turns out that in the period considered by these studies such an assumption corresponds to the belief that the median marginal tax rate is the relevant concept. We shall investigate alternative specifications in succeeding chapters.

Secondly, the value of θ measures the extent of fiscal discrimination between retained earnings and net dividends. We shall leave until Chapter 4 the question of how far this biases the firm's choice of financial policy, but it is already apparent that a 'non-discriminatory tax system' is not a clear-cut concept. To give it meaning we must decide for which particular class of shareholders discrimination should not exist. A system of continuously progressive personal income taxation (in which the marginal rate of tax was a continuous and increasing function of income) would imply that a situation of no discrimination could exist for only *one* level of income; there is no clear answer as to what should determine this particular level of income. When the imputation system of corporation tax was introduced in the U.K. in 1973 it was seen as a measure designed to remove the discrimination against dividends inherent in the previous classical system, and to encourage the issue of new shares. However, the arguments for this were based on a shareholder who paid the standard rate of income tax. This was justified by the Select Committee on Corporation Tax in the following terms:

> Your Committee note the difficulty but base their argument on the position of the standard rate taxpayer for want of any practicable alternative (House of Commons Paper 622, para. 21).

While sympathizing with the difficulty faced by the Committee, we can see that it is dangerous to base any argument about the effects of a change in the corporate tax system on the incentive afforded to any one group of shareholders, and in Chapter 4 we shall see that if the average marginal tax rate had been used the incentive effects of the switch to the imputation system would have looked very different.

The remaining aspect of the U.K. personal tax system to be examined is the taxation of capital gains. In Section 3.3 we examined the impact of capital gains taxation, and in equation (3.38) derived an expression for the average effective tax rate on accrued capital gains denoted by $\bar{e}$. This is a weighted average of the effective tax rates on individuals, $e(m)$, with the weights given by the distribution of accrued gains over income tax brackets. We have no data for this distribution, but we do have data for the distribution of dividends which was used above to calculate the mean and median tax rates on dividends, $\bar{m}$ and $\tilde{m}$ respectively. If we were willing to assume that the distribution of capital gains was the same as that for dividends, we might be able to compute the average and the median EAT Rates on capital gains from equations (3.37) and (3.38).

Appendix A, however, discusses evidence which suggests that the distribution of capital gains differs from that of dividends. Table A.8 contains estimates of the average and median tax rates on capital gains in the U.K. over the period 1965–71 (before 1965 there was no long-term capital gains tax). This shows that the average rate was around 22% and the median rate 30%, the reason for the median exceeding the mean being that there was an upper limit of 30% to the nominal rate of capital gains tax.

Given that we have no direct observations on the distribution function $a_2(m)$ for capital gains, we might proceed by estimating $\bar{e}$ by $e(\bar{m})$ and $\tilde{e}$ by $e(\tilde{m})$. However, as we pointed out in Section 3.3 the value of $\bar{e}$ is equal to $e(\bar{m})$ only if the function $e(m)$ is linear. Since it is nonlinear the average effective tax rate on capital gains is difficult to estimate, and taking a value of $e(\bar{m})$ will involve an error the size of which will depend upon the degree of nonlinearity. The median tax rate, however, is given exactly by $e(\tilde{m})$ since $e(m)$ is a monotonically increasing function of m. We shall use this approach to estimate the values for $\bar{e}$ and $\tilde{e}$, replacing m in (3.37) by the mean and median nominal capital gains tax rates in Table A.8. The final approximation is to choose an appropriate value for $\pi(m)$. In principle this will of course depend on the value of m (see Section 3.3), but our econometric estimates were for aggregate values of the realizations propensity, and in the light of these estimates we will take $\pi = 0.1$ for all shareholders. Given these assumptions, and values for the mean and median nominal capital gains tax rates, (from Table A.8), mean and median

Table 3.10 Mean and median EAT rates, U.K. 1965–71.

Year	$\bar{e}$	$\tilde{e}$
1965	0.184	0.225
1966	0.171	0.222
1967	0.174	0.223
1968	0.167	0.217
1969	0.154	0.206
1970	0.151	0.204
1971	0.149	0.206

Source: Own calculations.

Note: Before 1965 the tax rate was zero. The interest rate used to compute the values of $\bar{e}$ and $\tilde{e}$ from equation (3.37) was the rate on long-dated U.K. Government Securities.

income tax rates, (from Table A.5), and the rate of interest, we may calculate the values of $\bar{e}$ and $\tilde{e}$. These are shown in Table 3.10.

These effective tax rates are significantly lower than the corresponding nominal rates, and very much lower than the corresponding income tax rates. In 1971 the average effective tax rate on capital gains was 14.9%, and the mean income tax rate on all shareholders was 44.1%.

We saw in Section 3.3 that the benefit from taxing capital gains on realization is maximized for shareholders with an income tax rate of m^*, where m^* is given by equation (3.23). It is a function of the ratio of the realizations propensity to the interest rate. If we take a crude point estimate for this ratio of unity, then the value of the income tax rate which affords the maximum benefit from deferral is 58.6%. If we take a simple average of the average marginal income tax rates of personal shareholders over the period for which capital gains tax was in force (1966–71, leaving out 1965 when the tax was introduced during the year), then we find an average rate of 59.2%. This may suggest that those individuals who own shares are likely to be those for whom the tax concessions on capital gains have the greatest value.

We shall return to this matter in the next chapter when the tax rates examined in this chapter will be used to test hypotheses about the effect of taxation on corporate financial policy. It is to this question that we now turn.

Chapter 4

CORPORATE FINANCIAL POLICY

To tax and to please, no more than to love and to be wise, is not given to men (Edmund Burke, 1774).

One of the main reasons advanced by governments, at least in the U.K., for changing the corporate tax system is the desire to promote a different pattern of financing of productive investment. In turn, one of the principal questions raised by those who study the theory of finance is, how does the tax system affect the financial behaviour of corporations, and what is the optimal financial policy for a firm in the face of a variety of personal and corporate taxes?

The answers to these questions will provide a basis for analysing whether changes in the tax system have succeeded in their goal of influencing corporate financial policy, and may provide some clues to explain observed differences in the pattern of financing both over time and between countries. Later, in Chapter 8, we shall be concerned with the influence of the choice of financial policy on the investment decision, and the results of this chapter will be used to show that the optimal investment policy will, in certain circumstances, be a function of the financial policy of the firm. Investment in capital equipment is the link between society's consumption today and its consumption tomorrow. An appreciation of the determinants of the financing of this link can increase our understanding of the process by which intertemporal decisions are made and implemented. For the existence of markets for finance enables a large number of individual investors to share the risks of productive enterprise and participate both in risk-sharing and in the benefits accruing from the future profits of the economy. The means by which control over funds is exercised, whether through private individuals or institutional investors, influences the method by which real investment is financed.

In discussing the finance of investment and the alternative methods of raising capital open to the firm, we shall inevitably be drawn into an evaluation of the role of the stock market and an assessment of its efficiency in allocating resources between competing uses. Many writers have dismissed the stock market as unimportant simply on the grounds that empirical evidence suggests that a very small proportion of new investment is financed externally by issuing shares. Yet, if the use of internal finance is a profit-maximizing policy then the discipline of a perfectly functioning capital market would dictate the need to resort to internal finance to as great a degree as possible. So one of the questions we shall set ourselves below is whether a rational explanation of the observed preponderance of internal finance can be given in terms of optimizing behaviour, or is this phenomenon the result of some innate preference for internal financing on the part of managers?

Throughout the discussion we shall focus on the underlying determinants of the firm's financial strategy, and ignore the difficulties posed by the problem of fluctuating receipts and payments. The timing of money flows into and out of the company will give rise to a time-dependent pattern of corporate liquidity which will require its own policy, particularly with respect to the optimal level of cash balances, but which is different in kind from the long-run financial policy by which the firm decides how capital investment is to be financed. It is the latter with which we shall be concerned.

4.1 *Equilibrium in the capital market*

When examining the operations of the capital market, there are two problems which arise in the particular context of corporate finance. These are the effects of *taxation* on financing decisions, and the difficulty in finding a satisfactory way of modelling the behaviour of capital markets under *uncertainty*. With respect to the first of these, it was demonstrated by Modigliani and Miller (1958) that in the absence of taxes and transactions costs the firm will be indifferent to the method by which it finances its investment plans, because the value of the firm will be independent of the financial policy which it chooses. The existence of taxation will mean that companies will not, in general, be indifferent to the choice of finance. Much of the literature on this subject has been written with the U.S. tax system in mind, and cannot adapt to the question of the effects of a change in the *system* of taxing companies, as opposed to the effects of a change in the *rates* of tax. Since, as we have seen in the previous chapter, most European countries operate systems of company taxation which differ not only from that used in the U.S. but also from each other, we shall try to construct a model which is capable of handling all these different systems.

Uncertainty, however, raises rather deep and fundamental problems for economic analysis. Not the least of these is whether it makes sense to assume that firms maximize profits, (or, more formally, maximize the market value of their shares), in a world of uncertainty. If there is perfect certainty then maximization of the share price is the logical policy for a perfectly competitive firm pursuing the interests of its shareholders to follow, because, by maximizing their wealth this will give shareholders access to the largest possible consumption set. However, this argument does not hold when there is uncertainty about future profits. In this situation there is plenty of room for disagreement about which policy would provide the shareholders with the maximum consumption opportunities, and we shall see later that this poses serious difficulties for the conventional treatment of firms in economic theory.

For this reason Chapter 5 is devoted to the theory of the firm under uncertainty and the role of the stock market. We shall, however, in this chapter take a preliminary look at the relationship between uncertainty and share prices. We shall pursue this theme in the next chapter and also examine one aspect of risk and corporate finance which has attracted a great deal of attention, namely, the extent to which the use of debt finance is restricted by the impact of an increasing debt–equity ratio, known as leverage, on the probability of bankruptcy. Two effects are involved here. Firstly, the preferences of the shareholders, who are in effect the borrowers, may include the leverage of the company, and, secondly, the attitudes of the lenders towards the risk of the company going bankrupt and defaulting on the loan may result in the rate of interest at which the company can borrow being an increasing function of its debt–equity ratio. However, we shall see in Chapter 5 that the conditions under which the debt–equity ratio matters are the same as those under which the axiom that firms maximize profits becomes untenable, and so a mechanistic approach to the 'optimal' debt–equity ratio is inappropriate.

In order to isolate the effect of taxation on financial policy we shall begin by ignoring uncertainty and make use of the assumption of a perfect capital market, in which any firm or individual may either borrow or lend as much as they wish at the given market rate of interest. In reality, of course, the capital market is not an impersonal market in which an economic agent can transact at an externally given price, and the reasons for this are of fundamental importance in understanding the operations of the capital market in a world of uncertainty. The terms on which loans are made will depend very much on the relationship between borrower and lender, their respective wealth, and the latter's expectations of the prospects of the former. Nevertheless, it will prove helpful to sidestep these problems for the time being in order to focus attention on the role of the tax system.

The foundation of the analysis of the firm's choice of financial policy is the fundamental condition for equilibrium in the capital market. This says that in conditions of certainty the yield on investing a given sum of money in any particular asset will be the same as the yield on all other assets, taking into account taxes and transactions costs. For the time being we shall assume transactions costs to be zero. In this case the equilibrium condition is that the yield on investing the money value of a shareholding at the market rate of interest must equal the dividend and the capital gain, all quantities being measured net of tax. Let $V(t)$ be the market value of one of the firm's shares at the beginning of period t, and $d(t)$ the net dividend per share (i.e. cash in the hands of the shareholders after payment of income tax on dividends) which is assumed to be paid out at the end of period t. Capital gains on holding this share during period t are $V(t+1) - V(t)$, and are assumed to be taxed at a rate of capital gains tax given by z. As was commented on in Chapter 3 capital gains are usually taxed only when they are realized and not as they accrue, but we showed that it is possible to convert any given rate of capital gains tax charged on realized gains into an equivalent effective rate on accruals by making some assumptions about desired holding periods for shares. Therefore, we should be concerned with the *effective* rate of tax on accrued capital gains, and an expression for this was derived in equation (3.37). We shall return to this later, but for the moment to simplify the exposition we shall assume that accrued gains are taxed at the rate z.

If m denotes the marginal rate of income tax on unearned income and r the market rate of interest, then, assuming transactions costs are zero, the condition for equilibrium in the capital market is

$$(1 - m)r\,V(t) = d(t) + (1 - z)[V(t+1) - V(t)]. \qquad (4.1)$$

The use of a discrete time model raises the question of what determines the length of 'the period'. This is particularly important in connection with the analysis of announcement effects, where the government may announce certain tax changes in advance. If the period is one day, the announcement effects will be operative one day in advance and the optimal capital stock will be affected for only one day. Such effects would hold little interest. There are good grounds, however, for believing that it is reasonable to take the period as one year. Tax rates remain constant throughout the fiscal year, firms make up annual accounts, and their dividend policy, at least, is regarded as an annual decision. Moreover, the capital stock cannot be altered instantaneously and, although we make no explicit attempt at this stage to introduce costs of adjustment into the model, we shall allow for this by assuming that firms make financing and investment decisions once a year and are thus forced to hold any capital goods they may purchase for this length of time. These considerations will turn out to be of more consequence for the optimal investment decision than for the optimal financial policy of the firm. We may use the fundamental equilibrium condition of (4.1) to describe the firm's optimal financial policy.

4.2 *Taxation and the optimal financial policy*

The starting point of our analysis of the firm's optimal financial policy is the effect of taxation on the firm's decision. There are three ways in which investment can be financed: by retaining profits, by issuing new shares, and by borrowing. Before this century firms had either to rely on their own resources for finance or to borrow from the banks, usually on a short-term basis. New share issues were rare and the 'company promoter' was more interested in making speculative profits on one issue than in building up a continuing business out of managing issues of new shares. The use of long-term external finance and the growth of issuing houses are relatively recent phenomena, and the later development of the capital market has given companies a degree of flexibility in their pattern of financing.

In the analysis of Section 4.2.1 we shall make the following assumptions:

(1) Perfect certainty.

(2) A 'perfect' capital market, in the sense that both companies and individuals may either borrow or lend as much as they want at the given market rate of interest.

(3) Zero transactions costs; this assumption will be relaxed in Section 4.2.3.

(4) Tax rates are constant and uniform across individuals. Differences in tax rates between individuals are discussed in Sections 4.2.2 and 4.2.3.

(5) The firm will prefer policy A to policy B if the current share price corresponding to policy A is higher than the share price for policy B.

(6) The tax system makes no allowance for inflation, the effects of indexing the tax system will be examined in Section 4.2.5.

4.2.1 *Alternative methods of finance*

To examine the firm's choice of financial policy we shall compare in pairs the three alternative methods of finance open to it. Consider any *given* growth path (and its associated profit stream) and the various ways of financing the given level of investment expenditure. For the first comparison let the borrowing policy of the firm be fixed, and consider the choice in any given period (say, period 0) between financing the remainder of investment after borrowing by either retaining profits or issuing new shares. As above, $V(t)$ is defined as the price of a share at the beginning of period t, and dividends and taxes are paid at the end of each period. New shares are assumed to be issued, if at all, at the end of the period *ex dividend* and so are sold at a price equal to the share value at the beginning of the next period. Consequently, the alternative policies are to:

(1) Retain profits and hold the number of shares constant at N, say.

(2) Issue ΔN new shares at a price $V^2(1)$ and increase the net dividends per share (in the hands of the shareholders) from $d^1(0)$ to $d^2(0)$; superscripts refer to the policy being followed.

The proceeds of the new share issue under policy 2 amount to $\Delta N V^2(1)$. Since the two policies simply represent alternative ways of financing the same investment outlay, the amount raised by the issue of new shares under policy 2 must equal the increase in net dividends and tax paid on them implied by that policy. It was shown in Chapter 3 that the extra penalty taxation incurred by paying out an additional $[d^2(0) - d^1(0)]N$ of dividends is equal to $[d^2(0) - d^1(0)]N(1-\theta)/\theta$. Hence

$$\Delta N V^2(1) = [d^2(0) - d^1(0)]N/\theta. \tag{4.2}$$

From the assumption that both policies lead to the same future profit stream, we know that the total value of the equity in period 1 is the same in both cases;

$$V^1(1)N = V^2(1)\,(N + \Delta N). \tag{4.3}$$

Using equations (4.1), (4.2) and (4.3) we obtain

$$V^2(0) - V^1(0) = \frac{\Delta N}{N}\left[\frac{\theta + z - 1}{1 - z + (1 - m)r}\right]V^2(1). \tag{4.4}$$

If the term on the right-hand side of equation (4.4) is positive then policy 2 is the share-price maximizing policy, and if it is negative policy 1 is the optimal policy. The values of $V^2(1)$ and $[1 - z + (1 - m)r]$ are non-negative. Since the firm can choose the value of ΔN, the number of new shares issued, the optimal financial policy is to choose a positive value of ΔN, that is, to issue new shares, when the tax system is such that $\theta + z > 1$, and to choose a negative value of ΔN, in effect to buy back shares, when $\theta + z < 1$.

In the first case, when $\theta + z > 1$, the optimal financial policy is to issue new shares because the capital gains tax rate charged on the gains arising from retaining one unit of post-tax profits exceeds the additional taxation incurred by paying that unit out as dividends and financing investment by issuing new shares. Investment in excess of the fixed amount of new debt raised will therefore be financed from the proceeds of new share issues, and dividends will equal current profits after corporation tax and interest payments. This is not all, however, for equation (4.4) implies that the firm should go further and issue new shares in order to finance higher current dividends. In fact there are two reasons why this is unlikely to occur.

Firstly, new share issues whose purpose was to finance dividends in excess of current net profits would probably be declared illegal. A fundamental principle of company law designed to protect creditors is that the share capital must be maintained, and so it is illegal to pay dividends out of the issued share capital of the company. This constraint must be binding in the long run, although a company which has not capitalized all its reserves may have the freedom in the short run to increase dividend payments if a change in the tax system makes such a policy optimal. An example of a situation in which the revenue authorities would enforce this constraint is the following. Consider the imputation system of corporation tax, and imagine a firm owned by shareholders all of whom faced personal income tax rates below the rate of imputation. Then, when dividends were paid out, they would be entitled to a refund of tax, and if no further constraint were imposed they would be able to recoup all the corporation tax paid by the company by giving money to the company in the form of subscriptions to new shares which would then be returned to the shareholders as dividends. If this were to happen the authorities would either restrict dividends, or change the definition of θ applying to dividends in excess of profits.

Secondly, as more and more new shares are issued to finance dividends the effect of the policy will be to establish a capital loss on existing shares. Equation (4.4) allows us to establish the conditions under which the higher dividend will more than compensate for this capital loss provided that the capital loss is tax deductible. Most tax systems, however, do not provide for full loss offset and this introduces a nonlinearity into the tax system. If the shareholder has no gains on other assets against which he may offset the loss then the condition for further issues of new shares to be optimal becomes $\theta > 1$, which is more stringent than the original condition that $\theta + z > 1$. Hence, at some point it will no longer be optimal to issue new shares. We shall assume below that firms face the constraint that dividends must be less than, or equal to, current profits after tax and interest payments.

The second case is where $\theta + z < 1$, when the optimal policy is for the company to finance investment out of retained earnings rather than by issuing new shares because the capital gains tax rate is less than the penalty tax rate on dividends. In effect, the shareholders are receiving income in the form of capital gains in preference to income in the form of dividends. Again, this is not the end of the story because equation (4.4) shows that it is optimal for the firm to use any retained earnings surplus to its investment requirements for the purpose of repurchasing shares from the shareholders, instead of paying dividends. This policy has the effect of converting dividends to capital gains because the total value of the equity in equation (4.3) is divided between a smaller number of shares. It would even be optimal to pay a negative dividend and use the proceeds to repurchase shares.

These policies, however, would certainly be illegal for two reasons. Firstly, negative dividends, that is, a compulsory calling up of capital beyond the liability foreseen by the shareholder as represented by his original investment, are prohibited by law. Secondly, in some countries, the U.K. for example, it is illegal for a company to purchase its own shares unless a special Court Order is obtained (which would not be granted where the purpose was tax avoidance), and in other countries, such as the U.S., the proceeds from share repurchases are taxed as dividends where a policy of repurchase appears to be equivalent to paying a dividend. This removes the incentive for a company to buy back its own shares. The second set of constraints facing a firm, then, are that it may not repurchase its own shares, and its dividend must be non-negative. Legal constraints are necessary to prevent firms successfully pursuing policies of tax avoidance made possible by differential taxation of dividends, capital gains, and interest income. These possibilities would not arise in a tax system which was neutral with respect to the choice of financial policy, and so the conditions for neutrality will be examined below in Section 4.2.4.

Given the existence of these constraints we may summarize the results so far. For a given borrowing policy the optimal financing decision is:

(1) if $\theta + z > 1$, investment is financed entirely by new issues, all net profits being paid out as dividends

(2) if $\theta + z < 1$, investment is financed from retentions. Surplus retentions are distributed but if retained profits are inadequate then the firm resorts to external finance for the remainder.

The company is indifferent to its method of finance if and only if $\theta + z = 1$. Before exploring the implications of these results for particular tax systems, we shall complete our analysis of the effects of taxation on financial policy by proceeding to examine the other pairwise comparisons of policies.

The second pairwise comparison is between the two forms of external finance, borrowing and issuing new shares. For any *given* level of retentions the alternative policies are:

(1) Issue ΔN^1 new shares at the end of period 0 at a price of $V^1(1)$.

(2) Borrow an amount $\Delta N^1 V^1(1)$ at the end of period 0, repaying the principal and interest one period later.

In order to evaluate the desirability of using debt rather than equity finance in period 0, it is necessary to consider a one period loan the principal of which is repaid out of equity at the end of period 1. Since we are comparing two sources of external finance for a given level of retentions, the loan must be repaid by issuing new shares. This provides the appropriate basis for comparison. Furthermore, the fact that the two policies assume the same level of retentions means that they imply the same level of dividend payments in period 0. Hence from equation (4.1) we have

$$V^2(0) - V^1(0) = (1/\alpha)[V^2(1) - V^1(1)] \tag{4.5}$$

where $$\alpha = 1 + \left(\frac{1-m}{1-z}\right)r.$$

At the end of period 1 the interest payments on the loan taken out under policy 2 equal the difference in total dividends and taxes between the two policies.

$$(N + \Delta N^1)\frac{d^1(1)}{\theta} = N\frac{d^2(1)}{\theta} + \beta r \Delta N^1 V^1(1), \tag{4.6}$$

where
$$\beta = \begin{cases} 1-\tau & \text{if interest payments are deductible for corporate tax purposes,} \\ 1 & \text{if interest payments are not tax deductible.} \end{cases}$$

To repay the loan under policy 2, ΔN^2 new shares are issued at the end of period 1 at an issue price of $V^2(2)$. The amount raised is just sufficient to repay the loan, hence

$$\Delta N^1 V^1(1) = \Delta N^2 V^2(2). \tag{4.7}$$

Having paid off the loan the value of the equity in period 2 is the same for both policies and so we have

$$(N + \Delta N^1) V^1(2) = (N + \Delta N^2) V^2(2). \tag{4.8}$$

Some algebraic manipulation of equations (4.1), (4.5), (4.6), (4.7) and (4.8), yields

$$V^2(0) - V^1(0) = \frac{r}{\alpha^2}\cdot\frac{V^1(1)}{1-z}\cdot\frac{\Delta N^1}{N}(1 - m - \theta\beta). \tag{4.9}$$

If the right-hand side of equation (4.9) is positive, then policy 2 is the policy which maximizes the share price, and if it is negative policy 1 is the optimal policy. Consequently, we can see that investment will be financed by issuing new shares if

$$1 - m < \theta\beta. \tag{4.10}$$

The interpretation of this condition is clear. If a shareholder subscribes to an issue of new shares instead of lending his savings at the market rate of interest, then, by giving up $(1 - m)$ units of net interest payments he can receive $\theta\beta$ units of net dividends.

Moreover, if this condition holds it will be optimal to issue new shares not only to finance current investment, but also to wipe out existing debt. There is no legal obstacle to the issue of new shares in order to redeem outstanding debt provided that this is the stated purpose of the share issue. In fact it would even be optimal for the firm to issue new shares and lend out the proceeds at the market rate of interest thus accumulating financial assets in addition to physical assets. This possibility seems to call into question the very nature of the firm as a productive, as opposed to a financial, institution. If exercised on a large scale, such a policy might also be construed as being *ultra vires*, and hence in U.K. company law illegal.

In practice, however, we need not worry too much about this problem. Consider the case where interest payments are deductible against corporation tax so that $\beta = 1 - \tau$. Then the strict inequality (4.10) would never be satisfied – recall the definition of the ACID Test Statistic which by constraint (3.12) must be less than or equal to unity. In this case the problem would never arise, and since corporate tax systems in practice do allow interest payments as a deduction we would not expect to observe the phenomenon. However, suppose that the system were changed to remove interest-deductibility, then issuing new shares to finance lending operations by the firm would be profitable providing

(1) $\theta > 1 - m$, which is clearly possible (under the imputation system, for example), and

(2) the treatment of interest is symmetric so that interest income is not taxed to corporation tax if interest payments are not tax deductible.

There would be an incentive for individuals to form companies through which to channel all their lending, although such lending would have to be to other individuals or to the government, because by the same token companies would have no incentive to borrow. For example, consider the situation of an imputation system and a firm whose shareholders paid personal income tax at the rate of imputation (in the U.K. this would be the standard rate of tax). If corporate interest income were not taxed, the shareholders could give money to the company as a share subscription, and the company could lend the money tax free, and return the interest receipts to the shareholders in the form of dividends without either company or shareholder incurring any tax liability. In fact, if the shareholders paid lower rates of tax they would actually receive a refund. In these circumstances the revenue authorities would have to withdraw the benefits of imputation; indeed the whole concept of 'imputation' makes little sense if corporate income is not charged to corporation tax. We can therefore assume that condition (4.10) holds only in the range where new shares are issued to finance real investment and to repay existing debt.

If the inequality sign in equation (4.10) is reversed, the optimal policy is for the company to buy back shares but if, as before, we rule out such a policy, then the company will simply finance all investment by borrowing. When a new company is formed it will be started with the minimum equity stake and the remaining initial capital will be raised by borrowing.

This brings us to the final comparison which is between financing investment by retaining profits or by borrowing for a given level of new share issues (which for the sake of simplicity we shall assume to be zero). The alternative policies are:

(1) Retain profits, and pay a net dividend per share of $d^1(0)$ at the end of period 0.

(2) Borrow in period 0, paying a dividend of $d^2(0)$, and repay the principal and interest at the end of period 1. For this pairwise comparison, with new share issues taken as given, the loan is repaid by increasing retentions and hence lowering dividends in period 1.

Because the two policies finance the same investment outlay the amount borrowed under policy 2 is equal to $[d^2(0) - d^1(0)]N/\theta$, that is, the difference in dividends and taxes between the two policies. At the end of period 1 the cash flow constraint is that

$$\frac{d^1(1)}{\theta} = \frac{d^2(1)}{\theta} + (1 + \beta r)\left[\frac{d^2(0) - d^1(0)}{\theta}\right]. \tag{4.11}$$

The value of the equity in period 2 is the same in both cases, and hence $V^1(2)$ equals $V^2(2)$. Using both this result and equations (4.1) and (4.11) we have

$$V^2(0) - V^1(0) = \frac{[d^2(0) - d^1(0)]}{\alpha^2(1 - z)}[\alpha - (1 + \beta r)]. \tag{4.12}$$

Since policy 2 allows the firm to pay a higher dividend in period 0 than under policy 1, we can see that policy 2 will maximize the share price when $(\alpha - 1 - \beta r)$ is positive, that is when,

$$1 - m > (1 - z)\beta. \tag{4.13}$$

The explanation of this condition too is straightforward. By using retentions instead of debt a shareholder gives up $(1 - m)$ units of net interest payments, the effective cost of which to the company is β, and receives an amount $(1 - z)\beta$ in the form of capital gains.

If equation (4.13) is satisfied, the optimal policy is to borrow as much as possible, not only to finance investment but also to pay out higher dividends. This means that we must again impose the constraint that dividends cannot exceed current equity earnings after tax, in which case the optimal policy is to distribute all profits and borrow an amount equal to the value of desired investment.

When the inequality sign in equation (4.13) is reversed, the optimal policy is to finance investment from retained earnings and to use any excess retentions to redeem debt. There is also an incentive to use retentions to accumulate financial assets, at least for those shareholders with high marginal rates of tax on investment income. In this way the company can lend on behalf of the shareholders who may prefer to accept the combined burden of corporation tax and capital gains tax instead of full income tax on their investment income. Such avoidance possibilities are constrained by the authorities either by the prohibition of the accumulation of funds which are in excess of the needs of the business, or by the imposition of additional taxes on such funds. The need for these restrictions is likely to be particularly great for small, or 'close' companies which are owned and managed by a small group of individuals. In larger firms, with a dispersed body of shareholders, many shareholders will not have sufficiently high income tax rates to make this sort of financial operation attractive. We shall model the restrictions by assuming the following two legal constraints; firstly, that the level of debt must be non-negative, and secondly, that retentions cannot be increased by paying negative dividends.

It is clear, therefore, that the existence of differential tax rates on various forms of investment income creates a need for a number of legal restrictions on the financial policy of corporations. The model explored above suggests the sorts of restrictions which would be necessary, and many of these constraints can be found in existing corporate tax legislation.

4.2.2 *The optimal policy*

We may now draw together the results derived above, and describe

Table 4.1 Optimal financial policy: (a) assuming interest deductibility.

Source of funds	All corporate tax systems
Retentions	$m \geqslant \tau + z(1-\tau)$
Debt	$\tau + z(1-\tau) \geqslant m$
New issues	

Note: The firm would be indifferent to the choice between debt and new issues in the following two limiting cases, (1) under the imputation system when $s = \tau$, and (2) under the two-rate system when $c_d = 0$.

the optimal financial policy of the firm. Consider first the case where interest payments are deductible against corporation tax. This provision seems to be common to most corporate tax systems in practice. Given this assumption, and those set out at the beginning of Section 4.2, it turns out that the optimal financial policy is independent of the system of corporation tax. This is shown in Table 4.1 which illustrates the financial policy under each of the independent systems of corporation tax. We defer discussion of the fully integrated system until Section 4.2.4.

From the table it is apparent that for shareholders whose marginal rate of tax on unearned income is above a certain critical value, retentions are preferred to the use of debt finance. Shareholders whose income tax rates are below this value would prefer the company to borrow. It is interesting to note that it is never optimal to issue new shares (except in the limiting cases mentioned in the note to Table 4.1). This is because, as we have seen when discussing the interpretation of equation (4.10), the interest deductibility provision means that debt will always be preferred to new share issues.

The critical value of the personal income tax rate above which retentions are preferred to debt depends on the corporate tax rate and the system of capital gains taxation. We may distinguish three cases:

(1) No capital gains taxation ($z = 0$). In this case retentions are preferred to debt when $m > \tau$, that is, when the personal tax rate exceeds the corporate tax rate.

(2) Full capital gains taxation ($z = m$). When capital gains are taxed at the same rate as income, debt finance is always preferred to the use of retained earnings.

(3) Concessionary capital gains taxation ($0 \leqslant z \leqslant m$). If capital gains are taxed at all they are normally taxed at concessionary rates. For example, in the U.S. and the U.K. it is a reasonable approximation

to assume that capital gains are taxed at one half the rate of income tax. In the general case where $z = \lambda m$, retentions are preferred to debt when

$$m > \frac{\tau}{1 - \lambda(1 - \tau)}. \tag{4.14}$$

For the U.K. and the U.S. $\lambda = 0.5$ and the condition becomes $m > 2\tau/(1 + \tau)$. For example, if the corporate tax rate is 50% then for retentions to be used the personal tax rate must exceed two-thirds.

It should be remembered that z is the effective tax rate on accrued capital gains which, in general, will be less than the nominal rate on realized capital gains, and this can be considered as equivalent to a reduction in the value of λ. An estimate of the effective tax rate can be made using the model suggested in Chapter 3. We shall take up this point when we come to discuss the optimal choice of equity finance, but in order to illustrate the potential quantitative importance of this effect Table 4.2 shows, for several typical values of λ and the corporate tax rate, the critical values of the income tax rate above which shareholders facing this critical rate prefer the firm to finance investment from retentions instead of from debt.

Clearly, given the evidence on the distribution of marginal tax rates of U.K. shareholders discussed in Chapter 3, a substantial number of shareholders would prefer the firm to use internal finance rather than debt finance, *even if* there were no costs attached to a high debt–equity ratio. We shall defer discussion of the evidence on the actual pattern of finance used by firms until Chapter 7.

We turn now to consider the optimal financial policy in tax systems where interest payments by companies are not tax deductible. With this provision β takes on the value of unity in equations (4.10) and

Table 4.2 Critical values of the income tax rate above which retentions are preferred to debt.

τ \ λ	0	0.25	0.5	1.0
0.30	0.30	0.36	0.46	1.00
0.40	0.40	0.47	0.57	1.00
0.50	0.50	0.57	0.67	1.00
0.60	0.60	0.67	0.75	1.00

Table 4.3 Optimal financial policy: (b) no interest deductibility.

Source of Funds	System of company taxation		
	Classical	Imputation	Two-rate
Retentions	$m \geqslant z$	$m \geqslant s + z(1-s)$	$m \geqslant c_u - c_d + z(1 + c_d - c_u)$
Debt	Indifferent	—	—
New issues	when $z \geqslant m$	$s + z(1-s) \geqslant m$	$c_u - c_d + z(1 + c_d - c_u) \geqslant m$

Note: (a) See Chapter 3 for an explanation of the notation.
(b) The Table is constructed under the assumption that both the imputation system and the two-rate system alleviate part of the tax burden on dividends, in other words that $s \geqslant 0$ and $c_u \geqslant c_d$. If, on the other hand, these systems were designed to increase the tax burden on dividends by setting $s < 0$ or $c_d > c_u$, then the optimal policy would be to use retentions when $m \geqslant z$, and debt when $z \geqslant m$. New shares would never be issued.

(4.13). The optimal financial policy in these circumstances is shown in Table 4.3, and in this case it clearly depends on the system of corporation tax as measured by the variable θ, (the expressions for θ under different tax systems are given in Chapter 3).

The lack of any provision for interest deductibility removes the incentive to use debt finance which now disappears from the optimal financial policy altogether, except under the classical system where issuing new shares or borrowing is immaterial to the firm. This has the consequence that issuing new shares is the optimal policy for shareholders whose marginal tax rates are below the level shown in Table 4.3. In the absence of the interest deductibility provision the optimal financial policy is a choice between the two forms of equity capital, retentions or new issues. This choice is examined in more detail in the next section.

The general conclusions of this section are:

(1) the interaction between the personal and the corporate tax systems is important in determining the optimal financial policy.

(2) the optimal financial policy of a firm depends upon the marginal income tax rates of its shareholders.

(3) the use of debt finance is entirely the result of the tax deductibility provision for interest payments.

(4) the disincentive to the issue of new shares derives not from a system of company taxation which discriminates against dividends, but from the interest deductibility provision for debt finance.

4.2.3 *The optimal choice of equity finance*

We have seen that the interest deductibility provision for debt finance is, given the assumptions made above, a sufficient condition for new share issues never to be a strictly preferred form of financing. Since this provision is in practice very common, it suggests that the often-quoted stylized fact that new share issues are a relatively minor source of finance is not at all surprising, and is indeed the predictable result of profit-maximizing behaviour.

It is obvious, however, that there is a limit to the extent to which debt finance can be used, and it is the existence of a constraint on a firm's debt–equity ratio which creates a possible role for new share issues. We shall discuss the constraints on the use of debt below, and in this section we focus solely on the choice between the two methods of equity financing, taking the borrowing decision as given. We have seen above that retentions will be preferred to new share issues when

$$\theta + z < 1. \tag{4.15}$$

For the classical system this reduces to the condition that $m > z$, which is certainly satisfied except in those countries where in a few cases $m = z$. However, in no case would new share issues ever be preferred to retentions under the classical system. With the imputation and two-rate systems, however, the condition is more interesting. Since the two systems are equivalent when $s = c_u - c_d$, we shall develop the discussion in terms of the imputation system. Retentions will now be the preferred source of finance when

$$\frac{1-m}{1-s} < 1 - z. \tag{4.16}$$

The choice is illustrated in Figure 4.1. The line OB is a plot of z as a function of m (assuming $z = \lambda m$), and AC is a plot of $1 - \theta$ as a function of m. The two lines intersect at X at a value for m of m_c, say. At rates of income tax below m_c, AC lies below OB and new share issues are a cheaper source of finance than retentions. For income tax rates above m_c, OB lies below AC and retentions are the preferred method of financing. The value of m_c is the critical value of the income tax rate at which there is indifference between the two sources of finance. It is clearly at least as great as the rate of imputation (in the U.K. this is the standard rate of tax) because AC cuts the x axis at $m = s$. By rotating the line OB about the origin through the arc between the x axis and

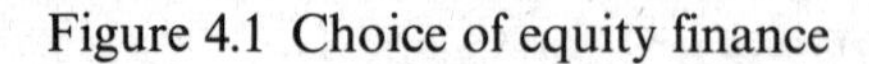
Figure 4.1 Choice of equity finance

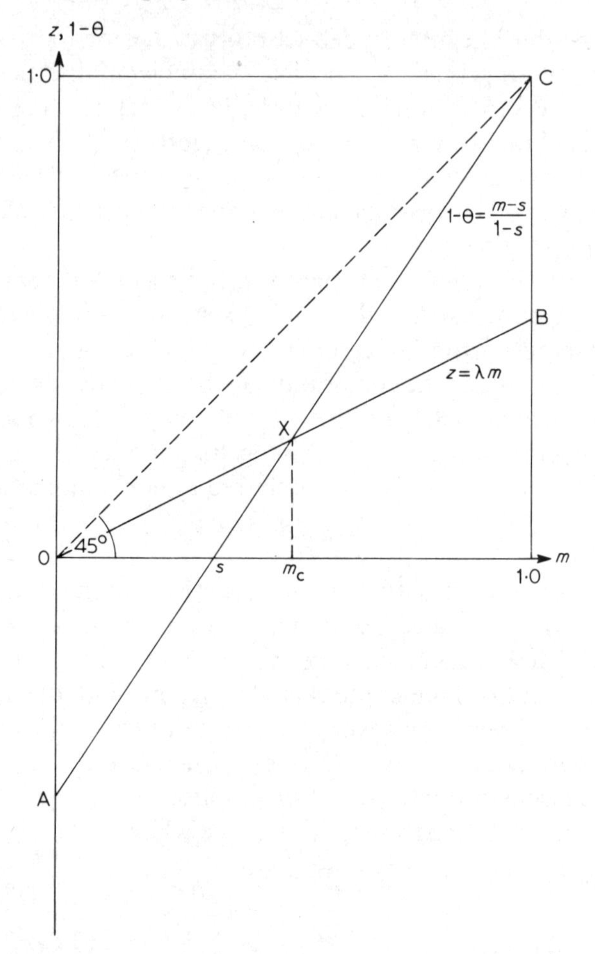

OC, (the 45° line), it is possible to trace out the values of m_c corresponding to different rate structures for capital gains tax lying between zero and taxation at full income tax rates.

For the sake of completeness we may note that under the classical system the graph of $1 - \theta$ is simply the 45° line, which never lies below the line OB, indicating that new share issues will never be preferred to retentions.

From equation (4.16) we know that the value of m_c is given by

$$m_c = 1 - (1 - s)(1 - z). \tag{4.17}$$

If we assume that $z = \lambda m$, then

$$m_c = \frac{s}{1 - \lambda(1 - s)}. \tag{4.18}$$

A numerical example may help to illustrate the meaning of this expression. In the U.K. the rate of imputation is about 1/3, and capital gains are taxed at one half the rate of income tax subject to an upper limit of 30%. Now if $s = 1/3$ and $\lambda = 1/2$, $m_c = 50\%$. Consequently, shareholders whose income tax rates are above 50% will prefer the firm to finance by retentions, and shareholders whose income tax rates are below 50% will prefer to see new shares being issued. The shareholders can be divided into two groups according to their tax position, one group preferring investment to be financed externally by new share issues and with profits paid out as dividends, the other preferring profits to be retained and investment financed internally. The value of m_c is the income tax rate forming the dividing line between these two groups.

So far we have ignored transactions costs. Yet transactions in shares may give rise to quite substantial transactions costs both for the company and for the shareholders. As far as the company is concerned a new share issue would normally be made through an issuing house which would charge a commission for its services. The new shares might be issued by tender, or the issuing house might arrange for the issue to be underwritten, in which case a number of financial institutions would undertake to purchase any shares left unsold after the public demand had been satisfied in return for a commission. Alternatively, there might be a rights issue of shares which is an issue to existing shareholders only, in proportion to the number of shares they already hold. This procedure reduces the transactions costs involved, and, not surprisingly, therefore, many new issues take the form of rights issues. Many of the costs involved are overhead costs (for example, commission fees, legal and advertising expenses, Stock Exchange fees), and there are substantial

Table 4.4 New issue costs, U.K. 1971 (per cent).

Size of issue (£ million)	< 0.5	0.5–1.0	> 1.0	All issues
Costs as % of issue size	9.77	8.05	4.94	6.91

Source: Davis and Yeomans (1974; Table IA.1).

Table 4.5 New issue costs, U.S. 1951–5 (average) (per cent).

Size of issue ($ million)	0.5–0.9	1.0–1.9	2.0–4.9	5.0–9.9	10.0–
Costs as % of issue size	10.24	8.00	3.33	1.53	1.33

Source: Benston (1969; Table VII).

economies of scale in new issue costs. This can be seen from the estimates of new issue costs as a percentage of the issue size for the U.K. and the U.S. shown in Tables 4.4 and 4.5. The figures relate to shares publicly offered for sale and probably represent an upper bound to average issue costs. The tables show clearly that in both countries there are significant economies of scale in transactions costs, which suggests that new issues are more likely to be used the larger the capital requirement of the firm.

Shareholders may incur transactions costs either when buying new shares, or when buying or selling existing shares if the payout ratio is either too high or too low to satisfy current consumption needs. The commission charges on transactions in shares, however, are relatively small and we shall ignore them. In the U.K. these charges range from 1.5% on the value of small transactions to 0.125% on large transactions.

The existence of new issue costs makes new share issues a less attractive method of raising finance. If the fraction of the proceeds of a new share issue which are absorbed by transactions costs is denoted by f, then in the analysis of the optimal choice of equity finance equation (4.2) becomes

$$(1-f)\,\Delta N\, V^2(1) = [d^2(0) - d^1(0)]\,N/\theta. \tag{4.19}$$

The condition for new issues to be the preferred source of finance is now

$$\theta(1-f) + z > 1. \tag{4.20}$$

As before, retentions are the optimal source of finance under the classical system, and under the imputation system the critical income tax rate at which there is indifference between the two sources of equity finance is given by

$$m_c = \frac{s-f}{1-f-\lambda(1-s)}. \tag{4.21}$$

In the example given above where $s = 1/3$ and $\lambda = 1/2$, the value of m_c in the absence of transactions costs was 50%. If we introduce transactions costs and take $f = 6.91\%$ (the average value for the U.K. given in Table 4.4) then the value of m_c falls to 44.2%. Transactions costs thus reduce the probability of observing issues of new shares.

A second factor producing a tendency in this direction is the taxation of capital gains only on realization, which means that the effective tax rate (the EAT Rate) is less than the nominal rate. This phenomenon was discussed extensively in Chapter 3 where estimates of the average EAT Rates in the U.K. from 1965 (when capital gains tax was introduced) to 1971 were presented. In 1971 the average EAT Rate on U.K. shareholders was 14.9%. If we substitute this value for z in equations (4.17) and (4.20) we obtain estimates of the critical income tax rate of 43.3% if we ignore transactions costs, and of 39.1% using a value for f of 6.91%. These compare with the following actual income tax rates of U.K. shareholders in 1971 which were discussed in Chapter 3; an average marginal rate of 44.1%, and a median marginal rate of 38.8%. It is clear from this comparison that for the 'average' shareholder the switch to the imputation system in the U.K. in 1973 still left retentions as the cheaper source of finance. The tax discrimination against new share issues was reduced by the change, but not eliminated for a large number of shareholders. There is, therefore, little reason to believe that the switch to the imputation system could have been expected to have led to a major change in the pattern of company financing. The policy chosen by the firm under the imputation system depends on how the conflicting wishes of the two groups of shareholders (those with income tax rates above and below the critical rate) are resolved.

Is there any way to reconcile the conflict that exists between two groups of shareholders whose desired policies differ? One solution would be to reward the group facing low tax rates with dividends, and the group facing high tax rates with capital gains. This was tried in the U.K. by some companies which offered shareholders the option of either a cash dividend or a number of shares with value equal to that of the cash dividend. The latter form of payment was called a 'scrip dividend'. However, in April 1975 these operations were described as tax avoidance and made illegal, and scrip dividends were deemed to be income for tax purposes. At the same time it was made illegal to issue a separate class of shares which could receive payment in the form of stock instead of cash. This means that management cannot adopt financial policies which satisfy all the shareholders, and some way must be found of reaching a satisfactory collective decision. These problems would disappear if the tax system were neutral.

4.2.4 *A neutral tax system*

From our previous discussion it is quite clear that a tax system which is not neutral with respect to the different sources of finance creates a need for legal constraints on financial policy to prevent tax avoidance, and encourages companies to devote real resources to discovering ways of converting one kind of income into another in order to minimize tax liabilities. This involves a real cost both on the part of companies and on that of the revenue authorities. The process is rather like an iterative game whereby companies devise new legal means of avoiding tax and then in their turn the authorities step in to impose a new legal constraint. In fact, in the U.K. such legislation became so complex that the authorities decided to adopt wide-ranging powers which provided that:

> where in consequence of any transaction in securities a person obtains a tax advantage, then unless it is shown that the transaction was undertaken for bona fide commercial reasons or in the ordinary course of making or managing investments the tax advantage may be counteracted by an additional assessment. The generality and subjectivity of this provision in its turn has occasioned a huge mass of conflicting case-law on the topic, and increasing confusion as to the likely incidence of tax liability (Hadden, 1972).

There is, therefore, a strong case for examining the conditions under which the tax system will be neutral. A tax system is defined to be neutral if it provides no incentive for the shareholders of a firm to prefer one method of financing to another. Furthermore, this must hold (a) for all three forms of financing, and (b) for all shareholders, which implies that the system must be neutral for all possible values of the personal income tax rate.

A firm will be indifferent towards its choice of financial policy when the inequalities (4.10), (4.13) and (4.15), are exact equalities, which occurs when

$$\begin{aligned} \theta + z &= 1 \\ 1 - m &= \beta\theta \\ 1 - m &= \beta(1 - z). \end{aligned} \tag{4.22}$$

Obviously, only two of these equations are independent, and, if we ignore the last equation, the first two can be solved to provide conditions for neutrality. These conditions are presented for each of the systems of company taxation distinguished in Chapter 3. It is clear from inspection of equation (4.22) that, given the assumptions of this chapter, a firm would not care about its financial policy in the absence of taxation, as the Modigliani and Miller (1958) result, referred to at the beginning of this chapter, states.

The classical system Substituting the value of $\theta = 1 - m$ in the above equations yields the conditions

$$\text{(a)}\ m = z \tag{4.23}$$

$$\text{(b)}\ \beta = 1. \tag{4.24}$$

For the classical system to be neutral capital gains must be taxed as income, and no deductibility provision extended to interest payments.

The imputation system In this case the two conditions become

$$\frac{1-m}{1-z} = 1 - s \tag{4.25}$$

$$\beta = 1 - s. \tag{4.26}$$

If we rule out the trivial case where $s = 0$ (which is where the imputation system reduces to the classical system), then the first equation demonstrates that in general an imputation system cannot be neutral, because the values of m and z depend upon the individual shareholder, whereas the value of s, the rate of imputation, is common to all shareholders. Only in the special case where all shareholders faced the same tax rate could a value for s be found which would produce neutrality. The second equation shows that a necessary condition for neutrality is that interest payments are deductible only against the rate of tax used to define the rate of imputation, not against the corporate tax rate (if the two rates are different, as, in general, they will be). In effect this means that the imputation system is extended to cover interest payments as well as dividends. Even if this were done, however, a neutral rate of imputation could be defined only in the special case where all shareholders faced the same personal tax rate, in which case the neutral value of s could be calculated from equation (4.25), and would depend upon both the rate of income tax and the rate of capital gains tax. For example, if the common rate of income tax was 40%, and capital gains were taxed at one half that rate, the appropriate rate of imputation would be 25%.

The two-rate system The conditions for neutrality are

$$\frac{1-m}{1-z} = 1 + c_d - c_u \tag{4.27}$$

$$\beta = 1 + c_d - c_u. \tag{4.28}$$

The results for the two-rate system are exactly parallel to those for the imputation system. Again, leaving aside the trivial case where $c_d = c_u$, neutrality can only be obtained in the case where shareholders face the same tax rate. Assuming this to be the case, the simplest version of a neutral two-rate system would be to set $c_d = 0$, maintain interest deductibility, and calculate the implied value of c_u from equation (4.27).

The integrated system Since the aim of the integrated system is to unify corporate and personal taxation we would expect to find that it satisfied the property of neutrality. It will be recalled that under the integrated system $\tau = m$, and $\theta = 1$ (equation (3.11)), so that for neutrality we require

$$z = 0 \tag{4.29}$$

$$\beta = 1 - m. \tag{4.30}$$

These conditions are satisfied if interest payments are allowed as a deduction for tax purposes ($\beta = 1 - \tau$), and if capital gains tax is not charged on gains arising out of retained profits. This can be achieved by increasing the acquisition cost of a shareholding by the imputed retained earnings allocated to the holding, and the adjusted acquisition cost can then be used to calculate the capital gains arising from other sources (for example, changes in 'goodwill' or interest rates).

Only the classical and integrated systems, therefore, are capable of achieving neutrality with respect to the choice of financial policy for any value of the income tax rate. The imputation and two-rate systems could be neutral only if there were a single rate of personal income tax.

The final remark to be made is that if the personal tax system were to be based on expenditure and not on income, (which is equivalent to setting $m = z = 0$), it is easy to see that the neutral corporate tax system which is appropriate for an expenditure tax consists of a classical system without an interest deductibility provision.

4.2.5. *An inflation-proof tax system*

So far we have assumed that the tax system takes no account of the rate of inflation, and it is evident from the preceding analysis that, in a system which is not indexed for inflation, the optimal financial policy is independent of the rate of inflation. When the tax system is indexed for inflation this result is still true, even though the benefits of indexation are given against different tax rates. For example, in the case of shares it is normally assumed that indexation would be given on capital gains, whereas with receipts of interest income the adjustment would take the form of taxing only those receipts representing the real rate of interest earned. If this were the case then with indexation equation (4.1) would become

$$rV(t) - m(r - \rho)V(t) = d(t) + V(t+1) - V(t) - z[V(t+1) - (1+\rho)V(t)], \quad (4.31)$$

where ρ is the rate of inflation. Income tax is charged only on real interest receipts and capital gains tax only on real gains, which are calculated by increasing the acquisition cost of the holding by the rate of inflation and subtracting this adjusted acquisition cost from the current market value. We can rewrite equation (4.31) as

$$V(t+1) = \alpha' V(t) - \frac{d(t)}{1-z}, \quad (4.32)$$

where $\alpha' = 1 + \rho + \dfrac{1-m}{1-z}(r - \rho)$, which reduces to $1 + r$ when $m = z$.

The remaining aspect of indexation to be considered is the deductibility of corporate interest payments. Under a fully indexed tax system in which individuals are taxed only on receipts of real interest payments, companies would be allowed to deduct for corporate tax purposes only their real interest payments and not the full nominal amount. One way of achieving this is to add to a company's taxable income the fall in the real value of its net monetary liabilities while retaining deductibility of interest payments. The effect of this is that the cost of borrowing one unit becomes, assuming interest deductibility, not $r - \tau r$ but $r - \tau(r - \rho)$.

The optimal financial policy under indexation can be found by replacing the nominal rate of interest, r, in Section 4.2.1 by the real rate of interest, $r - \rho$, and by altering equations (4.7) and (4.11) to allow the company to raise enough finance to meet the inflationary component of its interest charges. The reader may easily check that with these modifications the optimal financial policy is exactly the same as in the absence of indexation, provided that the real rate of interest is positive. Consequently, the analysis of this chapter applies to both indexed and unindexed tax systems.

4.2.6. *The decision to incorporate*

In the earlier sections we have seen how taxation affects the financial policy of an incorporated business. Can we now answer the question of what determines the decision to incorporate by a previously unincorporated enterprise such as a partnership? A number of factors might seem to make incorporation an attractive move:

(1) limited liability: at first sight it appears that the existence of limited liability might make it easier for a company to raise finance. This is at least partially illusory, however, for it takes no account of the response of creditors who may be less willing to extend facilities when shareholders are protected by limited liability, nor of the fact that it is quite common when lending to small companies for banks to require personal guarantees from the directors. The possibility of setting up as a limited liability company cannot transform the terms on which lenders are willing to supply finance to a particular well-defined business operation. Limited liability is, however, a very convenient form of contract between borrower and lender for risky business enterprises where the supplier of finance may find it extremely costly to monitor the performance of the management to ensure that the funds are being used wisely. In this sense limited liability provides some minimal protection against the exploitation by managers of their monopolistic access to information about the company's activities; the problem of 'moral hazard'.

(2) separation of the scale of ownership from control: only a company has the legal right to issue shares and this enables the ownership of the company to be transferred easily between individuals, and to be divided among individuals in any desired manner, without affecting the control of the enterprise which can remain in the hands of a single management team. For large firms this facility is essential

and probably overrides any other consideration about incorporation. This may explain why limited liability is a *necessary* provision for companies even if it is not an enormous advantage in itself. Suppose that limited liability did not hold. In certain circumstances the shareholders might then owe money to the company's creditors, and the market price of the shares would be negative. Individual shareholders would have an incentive to destroy any evidence that they were the owners of the shares. They would simply burn bearer shares, and might attempt to give registered shares away to gullible friends who were unaware that the price was negative. Clearly, once we accept a system in which the ownership of a single firm is represented by a very large number of paper claims, the smooth functioning of a market in these claims requires limited liability. Limited liability is, therefore, at least as much a consequence of corporate status as a prerequisite.

(3) pension provisions: for small firms contemplating the switch from unincorporated status to that of a private company, a major consideration in some countries (especially in the U.K.) is the generous nature of the tax concessions to pension contributions made by companies which are unavailable for self-employed entrepreneurs. Companies may make substantial tax-free contributions to an employees' pension fund, whereas self-employed traders face upper limits on the amounts which they are able to save free of tax. In practice this consideration appears to be an important factor for small businessmen in the U.K.

(4) taxation: the effects of taxation on the decision to incorporate do not seem well understood, and there is no clear account of this problem in the literature. In fact the same considerations that were analysed in Section 4.2.2 also apply to the decision to incorporate. However, we shall explore a somewhat different model in order to consider explicitly the position of an entrepreneur wishing to incorporate.

Consider an individual who has an idea, or a special talent which produces services that can be sold in the market for a cash flow of $c(t)$ at time t over the time interval from $t = 0$ until $t = T$, (we shall assume $c(t) \geqslant 0$ for all t). He has the choice of remaining as an unincorporated entrepreneur paying income tax on the proceeds of his invention as they accrue, or incorporating his idea receiving equity shares in return, and paying corporation tax on the cash flow. If he does incorporate, there is the further choice of whether to distribute the proceeds as dividends, or whether to accumulate them within the company and sell out at the end of the horizon at time T. In all then there are three alternatives. If we assume that the individual faces a perfect capital market then he will choose that alternative which produces the highest present discounted value of post-tax income, borrowing if necessary to finance his desired consumption stream. We shall assume that interest payments are deductible both against personal income tax and against corporation tax.

The present discounted value of the income stream under the three alternatives is given by the following expressions:

(i) The unincorporated business will discount the post-tax cash flow at the rate of interest net of tax, yielding a present discounted value equal to

$$P_1 = \int_0^T (1 - m) c(t) e^{-(1-m)rt} dt. \tag{4.33}$$

(ii) The incorporated business can distribute its earnings as dividends. We saw in Chapter 3 that if profits are $c(t)$ the post-tax dividend which can be paid to the shareholders is $(1 - m)$ACID $c(t)$, where ACID is the ACID Test Statistic. Hence the present discounted value of the dividend stream is

$$\begin{aligned} P_2 &= \text{ACID} \int_0^T (1 - m)\, c(t) e^{-(1-m)rt} dt, \\ &= \text{ACID} \times P_1. \end{aligned} \tag{4.34}$$

Since ACID $\leqslant 1$, this policy of distributions under incorporation would never be attractive from the tax point of view.

(iii) The alternative version of incorporation is to accumulate earnings within the company, investing them to earn the market rate of return and paying corporation tax on its income. Assuming that capital gains tax is levied only on realization, the individual may sell his shares at the end of the horizon thus incurring capital gains tax on the value of the assets of the company at time T. These assets have a value at time T of

$$\int_0^T (1 - \tau)\, c(t) e^{(1-\tau)(T-t)r} dt.$$

The present discounted value at time 0 of the post-tax capital gain is

$$P_3 = (1 - z)(1 - \tau) e^{(m-\tau)rT} \int_0^T c(t) e^{-(1-\tau)rt} dt. \tag{4.35}$$

Given this policy, incorporation will be desirable if $P_3 > P_1$, which is equivalent to the condition

$$\frac{(1 - z)(1 - \tau)}{(1 - m)} \cdot \frac{p(\tau)}{p(m)} > 1, \tag{4.36}$$

where $$p(x) = \int_0^T c(t) e^{rx(t-T)} e^{-rt} dt. \tag{4.37}$$

It is easy to see that $p(x)$ is a decreasing function of x because an increase in x is equivalent to an increase in the discount rate. Hence $m > \tau$ implies that $p(m) < p(\tau)$. If $m < \tau$ then condition (4.36) certainly does not hold (since $z > 0$). Hence a *necessary* condition for incorporation to be attractive for tax reasons is $m > \tau$, i.e. for the personal tax rate to exceed the corporate tax rate. However, this is not sufficient, as the reader can see by considering the case where $m = z$.

A *sufficient* condition, however, is that $(1 - z)(1 - \tau) > (1 - m)$, with which we are familiar from Section 4.2.2 where it appeared as the condition that retained earnings were preferred to debt finance. Moreover, suppose that capital gains tax were to be levied on an accruals basis, which was the assumption made in earlier sections. This is equivalent to looking at the relationship between P_1 and P_3 as $T \to 0$; in which case the necessary and sufficient condition for incorporation to be attractive is precisely the condition for retained earnings to be the optimal source of finance, namely $(1 - z)(1 - \tau) > (1 - m)$. So the analysis of the decision to incorporate runs parallel to that of the optimal financial policy for a corporation.

The tax advantages of incorporation are probably overstated by this analysis because the tax authorities may deem the pursuit of the third strategy outlined above as 'tax avoidance', and restrict the ability of companies to follow this policy. In the U.K. for example, provisions exist to compel 'close companies' (those companies under the control of five or fewer persons and where less than 35% of the shares are publicly held) to distribute a certain fraction of their income, and so the value of the incorporated business will be a weighted average of P_2 and P_3 where the weights will depend upon the fraction of income distributed. Since P_2 is necessarily less than P_1 these provisions clearly reduce the advantages of incorporation purely for tax reasons, and it seems evident that the main factors lying behind the decision to incorporate are considerations (2) and (3), the ability to separate the scale of ownership from control, and the tax concessions to pension contributions made by a company.

This conclusion is borne out by the negative results of attempts to relate the proportion of business gross product originating in the corporate sector to the value of the tax term $[(1 - z)(1 - \tau) - (1 - m)]$ for both U.S. and U.K. data. A variety of specifications were tried but the coefficients of the tax term were insignificant, and in many cases had the wrong sign (the results are not reported to save space).

4.3 *Share valuation and share ownership*

We have seen that differences in their personal tax position may lead to conflict among the shareholders over the choice of financial policy for the firm. We will now consider the question of whether shareholders differ in their valuation of the firm for a given financial policy?

The fundamental condition for equilibrium in the capital market can be interpreted as an implicit theory of share valuation, for equation (4.1) may be rearranged to give the following difference equation for the share price

$$V(t+1) - \alpha V(t) + \frac{d(t)}{1-z} = 0 \tag{4.38}$$

where α is the discount factor in period t and is equal to $1 + r(1-m)/(1-z)$.

This difference equation may be solved to give an expression for the current share price, $V(0)$.

$$V(0) = \sum_{k=0}^{t} \frac{1}{1-z} \frac{d(k)}{\alpha^{k+1}} + \frac{V(t+1)}{\alpha^{t+1}}. \tag{4.39}$$

We may replace $d(k)$ by $(1-m)\, g(k)$, where $g(k)$ is the gross dividend per share in period k and takes the same value for all shareholders, (whereas the net dividend $d(k)$ depends of course on the personal tax rate of each shareholder). If, as $t \to \infty$, the value of the share price increases at a slower rate than the discount factor, then the final term in the above equation tends to zero as $t \to \infty$, in which case

$$V(0) = \sum_{k=0}^{\infty} \frac{1-m}{1-z} \frac{g(k)}{\alpha^{k+1}}. \tag{4.40}$$

This looks like the familiar result that the value of a share is the present discounted value of the net dividend stream accruing to its owner. In this case, however, the share value is the discounted value of a weighted dividend stream, where both the market discount rate and the dividend are multiplied by the same weight, namely $(1-m)/(1-z)$.

Let us denote this factor $(1-m)/(1-z)$ by γ. It is easy to see that in general the only value of γ which ensures that the valuation of the share is independent of personal tax rates is unity. In other words, capital gains must be taxed at the same rate as income for the valuation to be independent of tax rates. This is the personal equivalent of the fundamental theorem of tax-rate invariance proved by Samuelson which states that:

> If, and only if, true loss of economic value is permitted as a tax-deductible depreciation expense will the present discounted value of a cash-receipt stream be independent of the rate of the tax (Samuelson, 1964).

In the case considered here, the loss of economic value allowed as a deduction is replaced by an increase in value to be taxed at full income tax rates. If γ does not equal unity it is still possible for individuals to accord identical values to a share provided they all face the same value for γ. This would be true, for example, in the special case where, although the income tax rate differed from the capital gains tax rate, all shareholders faced the same tax rate. Where tax rates vary across individuals, however, γ will be the same for each shareholder only where capital gains are taxed to the following unusual schedule (where $\eta = 1/\gamma$)

$$z = (1 - \eta) + \eta m. \tag{4.41}$$

For example, if we set $\eta = 0.5$, all shareholders would accord the same value to a share provided their capital gains tax rate was 50% plus one-half their rate of income tax! Although such a tax system is sufficient to ensure identical valuations, it is not necessary and the most desirable system would be simply to tax capital gains as income.

In most countries, however, capital gains are not taxed as income, and individuals will value shares at different rates. This phenomenon creates difficulties for the existence of an equilibrium in the market for shares. Suppose individual A values shares more highly than individual B; then A will attempt to buy an infinite amount of shares from B who will supply them by selling short. Equilibrium can be assured by ruling out short sales in which case the shares are held by those individuals who place the highest valuation on the shares. This is the 'clientele effect'. From data for individual firms in the U.S. in 1966–7, Elton and Gruber (1970) concluded that there was evidence of a clientele effect in that firms with low payout ratios did attract shareholders with significantly higher tax rates.

It is interesting to question which value of the tax rate leads to the highest valuation of a company's shares. In fact, the tax rate which maximizes the share price is a function of the time profile of the dividend stream. To see this we shall examine two simple examples. Consider, first, a company in steady-state growth with money dividends per share growing at a given constant rate g. We shall normalize by taking the gross dividend at time 0 to be unity (in which case the share price is equal to the price–earnings ratio). From equation (4.40) we have that in steady-state growth,

$$V(0) = \frac{1}{r - g/\gamma}. \tag{4.42}$$

It follows from this equation that

$$\frac{\partial V(0)}{\partial \gamma} = -\frac{g}{(\gamma r - g)^2}. \tag{4.43}$$

If we restrict our attention to firms with positive monetary growth rates, we can take this expression to be negative and so the share price is a decreasing function of γ. Now $\gamma = (1 - m)/(1 - z)$ and, if we consider tax systems in which $z = \lambda m (\lambda \leqslant 1)$, it is easy to show that γ is a decreasing function of m. Combining these two results we find that the share price is an increasing function of the rate of income tax, and hence shares will be valued most highly by those individuals in society facing the highest tax rates. This may be a contributory factor in explaining why the proportion of an investor's portfolio held in the form of shares tends to rise with income, a behavioural phenomenon which is well known (see, for example, Feldstein (1974)).

In the expression for γ used above we should really replace z by the EAT Rate to allow for the taxation of capital gains on realization. The Eat Rate falls short of the nominal rate of capital gains tax by an amount which we denoted in Chapter 3 by $R(m)$. This gives

$$\gamma = \frac{1 - m}{1 - m + R(m)}, \tag{4.44}$$

where $R(m)$ is given by equation (3.17). From equations (3.18) and (4.44) we may obtain

$$\frac{\partial \gamma}{\partial m} = -\frac{\left\{1 + \lambda + \dfrac{R(1 - m)(\pi + r)}{m[\pi + r(1 - m)]}\right\}}{[1 - m + R(m)]^2}. \tag{4.45}$$

Again γ is seen to be a decreasing function of the income tax rate, and, allowing for the benefit of deferral of capital gains tax, reinforces our result that for companies growing at a constant rate the shares will seem most attractive to individuals facing high rax rates. *Ceteris paribus*, they will be prepared to offer more for the shares in the stock market than will individuals facing lower tax rates. This is because of the *difference* in the tax rates charged on income and capital gains. As we have seen, if capital gains were taxed as income the valuation of the shares would be independent of the level of the tax rate.

The second example we shall consider is of a firm which pays no dividend for the first T years of its life from years 0 to $T - 1$, and then pays out all its income in year T. A case in point might be a mining company which invests all its capital in a mining venture in a distant land. The project has a long gestation period but finally the minerals emerge and within a year the mine is exhausted.

The price in period 0 of a share in this firm is given by (from equation (4.40))

$$V(0) = \frac{\gamma}{(1 + \gamma r)^{T+1}} \cdot g(T). \tag{4.46}$$

Differentiating with respect to γ yields

$$\frac{\partial V(0)}{\partial \gamma} = \frac{[1 + \gamma r - \gamma r(T + 1)]}{(1 + \gamma r)^{T+2}} g(T). \tag{4.47}$$

The value of γ which maximizes the share price is therefore given by

$$1 + \gamma r = \gamma r(T + 1) \tag{4.48}$$

$$\therefore \gamma = \frac{1}{rT}. \tag{4.49}$$

If we consider the simple case where $z = \lambda m$, then this solution gives a value for the income tax rate which maximizes the share price of

$$m = \frac{1 - rT}{\lambda - rT}. \tag{4.50}$$

The income tax rate given by this equation can take on a variety of values depending on the exact nature of the venture as measured by the length of the gestation period. Suppose that the interest rate is 10%, then for a project life of 10 years the value of m is zero, and the shares will seem most attractive to tax-exempt institutional shareholders. If, on the other hand, the project lasts 20 years and capital gains are taxed at one-half of income tax rates, the value of m is two-thirds and the shares will be bought by relatively wealthy individuals.

Consequently, it is impossible *a priori* to associate corporate securities with individuals in particular tax brackets without knowledge of the precise time profile of the future dividend stream. However, our results from the example of a company in steady-state growth combined with the relative stability of dividend payments in practice, suggest that it is likely that many, if not most, ordinary shares will be more attractive to high income individuals. They will offer a higher price and purchase a larger number of shares relative to their total portfolio than low income individuals. This prediction is certainly consistent with the evidence we have on the ownership of wealth.

At this point it would be fitting to return to basics and ask whether the foregoing analysis of share valuation conveys any real understanding of the way in which the stock market actually operates? This fundamental doubt about the economic role of the stock market stems from our failure so far to analyse the effects of uncertainty. We shall consider this problem in some detail later but at this point we may summarize our concern in the following question. Do share prices reflect either retained earnings or the present discounted value of the expected future dividend stream of the company?

There are two aspects to this question which are intimately connected but conceptually distinct. The first relates to our previous analysis of corporate financial policy where it was shown that, for a *given* level of investment, shareholders were indifferent between dividends and capital gains except for the effects of taxes and transaction costs. For the purposes of this argument we shall ignore taxes and transaction costs. To finance the given volume of investment the firm may either retain sufficient profits, or distribute those profits as dividends and at the same time issue new shares. The formal argument in Section 4.2 used the assumption of perfect certainty, but the same result holds even in a world of uncertainty. There may be a great deal of uncertainty about the future profits which will flow from the investment project, but this in no way alters the choice between financing a given level of investment by retentions or by issuing new shares. The uncertainty centres on the value of the project and hence on the total value of the equity, not on the share price itself. Whether the project is financed internally or by a new share issue will not alter the value which the market will place on the profit stream. The total value of the equity is independent of the method of financing, and the product of the share price and the number of shares will be the same for the two methods of equity finance (i.e. equation (4.3) will still hold even if there is uncertainty about future profits). Consequently, a policy which involves issuing new shares will reduce the share price in proportion to the number of shares issued relative to the share price which would obtain if the given investment project were financed internally.

This demonstrates that even if there is uncertainty about the future, there is no reason for shareholders to prefer dividends to capital gains. A desire for a stable level of dividends (an empirical phenomenon which we shall investigate in Chapter 6) cannot derive from an argument based on the effects of uncertainty about future profits as such (the 'bird in the hand' argument). It must be based on an alternative argument that either shareholders are unhappy with the amount of investment which the firm is undertaking, or that dividends have a special role to play over and above that which follows from their place in the financial flow of funds of the firm. For example, dividends may play an 'informational role' and provide management with a method of signalling to shareholders changes in their expectations about the future. We shall defer discussion of this possible role until Chapter 6, but there is one further aspect of uncertainty to be discussed at this point.

The second aspect of our question about the economic role of the stock market concerns the reaction of share prices to increased retentions which are made in order to finance a higher level of investment, not as an alternative to issuing new shares. In a world of perfect certainty the share price would reflect the value of the assets purchased, but in a situation of uncertainty the position is less clear-cut. Shareholders may differ in the value which they place on the assets of the company and many economists have doubted whether share prices do in fact reflect the economic value of a company's assets. This belief is based, at least partly, on the empirical observation that changes in share prices appear to occur randomly. However, this piece of evidence has been interpreted in two very different ways.

On the one hand, there are those who argue that investment in the stock market is first and foremost a speculative game, that prices are what they are today because of expectations about their value tomorrow. On the other hand, there are those who see the random behaviour of share prices as consistent with the view that the stock market is a perfectly efficient market in which all information about the future is capitalized in current prices, and where changes in share prices result from an immediate reaction to new information becoming available which, since by definition it is new information, accrues in an unpredictable fashion.

The former hypothesis was expressed most eloquently by Keynes in his famous description of the stock market as a game in which the idea is to guess what prices will be in a few months time knowing that everybody else in the market is facing the same problem.

> ... professional investment may be likened to those newspaper competitions in which the competitors have to pick out the six prettiest faces from a hundred photographs, the prize being awarded to the competitor whose choice most nearly corresponds to the average preferences of the competitors as a whole; so that each competitor has to pick, not those faces which he himself finds prettiest, but those which he thinks likeliest to catch the fancy of the other competitors, all of whom are looking at the problem from the same point of view. It is not a case of choosing those which, to the best of one's judgment, are really the prettiest, nor even those which average opinion genuinely thinks the prettiest. We have reached the third degree where we devote our intelligences to anticipating what average opinion expects the average opinion to be. And there are some, I believe, who practise the fourth, fifth and higher degrees (Keynes (1936); p. 156).

Keynes' contention is that individual investors and fund managers will have little incentive to evaluate the long term prospects of a firm in order to purchase shares in those companies which offer the best return, if they believe that share prices may be depressed in the near future because of a psychological wave of pessimism in the market. This begs the question of why share prices might be depressed. If it reflects less optimistic expectations about future dividends then although some investors may be concerned only with tomorrow's share price, that price will depend on the market's view of the long term prospects of the share. In which case the distinction between the short term and long term views becomes irrelevant. This is the contention of the 'efficient markets' school.

An 'efficient market' in this context is defined to be one in which prices always fully reflect available information (Fama (1970)). As it stands this statement does not represent an operational definition and an efficient market is usually redefined as one in which transactions take the form of a 'fair game', that is, expected excess profits conditional on current information are zero. In practice this implies that it is not possible to devise trading rules for buying and selling shares which give profits net of transactions costs greater than would have been obtained from a simple buy and hold policy. An example of such a rule is the filter rule, which says buy when the share price rises $x\%$ above a previous low (or, perhaps, a moving average of prices) and sell when the price falls $x\%$ below a previous high. Such a system is called an $x\%$ filter. There now exists a substantial body of empirical literature refuting the possibility of finding a trading rule of this kind based on past price information which enables supernormal profits to be made. (See, for example, Alexander (1961), Cootner (1964), and Fama and Blume (1966). The empirical literature on this whole problem is excellently surveyed by Fama (1970).) A special case of the 'fair game' model is the random walk model of share prices, which states that successive price changes are independently and identically distributed. Although it is more restrictive than the general model, it does seem to be supported by a large amount of empirical work. This is admirably surveyed in Brealey's book (1969).

The one reservation to the support which these results lend to the efficient markets hypothesis is that there is some evidence that insiders have exploited their monopolistic access to information to make profits by trading on the stock market. Studies of the New York Stock Exchange by Niederhoffer and Osborne (1966), and by Lorie and Niederhoffer (1968), found definite evidence of profitability on insider trading.

What does all this add up to, and, more precisely, despite their apparent contradictions, is there any substantive difference between the Keynesian view of the stock market as a casino, and the efficient markets hypothesis? After all, there is no more reason for expecting to be able to find a rule to beat the casino than to earn positive expected excess profits in an efficient market. Both views yield the same empirical prediction, that one cannot expect to make a fortune on the stock market without special knowledge or information. The differences arise in their interpretation of the evidence, and in particular in the inferences drawn about the economic efficiency of the stock market.

As an advocate of the efficient markets hypothesis, Fama (1970) identifies three possible impediments to the working of an 'efficient market', the existence of transactions costs, insider trading, and disagreement between shareholders. It is well known that transactions costs and exploitation of monopolistic access to information can lead to inefficiencies, but the last reason cited by Fama is puzzling. The key lies in the rather unusual use of the word 'efficiency'. Efficiency is conventionally described by economists in terms of Pareto-efficiency; an allocation of resources is said to be Pareto-efficient if it is not possible to make any one individual better off without making at least one other individual worse off. An allocation is efficient with respect to individuals' preferences, usually assumed to be defined over current and future consumption.

Whether the stock market produces a pattern of share prices which results in an efficient allocation of resources is a question that can be answered only within the framework of a well-specified theoretical model of how the market operates.

A discussion of theoretical models of the stock market is contained in the next chapter, but we may note here that the two views of the stock market recorded above implicitly use different models of the market. The 'efficient markets' school visualizes the purchase of a share as the purchase of a certain fraction of the profits of the firm, whatever those profits turn out to be. In this model expectations about such things as future technology are paramount. Keynes, however, envisaged a world in which the value of holding a share was primarily the right to resell it in the future, and where expectations were more concerned with future spot prices in the stock market than with the profitability of different business enterprises. This model is similar in spirit to the Hicksian 'temporary' equilibrium models which have recently begun to attract the attention of general equilibrium theorists. (See, for example, Hahn (1973) and Grandmont (1974).) The essential difference between these models and the traditional general equilibrium models is that once we allow spot markets to re-open in the future then price expectations enter the picture, and the resulting equilibrium, if it exists, will depend upon the way in which economic agents form their expectations about future prices. Analysis of these sequence economies is still very much in its infancy, but it seems clear that in general such equilibria as exist are unlikely to be efficient, and this seems to be what Keynes had in mind. A similar conclusion holds about the efficiency of stock markets, despite the fact that share prices may fully reflect available information.

Thus, the main lesson to be drawn from this preliminary discussion of efficiency in a world of uncertainty is that the observation that it is impossible to find a trading rule which gives positive expected excess profits, implies nothing about the economic efficiency of the stock market. We may interpret the evidence as showing that the stock market is *competitive*, not that it is efficient, and that the adjustment to a new set of equilibrium prices takes place very quickly. A competitive market may be a necessary condition for efficiency but it is certainly not a sufficient condition. Consequently, we are able to conclude from the empirical evidence neither that the stock market is totally irrational, nor that it results in an efficient allocation of resources. It follows from this that little is to be learnt from demonstrating yet again that share prices follow a random walk, and it is difficult to avoid the conclusion that much of the empirical work on the behaviour of share prices not founded on a theoretical model has led to a dead end.

Chapter 5

UNCERTAINTY, CORPORATE POLICY, AND THE STOCK MARKET

> In our most theoretical models we may be nearest to our most practical applications. (A.N. Whitehead, 1911).

Apart from a preliminary look in Chapter 4 at uncertainty and share prices, the analysis of the theory of the firm under uncertainty has been deferred until this chapter. Since business enterprise is inextricably bound up with risk-taking it may seem surprising that uncertainty was not introduced from the very beginning. The reason, however, for delaying the extension of the theory of the firm to allow for the existence of uncertainty is that the extension is non-trivial. In fact, uncertainty raises some deep and rather fundamental problems for conventional theories of the firm. It is to these problems that this chapter is addressed.

The requirements of large-scale production mean that some way must be found to share or pool the risks involved. The study of the firm begins with the different methods by which the risks may be shared among the participants in the enterprise. Traditionally, this has been seen as a question of sharing risks between the different providers of capital: equity shareholders, bond holders, and the government, the latter through its activities in taxing profits and subsidizing investment. Ideally, this concept of risk-sharing should be extended to include those in the labour force who bear risks by committing to the firm skills and expertise specially acquired for the operations of the particular business. Participation in risk bearing involves both capital and labour. The analysis of the role of labour in the sharing of risks is, however, beyond the scope of this book, and we shall restrict the discussion to the more conventional view that the members of the firm are its equity shareholders.

In this chapter we shall attempt to show that the existence of uncertainty is inconsistent with the fundamental axiom of the neoclassical theory of the firm that the firm maximizes profits, or, in its more general formulation, that it maximizes its stock market value. Once this point is grasped then the distinction between neoclassical and managerial theories of the firm appears rather artificial, and it is possible to develop models in which both management and the shareholders determine the eventual outcome and in which factors such as the composition of share ownership and the fear of take-over play a role.

The key to the problem lies in the importance attached to the operation of the stock market. The assumption of a perfectly competitive stock market has been implicit in much of our earlier discussion, and it is now time to deal with this matter explicitly. In confronting this problem, however, we face a major weakness in the existing state of economic theory, since few models have been advanced which purport to analyse the economic role of stock markets. On the one hand, as we have seen in Chapter 4, there is a wealth of statistical evidence on the behaviour of share prices which can be seen as consistent with either a perfectly competitive market or with the view of the market as a paradise for speculators along the lines of Keynes' analogy of the market with a casino.

On the other hand, the orthodox theory of the firm says very little about the workings of the stock market. As Leland (1974; p. 126) has put it

> Neoclassical production models have not needed stock markets because profit maximization provides a complete description of firm behaviour under certainty. Stockholders are invoked to justify profit maximization, but thereupon are hastily retired from the scene. Indeed, the existence of the stock market has been somewhat embarrassing, since traditional economic models are complete without it.

It seems important, therefore, to examine some simple models of economies in which stock markets do play a crucial part, and we shall look at this with particular reference to the determinants of corporate decisions and the way in which the stock market 'disciplines' companies. First, though, we shall review the elegant neoclassical approach to the introduction of uncertainty into economic theory.

5.1 *Uncertainty and economic theory*

Although many writers were concerned with the importance of risk and uncertainty, the rigorous extension of economic theory to a world of uncertainty was developed by Arrow (1964) and Debreu (1959). At the heart of their treatment of uncertainty is the redefinition of a commodity. In the Arrow–Debreu model commodities are distinguished not only by physical and spatial characteristics, and by the date at which the commodity is made available, but also by the 'state of the world' in which it is delivered. A 'state of the world' is defined by assigning values to all the uncertain variables which are relevant to the economy, (for example, the rainfall in the next year), and comprises a complete list of the values of all these variables. These states of the world are mutually exclusive, and together form an exhaustive set. To quote Malinvaud (1972a; p. 275), 'the complete characterisation of a commodity must specify the states in which it is available'. Commodities are now defined as contingent on the occurrence of certain events, and the market system comprises markets in all these contingent commodities. An example of a contingent commodity would be an umbrella to be delivered tomorrow only if it rains. Clearly, in a real economic sense this is a different commodity from an umbrella to be delivered tomorrow only if it does not rain, and different again from an umbrella tomorrow whatever the weather turns out to be.

This approach of redefining a commodity allows uncertainty to be formally incorporated into the neoclassical model of general equilibrium, and the standard results concerning the existence and Pareto-efficiency of equilibrium apply to the larger world containing an extended set of perfectly competitive markets, each market corresponding to one commodity, including of course markets for all contingent commodities.

The market equilibrium determines a set of prices for conditional contracts. Even if delivery of a commodity is contingent upon the outcome of an uncertain event, the market today for this contingent commodity results in a determinate price. This being the case a firm's profits are certain since they are the inner product of vectors of prices and quantities both of which are determined in current markets. We must assume that production sets are defined on contingent commodities, so that to sell a contingent commodity requires the purchase of contingent inputs. The possibility of selling a contingent commodity without making provision for purchasing the requisite inputs is disallowed. Since in the Arrow–Debreu model markets never reopen, this assumption prevents a firm from choosing a production plan which would be infeasible in certain contingencies. A production plan must be feasible in every state of the world. In the real world an inability to fulfil a contract will incur the wrath of the authorities, and the legal system specifies the penalties of non-fulfilment. The firm's behaviour will depend on these penalties, and we are led inevitably into a study of bankruptcy. We shall return to the consequencies of this in a later section. Even at this stage, however, we may note that the simple Arrow–Debreu model requires an external agency to enforce contracts. The matter cannot be left to economic agents alone.

Since a firm's profits are certain all shareholders of a perfectly competitive firm will wish the firm to choose that policy which maximizes profits, because this will allow shareholders access to the largest consumption possibility set. There is no room for debate as to the nature of the firm's objective function. Uncertainty affects only consumers who, although facing determinate budget constraints, must choose a consumption plan whose utility is uncertain, and we shall assume that individuals possess preference orderings over consumption bundles in different states of the world, and that their behaviour can be represented by the postulate of expected utility maximization.

The logical structure of the model and its incorporation of uncertainty is appealing in its simplicity and beautiful in its execution, but, as far as firms are concerned, there are serious weaknesses in this treatment of uncertainty. First, the assumption that there are as many contingent commodity markets as there are states of the world is unacceptable. While some futures and insurance markets exist, it is not unreasonable to say that to obtain a stake in the future profits of the economy, an individual must choose between the various ways of purchasing shares, directly or indirectly, in a limited number of joint-stock companies. As we have seen in Chapter 2, in both the U.K. and the U.S. a substantial fraction of the value added in manufacturing is produced by the largest 100 firms. Each stock or share of one of these firms consists of a claim on its future profits, and since there are only a limited number of corporations, the number of marketable contingent claims (or commodities) is far fewer than the number of states of nature. Consequently the proportionate claim on the firm's profits represented by a share is the same across all states of the world, and this is the reason for Diamond's description of corporate shares as a 'composite commodity', (Diamond, 1967). Each share is an entitlement to a bundle of contingent commodities.

The essential nature of a stock market economy with an incomplete set of Arrow–Debreu markets is that each firm has a monopoly of a particular pattern of returns across states of the world. Moreover, the lack of contingent commodity markets is not a superficial imperfection in the market system but the inevitable consequence of uncertainty. The costs of setting up a sufficient number of markets to insure against all business risks would be colossal, and would militate against the true spirit of entrepreneurship. As Arrow himself has said,

> In fact, it is not a mere empirical accident that not all the contingent markets needed for efficiency exist, but a necessary fact with deep implications for the workings and structure of economic institutions (Arrow, 1974).

Secondly, the Arrow–Debreu model distorts the firm as an economic institution beyond recognition. Those activities and functions most characteristic of a modern corporation are disregarded, and the model fails to capture the true nature of the joint-stock company with its complex interaction between its various constituent members, management, shareholders, and the labour force.

The third weakness in the conventional model is that it affords almost no role for the stock market. In fact, given the existence of the other markets the stock market is completely redundant.

These weaknesses in the conventional approach to uncertainty are closely related, and we shall argue that it is the development of a model of the stock market in a world with an incomplete set of markets (where there are fewer securities than states of the world) which enables a more realistic model of the firm to be constructed. The stock market is not only a market for shares in which individuals may spread risks or speculate, but is also the arena where we observe individuals and groups fighting for control of particular companies, a phenomenon ruled out by the conventional model. Consequently, when the stock market is incorporated into our analysis the firm no longer operates as a trust on behalf of its shareholders, but can be viewed as an institution in its own right with both shareholders and management influencing the choice of corporate policy. This framework is capable of integrating neoclassical and managerial theories of the firm and providing a fruitful source of theoretical and empirical ideas.

The question we shall attempt to answer is what is the appropriate representation of the behaviour of a firm in a world of uncertainty?

We know that if there are a complete set of contingent (and other) commodity markets, a perfectly competitive firm will maximize profits, but we have argued that a fundamental characteristic of a capitalist economy is the absence of a complete set of markets, and the consequent existence of a role for the 'entrepreneur' or management whose responsibility is to take 'business risks', which we may define as those risks against which it is impossible to completely insure by market transactions. Business risk is inextricably bound up with an incomplete set of markets.

5.2 *Stock market economies*

To examine the behaviour of firms under uncertainty we shall investigate a simple model of a stock market economy constructed with the aim of focussing attention on the main problems. We shall assume a two-period one-commodity world in which there are a given number of securities consisting of shares in a fixed number of firms J. Individuals in this world start life at the beginning of the first period with given initial endowments of shares in the firms. Firms announce their policies (or production plans) and individuals then exchange shares on the stock market in order to maximize their expected utility of consumption. The stock market then closes. Time goes by and in period two a particular state of the world comes to pass, thus determining the profits of each firm which are distributed to individuals in proportion to their shareholdings. Individuals enjoy this consumption and the world ends. There is no government and no taxation.

The profits accruing to a firm will be a function of the state of the world and the policy it has chosen. In this model uncertainty concerns only the amount of profits a firm will earn for a given choice of policy. This assumption means that we are considering purely 'technological' uncertainty; uncertainty as to which state of the world will occur. If the model were extended to more than two periods and the stock market allowed to reopen, or if there were several commodities, then individuals would be exposed also to uncertainty about future prices. Although, as we saw in Chapter 4, it has been argued that one of the weaknesses of the stock market is its reaction to price uncertainty and the role played by speculation, we shall see that a sufficient number of interesting questions about the behaviour of firms arise in the context of technological uncertainty, and so we shall not attempt an explicit treatment of price uncertainty.

Each individual has his own expectations about the state of the world likely to occur, and a utility function defined on consumption of the single physical commodity in the second period. Under the von Neumann–Morgenstern axioms of individual choice we may assume that each individual maximizes his expected utility of future consumption subject to (a) his budget constraint, (b) his subjective probabilities of different states of the world, and (c) the assumption that he faces given prices in the stock market. The solution to this problem will determine the composition of an individual's portfolio.

So far we have said nothing about how firms decide on their initial choice of policy. The obvious criterion would appear to be to select that policy which maximizes the share price, but is this necessarily in the shareholders' interests? We shall explore an example of the simple world we have described (taken from King, 1975b) to show that even in this case shareholders might be opposed to maximization of the share price.

Consider a world in which there are two securities and three possible states of the world. One security is a safe asset, or bond, which gives one unit of the commodity in all states, and the other consists of shares in a firm which has two policies open to it. This is the only risky firm in the economy. The profits matrix of the firm which describes the profit in each state of the world corresponding to the policy adopted is shown below

	State of the world		
Policy	1	2	3
1	0	0	k_1
2	k_2	0	0

k_1 and k_2 are assumed to be non-negative. No inputs to production are required and profits are determined by the choice of policy and the state of the world which materializes in the second period. The firm must choose which of the two policies to pursue.

There are three individuals in the world indexed by $i (i = 1, 2, 3)$ who have subjective probability assignments $\pi_i(s)$ over the states of the world $s(s = 1, 2, 3)$. The initial endowments of the individuals are identical and so initially they each own one third of the equity of the firm and one third of the safe securities.

The firm chooses its policy and announces the decision. Individuals exchange shares for bonds and we assume that each individual is a price-taker in the stock market with trading taking place only at equilibrium prices. Let n_i and w_i denote respectively the equilibrium holdings of shares and bonds of individual i, where we normalize so that they represent the fractions of the firm and the safe asset owned, i.e. $\sum_i n_i = \sum_i w_i = 1$. If we define the price of bonds to be unity and the equilibrium share price to be p, then the budget constraint of individual i is that the value of his initial endowment calculated at equilibrium prices equals the value of his chosen portfolio evaluated at the same prices. Formally the constraint is

$$\frac{1}{3}(p + 1) = pn_i + w_i. \tag{5.1}$$

Consumption by the ith individual in state s, $C_i(s)$ is therefore given by

$$C_i(s) = \frac{1}{3}(1 + p) - pn_i + n_i y^k(s) \tag{5.2}$$

where $y^k(s)$ is the firm's profit in state s under policy $k(k = 1, 2)$.

The first two terms represent consumption financed out of the interest on his bonds and the last term is the dividend on his shareholding.

Each individual maximizes his expected utility of consumption taking the policy of the firm and the share price as given. For our example we shall assume a particular functional form for the utility function and the preferences of each individual will be represented by the utility function

$$U(C) = \log C \tag{5.3}$$

Individuals, therefore, exhibit identical preferences (which in the particular case examined here happen to display constant relative risk aversion) but they differ in their subjective expectations about which state of the world is going to occur. The form of the utility function in equation (5.3) is chosen solely for simplicity, and the qualitative nature of the results does not depend upon the particular functional form assumed.

In period 1 the ith individual will maximize his expected utility, EU_i, which is given by

$$EU_i = \sum_j \pi_i(s) \log [C_i(s)] \tag{5.4}$$

where $C_i(s)$ is given by equation (5.2). The individual maximizes the above expression by an appropriate choice for n_i, his equity holding. The first-order condition for an optimum is

$$\sum_j \frac{\pi_i(s)[y^k(s) - p]}{\{\frac{1}{3}(1+p) + n_i[y^k(s) - p]\}} = 0, \quad i = 1, 2, 3. \tag{5.5}$$

Suppose that before the stock market opens the firm announces that it will pursue policy 1. Substituting from the profits matrix, equation (5.5) becomes

$$\frac{p[\pi_i(1) + \pi_i(2)]}{\frac{1}{3}(1+p) - pn_i} = \frac{(k_1 - p)\pi_i(3)}{\frac{1}{3}(1+p) + n_i(k_1 - p)} \tag{5.6}$$

$$\therefore n_i = \frac{(1+p)[k_1\pi_i(3) - p]}{3p(k_1 - p)}. \tag{5.7}$$

This equation gives each individual's demand for shares as a function of the share price, and it can be shown quite easily that for any given policy both individual and the aggregate demand for shares are decreasing functions of the share price, and so the firm faces a downward sloping demand curve for its shares.

The equilibrium share price is given by the condition that in total the individuals wish to hold the total outstanding equity (that is, $\sum_i n_i = 1$). This has a unique solution and the equilibrium share price corresponding to policy 1, $p^*(1)$, is given by

$$p^*(1) = \frac{k_1 \sum_i \pi_i(3)}{k_1[3 - \sum_i \pi_i(3)] + 3}. \tag{5.8}$$

Similarly it can be shown that the equilibrium share price corresponding to policy 2 is

$$p^*(2) = \frac{k_2 \cdot \sum_i \pi_i(1)}{k_2[3 - \sum_i \pi_i(1)] + 3}. \tag{5.9}$$

To proceed further we shall make some assumptions about the values of the parameters. Suppose that $k_1 = k_2 = 10$, and that the individuals' subjective probabilities can be described by the following matrix.

	State of the world		
Individual	1	2	3
1	0.5	0.1	0.4
2	0.5	0.1	0.4
3	0.1	0.05	0.85

With these values the two equilibria corresponding to the two policies are

$$\text{Policy 1} : p^* = 1; n_1 = n_2 = 2/9, n_3 = 5/9$$

$$\text{Policy 2} : p^* = \tfrac{1}{2}; n_1 = n_2 = 9/19, n_3 = 1/19. \tag{5.10}$$

If the firm knew that these would be the outcomes of its decisions, then it would know that to maximize its share price it should choose policy 1. As yet, however, we have not specified any institutional mechanism for decision-making within the firm. Would policy 1 be chosen by the shareholders? If we allow the shareholders to know what equilibrium share prices would be associated with each policy then they would be able to calculate from equations (5.2), (5.4) and (5.7) that their levels of expected utility resulting from the two policies would be

Individual	Policy 1	Policy 2
1 and 2	− 0.0942	+ 0.1372
3	+ 1.1448	− 0.6726

Consequently, if the policy decision is made by majority voting of the original shareholders then two-thirds of the votes will be cast by individuals 1 and 2 for policy 2 and one-third by individual 3 for policy 1. Majority voting results in the choice of policy 2, whereas share price maximization requires policy 1. Thus the *ex ante* shareholders would *reject* a policy of share price maximization.

After the stock market has closed the company is owned by a new set of shareholders which differs from the original owners because trading in the firm's shares has taken place. Suppose that the firm had announced policy 2 and that trading had taken place subject to the belief that policy 2 would be pursued. We now imagine that a survey of shareholder opinion is taken immediately after the stock market has closed.

The *ex post* shareholders will vote for that policy which maximizes their expected utility, but since the stock market has closed precluding any opportunities for further trading, this is equivalent to voting for the policy which gives profits in the state of the world which the shareholder believes is more likely to occur, state 1 or state 3. Individuals 1 and 2 will therefore vote for policy 2 and individual 3 for policy 1. Since individuals 1 and 2 now hold 18/19 of the equity between them, majority voting by the *ex post* shareholders would again produce a vote in favour of policy 2. If, however, policy 1 were announced initially and a vote taken after the stock market had closed, then since individual 3 would now hold 5/9 of the equity a vote by the *ex post* shareholders would this time go in favour of policy 1. Thus, whichever policy is announced, it will be sustained by majority voting of the *ex post* shareholders, but only policy 2 will be supported by a majority of both *ex ante* and *ex post* shareholders. In this example share price maximization would be rejected by a majority vote of the *ex ante* shareholders, but would be supported by a majority of the *ex post* shareholders. By altering the subjective probability matrix slightly, however, it is possible to produce an example in which the policy which maximizes the share price would be rejected by a majority of both the *ex ante* and *ex post* shareholders. Let the subjective probability matrix be

	State of the world		
Individual	1	2	3
1	0.5	0.05	0.45
2	0.5	0.05	0.45
3	0.1	0.15	0.75

The new equilibria for the two policies are

$$\text{Policy 1} : p^* = 1; n_1 = n_2 = 7/27, n_3 = 13/27$$

$$\text{Policy 2} : p^* = \tfrac{1}{2}; n_1 = n_2 = 9/19, n_3 = 1/19. \tag{5.11}$$

The share price maximizing policy is again policy 1, but the *ex ante* shareholders would vote for policy 2 because, assuming that they correctly foresaw the equilibria which would emerge, their expected utility levels corresponding to the two policies would be

Individual	Policy 1	Policy 2
1 and 2	+ 0.0005	+ 0.1372
3	+ 0.7854	– 0.6726

By the same argument as before, a vote among the *ex post* shareholders would result in individuals 1 and 2 voting for policy 2 and individual 3 voting for policy 1. Since, whichever policy is announced, individuals 1 and 2 command a majority of the *ex post* shareholders, a poll of the shareholders after the stock market had closed would always reveal majority opposition to the share price maximizing policy.

We have identified two phenomena which are often ignored or disregarded. Firstly, there may be a conflict of interest between different groups of shareholders and so unanimity as to the firm's choice of policy will not exist. Secondly, there is no presumption that the policy which maximizes the share price is in the shareholders' interests. In our example the shareholders would have voted to oppose a policy of maximizing the share price, but why would they object to a policy which would maximize their wealth? Clearly, there must be an externality, or indirect benefit, accruing to the shareholders from pursuing a policy which lowers the market value of their wealth. This benefit arises because the firm can alter the effective prices of the goods which the shareholders are implicitly purchasing. When buying a share an individual is buying a bundle of three contingent commodities which are units of the commodity to be delivered in one of the three states of the world. These commodities cannot be purchased directly but only indirectly through the purchase of the firm's shares (which can be interpreted as a 'composite commodity').

Consequently, when choosing a policy the shareholder must bear in mind the repercussions not only on the value of his wealth but also on the prices of the goods he wishes to purchase. The argument for share price maximization is that this will push the consumer's budget line outwards parallel to itself thus unambiguously increasing his welfare. However, if the slope of the budget line changes at the same time then it is clear that share price maximization is not necessarily the best policy.

To demonstrate this proposition formally we leave our example and return to the general two-period one-commodity model we described above in which there are J firms and M individuals. Individual i has an initial endowment of a fraction $\bar{n}_{ij}$ of the shares in firm j and the total number of shares in firm j is defined to be unity. We shall assume that the output of firm j depends upon the state of the world, represented by a continuous random variable s, and some organizational decision of the firm denoted by a continuous policy variable u_j. Inputs are not required, and there are no externalities in production. Hence the profits of firm j which will materialize in the second period, y_j, may be written as

$$y_j = f_j(u_j, s). \tag{5.12}$$

In this model a safe bond may be interpreted as equivalent to a share in a firm whose profits are determinate and independent of the state of the world. The policy decision is the redemption value of the bond issue, and the price at which the bonds will sell in the market will determine the rate of interest on safe bonds.

The utility of individual i is defined over his consumption in the second period and is assumed to be an increasing and concave function of consumption. Using previous notation his expected utility level may be written as

$$EU_i = \int_s U_i [C_i(s)] \pi_i(s) \, \mathrm{d}s. \tag{5.13}$$

If we denote the equilibrium share price of firm j by p_j then the budget constraint of individual i is

$$\sum_j p_j \bar{n}_{ij} = \sum_j p_j n_{ij}. \tag{5.14}$$

The consumption by individual i in state s is given by

$$C_i(s) = \sum_j n_{ij} f_j(u_j, s). \tag{5.15}$$

If we attach a positive multiplier λ_i to the budget constraint of individual i (which will measure his marginal utility of money wealth), then the necessary conditions for the maximization of his expected utility are

$$\int_s U_i'[C_i(s)]f_j(u_j, s)\pi_i(s)\mathrm{d}s = \lambda_i p_j \qquad j = 1\ldots N \tag{5.16}$$

where U' denotes the first derivative of U with respect to its argument.

Concavity of the utility function ensures that these conditions, together with the budget constraint, determine an individual's optimal portfolio.

As we argued above, when an individual buys a share in a firm he is effectively purchasing a bundle of different commodities, each commodity being a unit of the consumption good to be delivered in a particular state of the world. Underlying the set of share prices which he faces in the market is another set of 'implicit prices' for the different contingent commodities. These are the important prices because the individual's expected utility is defined on his consumption bundle of contingent commodities, not on his holdings of shares directly. The implicit price of the consumption good in state s is the amount which an individual would be willing to pay for a unit of consumption to be delivered in state s. In the Arrow–Debreu world with a complete set of contingent commodity markets, this amount would be equal to the market price for the particular contingent commodity. In the absence of these markets the implicit price is given by the individual's marginal valuation. In money terms the implicit price of consumption in state s faced by individual i, which we denote by $v_i(s)$, is

$$v_i(s) = \frac{1}{\lambda_i}\frac{\partial EU_i}{\partial C_i(s)} = \frac{\pi_i(s)U_i'[C_i(s)]}{\lambda_i}. \tag{5.17}$$

This enables us to rewrite equation (5.16) as

$$\int_s v_i(s) f_j(u_j, s)\mathrm{d}s = p_j. \tag{5.18}$$

This equation says that the individual values an extra share as the sum over states of the dividend he would receive in state s multiplied by his implicit price of consumption in state s.

As in our example we now ask the question, how would the expected utility level of each shareholder change in response to a change in the policy of one firm, say firm r, holding the policies of all other firms unchanged? A change in policy will change the profits of firm r in every state of the world, and will alter the wealth of individual i because a new set of equilibrium prices will clear the stock market. A small change in the policy of firm r will produce a change in the expected utility of individual i of

$$\frac{dEU_i}{du_r} = \int_s \left[\sum_j \frac{dn_{ij}}{du_r} f_j(u_j, s) + n_{ir} \frac{\partial f_r(u_r, s)}{\partial u_r} \right] \times U'[C_i(s)]\pi_i(s)ds \quad (5.19)$$

$$\therefore \frac{1}{\lambda_i} \frac{dEU_i}{du_r} = \sum_j p_j \frac{dn_{ij}}{du_r} + n_{ir} \int_s v_i(s) \frac{\partial f_r}{\partial u_r} ds. \quad (5.20)$$

The change in expected utility is thus equal to the sum of two terms, the first reflecting the desired change in the individual's portfolio and the second measuring his valuation of the change in the profit stream of firm r. From the budget constraint (5.14) we have

$$\sum_j p_j \frac{dn_{ij}}{du_r} = \sum_j (\bar{n}_{ij} - n_{ij}) \frac{dp_j}{du_r}. \quad (5.21)$$

From equation (5.18) we have

$$\frac{dp_j}{du_r} = \int_s \left[\frac{dv_i(s)}{du_r} f_j(u_j, s) + v_i(s) \frac{\partial f_j}{\partial u_r} \right] ds. \quad (5.22)$$

Hence from the last two equations

$$\sum_j p_j \frac{dn_{ij}}{du_r} = (\bar{n}_{ir} - n_{ir}) \int_s v_i(s) \frac{\partial f_r}{\partial u_r} ds + \sum_j (\bar{n}_{ij} - n_{ij}) \int_s \frac{dv_i(s)}{du_r} f_j(u_j, s) ds. \quad (5.23)$$

Suppose that the implicit prices are *independent* of the policy of the firm. In this case

$$\frac{dv_i(s)}{du_r} = 0 \quad \text{for all } s \quad (5.24)$$

and so

$$\frac{1}{\lambda_i} \frac{dEU_i}{du_r} = \bar{n}_{ir} \int_s v_i(s) \frac{\partial f_r}{\partial u_r} ds \quad (5.25)$$

$$= \bar{n}_{ir} \frac{dp_r}{du_r} \text{ (from 5.22).} \quad (5.26)$$

This equation shows that for all individuals who start life with positive holdings of the firm's shares, their expected utility is positively related to the firm's share price (remember that the multiplier λ will be positive for all individuals who are non-satiated). All shareholders will be unanimous in wanting the firm to choose that policy which maximizes the share price because, given the policies of other firms, this policy will maximize their expected utility. Clearly, a *sufficient* condition for share price maximization to be in the interests of all shareholders is that the implicit prices be unaffected by changes in the firm's policy. In the general case where the implicit prices do change, we have

$$\frac{1}{\lambda_i}\frac{\mathrm{d}EU_i}{\mathrm{d}u_r} = \bar{n}_{ir}\frac{\mathrm{d}p_r}{\mathrm{d}u_r} - \bar{n}_{ir}\int_s \frac{\mathrm{d}v_i(s)}{\mathrm{d}u_r} f_r(u_r, s)\mathrm{d}s + \sum_j (\bar{n}_{ij} - n_{ij})\int_s \frac{\mathrm{d}v_i(s)}{\mathrm{d}u_r} f_j(u_j, s)\,\mathrm{d}s. \tag{5.27}$$

This shows that if we do not wish to impose any further constraints on either the firm's technology (as given by the function f_r) or individual preferences then it is also a *necessary* condition for all shareholders to support share price maximization that the implicit prices be independent of the firm's policy. For if this does not hold we may choose a particular technology and a pattern of preferences such that individuals would support an alternative policy, and we saw this occur in the 3-shareholder example presented above. For the sake of completeness we shall derive the implicit prices of consumption in the three states of the world in our example to illustrate how the policy of the firm affects the prices.

The equivalent equations to (5.18) for our example are for shares and bonds respectively.

$$\sum_j v_i(j)y^k(j) = p^*(k) \quad k = 1, 2 \tag{5.28}$$

$$\sum_i v_i(j) = 1. \tag{5.29}$$

The equivalent to equation (5.17) for our assumption of logarithmic utility functions is that for any two states of the world g and h

$$\frac{v_i(g)}{v_i(h)} = \frac{\pi_i(g)C_i(h)}{\pi_i(h)C_i(g)}. \tag{5.30}$$

These equations give the numerical values of the implicit prices corresponding to the first subjective probability matrix as

	Policy 1 Individuals		Policy 1 Individuals	
State of the world	1 and 2	3	1 and 2	3
1	0.75	0.60	0.05	0.05
2	0.15	0.30	0.19	0.0528
3	0.10	0.10	0.76	0.8972

This table shows, first, that the implicit prices of contingent commodities differ between individuals and, secondly, that the prices depend upon the choice of policy. The first result occurs because the economy does not have a complete set of contingent commodity markets and hence the prices are only implicit. The second result is the one which produces the fundamental problem for the theory of the firm because it means that in general:

(1) the shareholders of a firm will disagree about its choice of policy (equations (5.26) and (5.27) show that for arbitrary preferences and technology a necessary and sufficient condition for unanimity is that the implicit prices are independent of policy)

(2) even if the shareholders did by some chance all agree (if all individuals were identical, for example), then there is no presumption that they would want the firm to maximize its share price.

It is clear that even in the case where prices are independent of the firm's policy, only shareholders with positive holdings will want the firm to maximize its share price. Those with zero holdings will be indifferent, and those with negative holdings will want the firm to minimize its share price. This is because their holdings are liabilities rather than assets. A negative shareholding, known as 'short sales', is technically possible but individuals in this position do not normally have any say in the determination of the company's policy and so we can safely neglect their wishes. Moreover, it does not make sense to treat short sales as simply a negative holding, because the shares involved are the liability not of the company but of the individual who has sold them, and if there is a possibility that the individual might go bankrupt then the shares in question will not be a perfect substitute for the firm's shares but will be regarded by the market as a new asset.

Our principal conclusion is that if by altering its policy the firm can influence the implicit prices of the contingent consumption goods which its shareholders purchase, then it is wrong to assume that the firm will necessarily maximize its share price. There is scope for specifying alternative objective functions for the firm which will reflect the composition of its ownership and the fact that its shareholders will disagree about which policy the firm should pursue. This result derives not from uncertainty in itself but from the monopoly position of the firm in markets in which the shareholder makes purchases. In any circumstances in which the firm can affect the prices of commodities which its shareholders buy or sell, directly or indirectly, we cannot assume that the shareholders would support a policy of share price maximization. In general, therefore, it is by no means obvious that a monopolistically competitive firm in a world of perfect certainty would wish to maximize its profits, although this is often overlooked because the 'firm' is regarded as a black box and the composition of its owners ignored.

The shareholders of a firm cannot be assumed to forget their role as consumers of the firm's products or suppliers of its inputs. This consideration has some relevance to the analysis of the behaviour of firms controlled, at least partially, by their employees. Many firms are able to influence both the wage rates for the specific skills they employ and the working conditions of their employees. Making the employees shareholders would not necessarily lead them to advocate the same policy for the firm as would be supported by the other shareholders, even if the employees could voice their opinion only in their capacity as shareholders.

As we saw in Chapter 2 monopoly is not simply an occasional aberration from a competitive norm but a characteristic feature of an industrialized society. Moreover, when we consider uncertainty we see why monopoly, in the sense used in this chapter, is almost inevitable. In a world of uncertainty the commodity space must be enlarged to distinguish between physical commodities to be supplied contingent upon different states of the world. With such a large number of commodities we would require an enormous number of very small firms if we were to avoid a situation of monopolistic competition. Given the existence of even a limited degree of set-up costs it is not surprising that we observe a finite number of firms, and these firms will have some degree of monopoly power. The very nature of business risk is that the firm has open to it projects which have a unique pattern of returns across states of the world, and it is the role of the entrepreneur or of management to take such risks in the knowledge that no insurance market can offer them complete protection against failure. Whereas monopoly in current product markets can be legislated against, a situation in which firms exercise a monopolistic influence on future contingent commodity prices, which are not even market prices but only implicit prices because the markets do not exist, is an inevitable characteristic of a capitalist economy. Monopoly is the essence of uncertainty. In these circumstances the assumption of share price maximization is an unappealing axiom for corporate behaviour.

5.3 *A managerial model with take-overs*

The doubts which the results of the last two sections cast on the assumption of share price maximization suggest that we examine alternative specifications of the objective function of the firm. Although in a stock market economy the level of profits is uncertain, the firm could maximize the expected value of profits and this motive has been examined by Zabel (1967), Smith (1969) and Malinvaud (1972b). If share price maximization would be rejected by some shareholders, the same problems will arise with expected profit maximization, and this objective is only well defined in the highly restrictive case where all shareholders have the same expectations. If they differ in their subjective probability assessments, then we need a rule for deciding whose probabilities should be used to calculate expected profits.

Similar objections may be raised to the proposal that the firm should be assumed to have its own utility function defined on profits in each state of the world. The shape of the function is supposed to indicate the degree of the firm's aversion to risk-taking. This approach has been adopted by Sandmo (1971), Leland (1972), and Radner (1972). One of the weaknesses of the approach is that the concept of risk aversion describes the preferences of an individual and is inappropriate when applied to an organization the very rationale of which is to enable the scale of management and production (and hence profits) to be separated from the scale of ownership. The riskiness of the firm's profits will be very different from the riskiness of its shareholders' consumption level because the latter will depend upon how much of their wealth individuals choose to invest in the firm. If we try to avoid this difficulty by identifying the 'firm' with the management, we lose much of the richness of the problem by ignoring the interplay between shareholders and management.

For this reason the view that firms should be assumed to operate in their shareholders' interests has remained an idea of great appeal. However, this provides a well-defined objective function for the firm only when shareholders are unanimous in their choice of policy, and, although several authors have attempted to find general sets of conditions for shareholder unanimity (Ekern (1973), Ekern and Wilson (1974), and Leland (1974)), as we saw in the last section unanimity will be obtained only in very special cases.

In the face of a dilemma of this kind institutional arrangements will emerge or will be devised in an attempt to resolve some of the conflicts between economic agents, and to ensure that an equilibrium of a stock market economy is at least possible. We shall give examples of two of these institutional factors, the legal system and the take-over bid.

It may be possible to use the law to solve some of the conflicts between shareholders by trying to internalize the externalities which give rise to disagreement between shareholders. In some respects company law does attempt to do this by preventing 'abuses' of an individual's ability to determine company policy. In a case in the U.K.,

> Three of the four controlling members of a railway construction company wished to exclude a fourth from further participation. Instead of winding up the company, as they might have done, they diverted contracts which would otherwise have been granted to the company to a firm which they set up in their own names. The remaining member was held entitled to require the others to account to the company for the profits made on the contracts. *Cook v. Deeks* (1916) 1 A.C. 554.

Decision-making by majority voting of shareholders offers one possible solution, although a voting decision rule of this sort is open to the objections that a unique decision may not emerge (Condorcet's voting paradox described in Arrow (1951)), and that it takes no account of the intensity of shareholders' preferences. This means that we must consider situations in which either a minority of shareholders would like to buy out the majority in order to change the firm's policy, or a majority might abuse its position of control to persecute the minority, thus undermining the whole system by making individuals or groups unwilling to hold a minority stake in any company. On this latter point a number of rules exist to prevent a majority of the shareholders from 'oppressing the minority' by which is meant a policy of exercising majority power to discriminate in favour of one particular group of shareholders. This does not, however, mean that the majority cannot pursue a course which appears to damage the interests of all shareholders,

> A small minority shareholder in a car washing company complained that the controlling shareholder and director was acting oppressively, for instance by issuing car wash vouchers at a discount in order to secure a rapid cash inflow, though the price of the vouchers was less than the cost of washing, and more generally by not attending to the payment of the company's creditors so as to make the continuance of its business difficult. It was held that such allegations of mismanagement or inefficiency were not sufficient to establish oppression. *In re Five Minute Car Wash Service Ltd* (1966) 1 W.L.R. 745.

This example shows that a minority of shareholders may well disagree with the majority and it is not inconceivable that they could bribe the majority into changing the firm's policy. To allow for behaviour of this kind it has been suggested that the process of determining the firm's policy be modelled as a co-operative game between the shareholders (Drèze 1974, Hart 1976). In this approach coalitions of shareholders are formed which exchange both shares and commodities (or money) to achieve a reallocation of control of the firms in the economy. Unfortunately, as Hart shows, if control of a firm can be exercised by holding less than than 100% of the shares, (which it clearly can in practice because company law embodies majority control), then there may be no equilibrium solution to the game. This approach also assumes that coalitions of shareholders may be formed easily and costlessly, and it ignores the costs involved in obtaining information about the firm's activities and about the consequences of changing its policy. We shall suggest a somewhat different approach which introduces the existence of management teams and stresses the role of information.

In the model of a stock market economy analysed in the previous section, the informational requirements of economic agents were quite stringent. When deciding on which policy a firm should pursue individuals were assumed to know, first, the consequences of different policies for the firm's profits in each state of the world (the functions $f(u, s)$), and secondly, the values of the equilibrium prices which would emerge in the stock market corresponding to any given set of policies which had been announced by firms. Knowledge of the latter is a particularly stringent requirement because it means that individuals must be able to compute the general equilibrium solutions of a stock market economy. Past experience may offer a guide, but will not provide a complete answer. In the same context we may note that for a firm to be able to maximize its share price, even if this were agreed to be desirable, it too would need the ability to compute equilibria. This requirement places much greater demands on economic agents than is required in the simple complete markets model in which all external information needed by individuals is conveyed in the values of market prices. In practice individuals and firms will have expectations about how changes in policy would affect share prices, and these may be represented by 'perceived' demand curves for firms' shares.

The first informational requirement to which we drew attention was knowledge of the effects of a policy change on the firm's profits. Each shareholder has a set of beliefs about the effects of different policies on profits, but he may well have little confidence in these beliefs. Unfortunately for him to obtain further information is unlikely to be a costless operation, and it makes more sense for him, along with all the other shareholders, to rely on management to exercise its judgment. One of the primary roles of management is not just the organization of production but the collection and analysis of information regarding potential future projects. Since shareholders rely on management for this purpose there is clearly room for management to exploit its position and pursue to some extent its own objectives. The threat to management and the constraint on its discretionary behaviour is its possible replacement by an alternative managerial team. Shareholders who lack adequate information are constrained to choose between alternative managerial teams, not between alternative policies. The process by which shareholders learn is the receipt and absorption of information, and their behaviour will be affected by the credence they give to various reports. Thus one of the roles of company law is to prevent shareholders being given false information which it would be impossible or expensive for them to check. The following case illustrates the point:

> A company issued a prospectus inviting subscriptions for the purpose of buying a rubber estate in Peru. The prospectus contained extracts from the report of an expert on the spot, which gave the number of matured rubber trees on the estate, and other information. The report was false. *Held*, the accuracy of the report was *prima facie* the basis of the contract and, therefore, if the company did not intend to contract on that basis, it should have dissociated itself from the report in clear and unambiguous terms, and warned the public that it did not vouch for the accuracy of the

report. As there was no such warning the contracts to take shares could be rescinded *Re Pacaya Rubber and Produce Co. Ltd.* (1914) 1 Ch. 542.

The model analysed above assumed also that the shareholders took the price of shares as given when making their portfolio decisions. It may be possible for some shareholders to influence the market price either by the size of their transactions or by circulating information which leads other shareholders to revise their plans and gives rise to a new set of equilibrium prices. Again the law does not permit the circulation of false information for this purpose, a decision emanating from a case of 1814.

A number of people arranged for false reports of the death of Napoleon to reach London. The price of Government securities, of which they had recently made large purchases, rose sharply. Those involved sold out and made a handsome profit. The ring leaders were subsequently indicted and convicted of conspiring to cause a rise in the price of the public funds by false rumours. The conviction was upheld on appeal as a fraud on the public: it was a conspiracy to effect a public mischief by giving a false price to a vendible commodity on the market by means of false rumours' *R. v. de Berenger* (1814) 3 M. & S. 67.

These cases demonstrate the close relationship between the theory of the corporation in a world of uncertainty and the institutional and legal forms of control which have grown up to monitor its behaviour.

Because of the cost of obtaining information it is difficult for a shareholder to evaluate the merits of the current management's performance, and even more difficult to persuade his fellow shareholders to form a coalition in order to change the firm's policy. In the light of such costs we suggest the following managerial model for a stock market economy. In addition to the given number of firms there are a number of managerial teams which compete for the right to run particular firms. The teams own shares and obtain utility both from consumption and from being in power. There is an initial assignment of teams to firms (some teams may initially be unemployed, at least as managers). Any team can challenge an existing management by proposing an alternative policy than the one currently proposed. The shareholders then vote between the existing management team and the rival team, the outcome being determined by majority vote. The teams will also be able to cast their votes and will obviously have an incentive to buy shares in firms they would like to control. Individuals trade on the stock market, given the policy in force, and vote between teams in proportion to their holdings. Equilibrium is characterized by a set of market-clearing share prices, a policy for each firm, and an assignment of managerial teams to firms. In the equilibrium position the following conditions must hold.

(1) Given the policies adopted by firms, each shareholder must be holding his optimal portfolio.

(2) Given these equilibrium shareholdings no policy put up by a management team other than the existing management would attract majority support.

(3) Given the policies and the shareholdings of existing management teams, no rival team has an incentive to simultaneously trade on the stock market and propose an alternative policy for consideration by the shareholders.

The interpretation of this model is that the individual shareholders behave as conventional price-takers and policy-takers, but that the management teams are involved in a non-co-operative game. Although it raises the usual problems associated with majority voting, the model does contain a number of realistic features. In a sample survey of shareholders of a large company Vernon, Middleton and Harper (1973) found that the most important factor in the minds of shareholders when assessing the company's performance was not its financial record but the 'quality of the management team'. Take-over activity also has a place in the model. A take-over bid may be defined as the proposal of an alternative policy by a rival management team, and a take-over takes place if the proposal is accepted by a majority of the shareholders.

We have not so far discussed the dynamics of the managerial model and it is evident that this creates a further problem for the shareholders to consider. In the three-shareholder example it was apparent that a vote of the *ex ante* shareholders produced a different outcome from a vote of the *ex post* shareholders. Underlying this phenomenon is a dynamic problem. In our model individuals can do two things. Firstly, they can buy or sell shares at known equilibrium prices, and knowing the policy decision of the firm. Secondly, they may vote between policies by casting a number of votes in proportion to their shareholding. As long as these two aspects can be kept as separate decisions in the minds of the shareholders the outcome is determinate. However, as soon as shareholders realise the myopic nature of this attitude the situation changes. In our example there would be no problems if the decision were made by *ex ante* shareholder voting and could not be changed. However, if the vote were to be taken after the stock market had closed then shareholders' demands for shares would be affected by their expectations about which policy was likely to win. This would depend upon their estimate of other shareholders' demands for shares which in turn would depend upon their expectations about the outcome of the vote, and so on. The sequential nature of decisions on policies on the one hand, and trading in the stock market on the other, is an additional complication in reaching an equilibrium in stock market economies. Just as in sequence economies of the traditional type, where the fact that the spot markets re-open creates a role for price expectations, in stock market economies policy expectations are important even when the stock market itself does not re-open.

Take-over bids in practice usually involve the offer to purchase from the existing shareholders any shares they may wish to sell at a fixed offer price. This brings to the fore the difference between individuals who buy and sell shares in the market taking the policies of companies as given, and those traders who buy and sell in order to change a firm's policy. The latter may be described as take-over raiders and in our model only managerial teams can be take-over raiders. This distinction is precisely that used by the authorities in defining what actions should be subject to the controls imposed on those making take-over bids, in that any attempt to buy control of a company through the market or otherwise is deemed to constitute a take-over bid, and is subject to the same controls on disclosure as other more formal bids. Since the demand curve for a firm's shares will be downward-sloping (as was demonstrated in the last section) it is clear that a premium over the current share price must be paid in order to buy sufficient shares to take over the company. The market share price measures the valuation of the marginal shareholder, whereas to buy control a raider must persuade a good number of the intra-marginal shareholders to part with their shares. This shows immediately that there is no necessary relationship between the market valuation of a company and its probability of being taken-over. A raider cannot purchase a company at its current share price and the probability of a bid being successful is related not to the share price but to the valuation of the firm under the existing management of the intra-marginal shareholders. We should not be surprised therefore to find that the empirical correlation between take-over and share prices or valuation ratios is weak. This finding (see, for example, Singh (1971)) runs counter to the arguments advanced by Marris (1964). The real test of the relevance of a managerial model is not whether a firm maximizes its share price but whether managerial behaviour is influenced or modified by the threat of take-over. We shall investigate this issue in the context of an econometric study of corporate dividend and financial behaviour in Chapters 6 and 7.

We may now extend our definition of a take-over bid to include an offer by a rival management team to purchase any number of shares at a fixed price together with a proposal of the policy it would pursue if the offer were successful. The take-over takes place if a majority of the shareholders agree to the offer. This involves no bargaining by the individual shareholders who react to the offer as individuals. Their willingness to sell will depend upon their valuation of the shares relative to the offer price, and their valuation will depend upon whether they think the bid is likely to succeed. The participants in the bid have an incentive to influence shareholders' expectations about the outcome of the bid. Although in the model we have suggested a take-over bid can be made only by a rival management team, it can be financed by individuals who may purchase shares in a company controlled by the rival team. This provides an indirect route by which a minority of shareholders can pay another management team to buy out the majority in order to change the firm's policy. For this to happen, however, the initiative must come from the rival team and since it is involved in a game with the existing management, and indeed other rival teams, it is not necessarily always in its interests to take up the cause of the minority and make a take-over bid. One reason for this is that both shareholders and management teams are uncertain about the preferences of shareholders (as we argued above, current market prices do not convey sufficient information) and hence cannot be sure whether any given bid would be successful. Since a take-over bid is not a costless operation, management teams will think carefully before making a public bid for another firm. A major cost of an unsuccessful bid by a team is the possible adverse impression of the team's judgment which may be given to its own shareholders, thus making *itself* more exposed to a take-over bid.

In this section we have suggested that to understand the behaviour of joint-stock companies it is perhaps best to consider them as being run by a number of management teams which are empowered to select a set of policies subject to the constraint that they may be dismissed by their shareholders and replaced by a rival team. Such a formulation seems to correspond more to the reality of a stock market economy in which management takes the initiative in formulating policy, and in which the main threat to its security comes from take-over bids. A general model might endow the management team with its own utility function of which the perceived risk of take-over would be one argument, but which would also contain other variables from which management derived utility, such as growth or size. It is the lack of information possessed by, and the difference of opinions between, shareholders which create the discretionary power for management to pursue their own goals. A serious weakness of conventional managerial models of the firm is that they often ignore shareholders altogether, thus disregarding the problems which provide the rationale for the concept of managerial discretion. The composition of share ownership may still have an influence on the firm's behaviour, even though it is controlled by a management team.

If share price maximization is to be retained as an objective function for the firm, then its justification must surely be as a *rule of thumb*, to be adopted in the absence of information about the preferences of shareholders.

5.4 *Uncertainty and the debt–equity ratio*

In Chapter 4 we demonstrated that in the absence of taxes and transaction costs the market value of a firm facing a perfect capital market would be independent of its debt–equity ratio, or indeed any other aspect of its financial policy such as the dividend payout ratio. Hence the firm would be indifferent to its choice of financial policy. The assumptions which were responsible for this result were that both individuals and firms could borrow or lend as much as they wanted at a common market rate of interest, and that it was certain that interest payments would always be made, that is there was no risk of default.

A great deal has been written by economists about how far this result survives the introduction of uncertainty into the model. This interest was inspired by the work of Modigliani and Miller (1958) who showed that, even in the presence of uncertainty, the value of a firm would be independent of its debt–equity ratio under certain conditions. The precise nature of the assumptions necessary for the result to hold have been the subject of much debate since (for example, Hirshleifer (1966), Robichek and Myers (1966), Stiglitz (1969), (1972), (1974), Smith (1970), (1972), Fama and Miller (1972), Milne (1975), Baron (1976) and Hagen (1976)).

In fact the general conditions which are both necessary and sufficient for the firm to be indifferent to its financial policy are provided by the results of Section 5.3. This is because we may interpret the policy variable of firm j, u_j, as its debt–equity ratio. Since a change in the debt–equity ratio cannot affect the profits of the firm in any state of the world, but only the division of those profits between the shareholders and the bondholders, the effect of a change in the debt–equity ratio of firm j (denoted by d_j) on the value of the firm to its shareholders is given by equation (5.22) as

$$\frac{\mathrm{d}p_j}{\mathrm{d}d_j} = \int_s \frac{\mathrm{d}v_i(s)}{\mathrm{d}d_j} f_j(u_j, s)\,\mathrm{d}s. \tag{5.31}$$

This shows that without making any assumptions about bankruptcy or the existence of similar firms in identical 'risk classes' (as assumed by Modigliani and Miller (1958) in their original paper), or the number of markets, the general necessary and sufficient condition for the firm's value to be independent of its debt–equity ratio is that the implicit prices of the contingent commodities bought or sold by its shareholders are independent of its debt–equity ratio.

The proof of this theorem is appealing in its simplicity, and it enables the basic result to be derived without the need for any of the special assumptions made by other writers (see the contributions listed above) which make it difficult to compare their results. Nevertheless, we shall present an alternative proof to throw further light on the nature of the problem. We shall formally introduce bonds into the model of a stock market economy analysed in the previous section. Before the stock market opens firm j announces both a production policy u_j and its intention of issuing bonds to the value b_j at an interest rate r_j. There are no bonds initially and endowments consist only of shares. The stock market opens and individuals exchange shares and bonds. Since no inputs to production are required, the proceeds of the bond issue are returned to the shareholders immediately the stock market has closed. This means that the effective price of a share of firm j in the stock market is $p_j - b_j$. In period 2 the state of the world is known and the profits of firm j are either sufficient to meet the repayment of interest and principal, or they are not in which case the firm is said to be bankrupt. Let the set of states in which firm j does not go bankrupt be denoted by s_1, and the set of states in which it does go bankrupt by s_2. Clearly s_1 and s_2 form a complete partition of the states of the world, and the partition will depend upon the firm's debt–equity ratio. We shall assume that the firm has limited liability so that in s_1 the returns to shareholders are the firm's profits minus its debt commitments, and in s_2 the shareholders receive nothing. Then we know from equation (5.18) that the effective share price is the inner product of the vectors of the shareholder's implicit contingent commodity prices and the returns to shareholders in different states of the world.

$$\int_{s_1} v_i(s)\,[f_j(u_j, s) - b_j(1 + r_j)]\,ds = p_j - b_j \qquad \text{(for all } i\text{).} \quad (5.32)$$

The bondholders receive full repayment of their loans in states belonging to s_1, and receive the firm's profits in s_2. Hence

$$\int_{s_1} v_i(s)\,b_j(1 + r_j)ds + \int_{s_2} v_i(s) f_j(u_j, s)ds = b_j \qquad \text{(for all } i\text{).} \quad (5.33)$$

If we add these two equations we obtain

$$p_j = \int_s v_i(s) f_j(u_j, s)\,ds \quad \text{(for all } i\text{).} \qquad (5.34)$$

Hence the share price, or market value, of the firm is completely independent of its debt–equity ratio if, and only if, (for an arbitrary specification of technology and individual preferences) the implicit prices of contingent consumption goods are independent of the debt–equity ratio. If we differentiate equation (5.34) with respect to the debt–equity ratio we obtain equation (5.31).

Since the condition that the implicit prices be independent of the firm's policy is also the necessary and sufficient condition for shareholders to agree on the choice of policy and to agree on share price maximization, we immediately have the following result: *either* the implicit prices are independent of the firm's debt–equity ratio, in which case all shareholders agree on share price maximization but are quite indifferent to the firm's financial policy because this cannot affect the share price; *or* the choice of debt–equity ratio will alter the implicit prices, in which case the shareholders will care about the choice of the firm's debt–equity ratio but will not in general agree that the firm should maximize its share price. Hence the idea of an 'optimal' debt–equity ratio based on the assumption that the firm will maximize its share price or market value is a contradiction in terms. The very situations in which the debt–equity ratio matters are those in which the assumption of share price maximization breaks down and there is no well-defined objective function for the firm. To discuss the determinants of the debt–equity ratio would require the specification of an alternative objective function for the firm.

In terms of the managerial model suggested above the choice of a firm's debt–equity ratio is one element of a strategy in a game being played between the current management of the firm and rival management teams. Seen from a game-theoretic point of view there is no such thing as an 'optimal' debt–equity ratio because the management is not optimizing subject to externally given constraints. If we suppose that the main threat to management comes from a take-over bid by one of its rivals then it is not unreasonable to believe that the management would aim for an 'acceptable' debt–equity ratio which would be influenced by changes in management's subjective fear of being taken-over. The danger, of course, is that a rival team need only buy out, or obtain the support of a majority of the equity holders and for a given firm size the higher the debt–equity ratio, the easier it is for a rival team to do this. Also there is evidence that in the U.K. at least, management does think in terms of an 'acceptable' rather than an 'optimal' debt–equity ratio (HMSO 1975; paragraph 195). In Chapter 7 we shall test an econometric model of the determinants of the debt–equity ratio which incorporates the effect of take-over activity.

Two further considerations may influence the firm's choice of debt–equity ratio. The first is the effect of taxation, which we have analysed theoretically in Chapter 4 and to which we shall return in the empirical investigation of Chapter 7. The second is the legal consequence for the management of bankruptcy. If the firm goes bankrupt then the management loses its position and control of the firm switches from the representatives of its shareholders to those of its creditors and debt-holders. In our two-period model this was of no consequence because there were no decisions to be taken in period 2; but, in a model with many periods, bankruptcy itself becomes an elusive concept because in principle the firm may always borrow to meet its current debt obligations thus postponing the day of reckoning. If the situation improves this day will never come but it is clear that both the definition of bankruptcy and its consequences are dependent upon the confidence which the firm's creditors, and the market in general, have in the current management. Although this might suggest that in the absence of taxation the management would try to minimize the debt–equity ratio such an argument ignores the wishes of the shareholders who in general will care about the ratio, and there is no presumption that they will want a very low debt–equity ratio. It does suggest, however, that in economies with highly developed capital markets where take-overs are a normal part of stock market activity, there will be a risk entailed in adopting a debt–equity ratio which is higher than is necessary to keep the shareholders satisfied. The major reason for shareholders wanting a high debt–equity ratio is the existence of tax incentives to debt finance. Provided that this constraint is not violated and that there is no imminent threat of take-over, management will be free to operate independently of its creditors and debt-holders. In other economies with less developed stock markets the influence of shareholders and rival management teams will be less, and the firm will be free to raise its debt–equity ratio and will need to do so to obtain sufficient finance. If it pursues this policy, however, in order to build up confidence it will need to inform its creditors regularly about its policy, so that if in a bad year it finds difficulty in meeting its debt obligations the creditors will be willing to extend further loan facilities. With high debt–equity ratios the creditors are becoming more like shareholders, but without formal control, and this fact is likely to be reflected in the growth of consultation between the management and its major creditors.

The basic condition for a firm to be indifferent to its choice of debt–equity ratio is that the implicit prices of contingent commodities be independent of the ratio. In general these prices will be dependent upon both the firm's financial policy and its real policy, although there are a number of special cases in which the prices will be independent:

(1) The Arrow–Debreu world in which markets exist for all contingent commodities. If each firm is *small* in relation to the size of the market then it will be unable to affect the equilibrium contingent commodity prices. This result depends crucially on each firm being small.

(2) Similar to case (1) is the situation in which, although there are no markets in contingent commodities themselves, there are as many firms as there are states of the world and each firm has a profit vector which is linearly independent of the profit vectors of all other firms. Then equation (5.34) can be seen to be the jth equation in a system of simultaneous equations which for given real policies of each firm and for a given set of share prices determine the values of the implicit prices which will be the same for all individuals. Another firm may be set up, and whatever real or financial policy it chooses, provided it believes its choice will have no effect on other firms' share prices or

choice of policy, the set of simultaneous equations will remain the same and its solution will produce the same values for the implicit contingent commodity prices. In principle, however, there is no reason for a firm operating in an economy, comprising a finite number of firms, to believe that its policy will not influence the equilibrium set of share prices.

(3) Similar to case (2) is the situation in which a potential new firm has the ability to produce only those profit vectors which are linearly dependent on the profit vectors of the existing firms (the so-called 'spanning' property discussed by Ekern and Wilson (1974)). If the firm believes that it cannot influence the share prices of other firms (in some sense each firm is 'small') then it cannot alter the set of equations which determine the implicit prices because it is adding an extra linearly dependent equation which is therefore redundant. For the new firm to believe that it cannot influence other share prices requires it to supply a quantity of the particular 'pattern of returns across states of the world' which is very small in relation to the total supply by other firms. In a world of uncertainty with an extremely large number of contingent commodities this is unlikely to be the case. Consequently, even if the 'spanning' property holds, both the real and financial policies of a new firm are likely to affect the implicit prices giving rise to all of the problems that we have discussed above in connection with the firm's objective function and debt–equity ratio. The 'spanning' property is not sufficient to ensure that the implicit prices are independent of the firm's policy.

(4) The remaining special case where the debt–equity ratio does not matter is where bankruptcy never occurs and is never expected to occur whatever the amount borrowed by either firms or individuals. In the absence of bankruptcy equation (5.33) becomes

$$\int_s v_i(s)\mathrm{d}s = \frac{1}{1+r_j} \qquad \text{(for all } i \text{ and } j\text{).} \tag{5.35}$$

This equation shows that in the absence of bankruptcy all firms may borrow or lend at the same market rate of interest. We may note that this statement makes no assumption about whether the firm can influence the market rate of interest through its borrowing policy. The same holds true for individuals who may borrow by selling bonds short, a possibility which we have not so far ruled out. Thus an implication of the no bankruptcy assumption is that both firms and individuals may borrow or lend at a common interest rate.

The budget constraint of individual i in the model in which firms may issue bonds is given by

$$\sum_j p_j \bar{n}_{ij} = \sum_j (p_j - b_j) n_{ij} + \sum_j b_{ij}. \tag{5.36}$$

The consumption possibility set of individual i is described by

$$C_i(s) = \sum_j n_{ij} f_j(u_j, s) + (1 + r) \sum_j p_j(\bar{n}_{ij} - n_{ij}) \tag{5.37}$$

where r is the market rate of interest. For a given set of market prices the individual may choose any point in the space described by (5.37) by choosing any values he likes for n_{ij}. Suppose we start in an initial equilibrium and then a particular firm (or group of firms) changes its debt–equity ratio holding real policies constant. The question is, what will the new equilibrium look like? Imagine that immediately after the change the same set of prices prevailed in the share and bond markets as characterized the initial equilibrium. We know that if all the share prices p_j and the interest rate r remain the same then each individual's consumption possibility set is unaltered, and hence they will choose the same values for the n_{ij} as before. Since their planned equity holdings are unchanged the markets in shares will again be in equilibrium. It is now trivial to show that the bond market also remains in equilibrium. Since the interest rate is common to all we may write down the net excess demand for bonds as

$$\sum_i \sum_j b_{ij} - \sum_j b_j \tag{5.38}$$

$$= \sum_i \sum_j \{p_j(\bar{n}_{ij} - n_{ij}) + b_j n_{ij}\} - \sum_j b_j$$

$$= \sum_j p_j \sum_i (\bar{n}_{ij} - n_{ij}) + \sum_j b_j \sum_i n_{ij} - \sum_j b_j$$

$$= 0 \qquad \left(\text{since } \sum_i n_{ij} = 1\right). \tag{5.39}$$

Even though the debt–equity ratio of one or several firms has changed, the equilibrium share price and interest rate remains the same and the proportion of each firm owned by each individual is the same. The consumption of each individual is also unaltered and so the implicit prices given by equation (5.17) will be unchanged. The debt–equity ratio of the firm is a matter of complete indifference to the firm and its shareholders.

The assumption that bankruptcy never occurs is, however, quite ridiculous as the following story shows. A small entrepreneur experiences a dream which convinces him that a Great Drought is soon to descend on the world drying up all known sources of water. It so happens that current storage facilities for water are non-existent. The entrepreneur decides to invest in a huge project of constructing and filling storage tanks all round the world which, in the event of a drought, would give him a world monopoly of water. This power, so he reckons, would be enough to earn him fabulous riches beyond belief, beautiful women beyond description, and power beyond his imagination. To finance this project he simply issues bonds and because there is assumed to be no risk of bankruptcy the market is quite indifferent to his firm's debt–equity ratio.

Alas, few entrepreneurs are in the position of this fortunate individual for the simple reason that most of the lenders in the market have not experienced the same dream and believe that there is an exceedingly high probability that 'crackpots' of this kind will go bankrupt. This means that they will either demand a much higher rate of interest from the risky entrepreneur or refuse to offer credit facilities above some upper limit. In this situation where there is a positive probability of default a firm's debt–equity clearly will matter. This is not simply a question of differing expectations about the likelihood of bankruptcy. If our daring entrepreneur had planned to finance 99% of his project by debt his local bank manager might have been more than a little alarmed to discover that before his dream the entrepreneur had been a manufacturer of storage tanks and had been unable to sell all his production. The uncivil thought that his prospective client might solve all his financial problems, enjoy an expensive foreign holiday, and then disappear, might cause the bank manager to hesitate.

The institution of limited liability for his firm may mean that our entrepreneur is quite willing to plan for the firm to go bankrupt in certain states of the world. If he believes that in certain states he will go bankrupt he has an incentive to go bankrupt in a big way. For example, if his profits may take the values of either 10 or 20 and he has an existing debt of 10, then the entrepreneur might try to raise a further loan of 10 by concealing the existence of the first loan. If he can do this then there may be an equilibrium level of planned criminal behaviour.

The above arguments are no less true for an individual than for a firm. The model was developed on the assumption that there was no limit on an individual's ability to sell bonds short, but selling bonds short is equivalent to borrowing. Like a firm, an individual may go bankrupt in some states of the world and this will mean that he will not be able to borrow on the same terms as firms or other individuals. Consequently, we must either drop the assumption of price-taking behaviour in the bond market, or impose credit limits on individuals which would mean that the first-order conditions for the maximization of his expected utility would no longer be given by equations (5.32) and (5.33). Individuals will certainly now care about the debt–equity ratios of the firms in which they invest.

It might be argued that an individual would never choose to go bankrupt in any state of the world because he is not protected, as firms are, by limited liability. This argument is false for two reasons. First, an individual may sincerely believe that there is a zero probability of his going bankrupt while others believe that there is in fact a positive probability. It is the opinions of the others which matter. Secondly, we have not yet defined the consequences of bankruptcy for an individual. Negative consumption is infeasible and few societies are willing to impose mandatory death sentences on bankrupts through either starvation or more positive action, although even this might not be sufficient to ensure that an individual never plans to go bankrupt in any state of the world. The institutional and legal consequences of personal bankruptcy will be a determinant of the resulting equilibrium.

The upshot of all this is that shareholders will care about both the real and financial policies of firms. Moreover, the ability of any one individual to put into effect an idea or production plan will depend critically on his initial wealth. A wealthy individual will be freed from the necessity to borrow in order to finance a project and he may also be able to buy control of existing companies. A poor man with bright ideas will have to persuade his wealthier colleagues that his ideas are worth supporting. In this sense wealth is power, for it means that the investment decisions which are taken will reflect the views of those with wealth. In an economy in which the establishment of a new firm entails a certain minimum level of initial set-up costs not only will there be a finite number of firms (because the economy's total resources are limited), but an individual who starts life with a small initial endowment will find it difficult to start his own firm unless he can persuade a sufficient number of other individuals to buy equities or bonds in his idea. He will need to establish a concensus that the project is worthwhile. A rich man can simply go ahead and back his own judgment..

5.5 *A model of shareholder influence*

We have shown above that the assumption that firms maximize their share price loses much of its force in a world of uncertainty. Nevertheless, at least some firms may continue to pursue a policy of share price maximization in the absence of a clear alternative, and we shall examine the consequences of this kind of behaviour for the influence of shareholders on corporate policy.

We shall use the same model as before. Consider a particular firm pursuing a policy denoted by u and whose shares sell at a price p (in this section subscripts will appear only when denoting individuals). The demand by individual i for the shares of this firm will be a function of the share price of each firm, the policy of each firm, and his initial endowment. The share prices of other firms will be a function of initial endowments and policies chosen by firms, and so we may write the aggregate demand function for the shares of the firm as

$$n = \sum_i n_i(u, p). \tag{5.40}$$

where the parameters of this function are the initial endowments of each individual, and the policies followed by the other firms in the economy. We shall now assume that the firm acts *competitively*, in that it takes the policies of other firms as given. This implies that when announcing a new policy, the firm ignores any repercussions which this may have on the decisions of other firms.

If we suppose that the firm maximizes its share price p subject to the constraint that the demand for its shares must equal the supply, we may set up the following Lagrangian

$$\mathscr{L} = p + \lambda[\bar{n} - \sum_i n_i(u, p)]. \tag{5.41}$$

The first-order conditions for a maximum are

$$\lambda \sum_i \frac{\partial n_i}{\partial p} = 1 \tag{5.42}$$

$$\lambda \sum_i \frac{\partial n_i}{\partial u} = 0. \tag{5.43}$$

The second-order conditions require that the total demand for shares be a concave function of the policy variable.

The first equation says that if we draw the aggregate demand function for the firm's shares (as a function of price) corresponding to the optimal choice of policy, then its slope is measured by λ. The second equation gives the choice of optimal policy, u^*. To explore the determinants of u^* further, we shall construct the following quadratic distance function for each shareholder

$$d_i = \tfrac{1}{2}(u - u_i^*)^2 \tag{5.44}$$

where u_i^* is the optimal policy for the firm in the opinion of shareholder i. It is the solution obtained by setting equation (5.19) equal to zero, and is given by the maximization of the expected utility of shareholder i on the assumption that the policies pursued by the other firms remain unchanged. The value of d_i measures the distance between the actual policy being pursued by the firm, and the policy which shareholder i would like to see pursued. We shall now make the strong assumption that the demand for shares by individual i may be written as a function of the distance between his desired policy and the actual policy

$$n_i = n_i(d_i, p). \tag{5.45}$$

In this case equation (5.43) becomes

$$\sum_i \frac{\partial n_i}{\partial d_i}(u - u_i^*) = 0. \tag{5.46}$$

The optimal policy for the firm, u^*, is the solution to this equation and is given by

$$u^* = \frac{\sum_i (\partial n_i/\partial d_i) u_i^*}{\sum_i \partial n_i/\partial d_i}. \tag{5.47}$$

If we put $\alpha_i = \dfrac{1}{n_i}\dfrac{\partial n_i}{\partial d_i}$, we have

$$u^* = \frac{\sum_i \alpha_i n_i u_i^*}{\sum_i \alpha_i n_i}. \tag{5.48}$$

The optimal policy is a weighted average of the policies desired by each individual shareholder, where the weights are the product of two terms. The first is the value of α_i which is the proportionate change in his holding which shareholder i makes per unit change in the distance between the actual and desired policies, and so α could be described as the 'coefficient of sensitivity'. The second term is simply the fraction of the equity owned by shareholder i. His influence on the choice of corporate policy is then given by the interaction between the size of his holding in the company, and the sensitivity with which that holding is altered in response to a change in company policy.

In the special case where the value of α_i, the coefficient of sensitivity, is the same for all shareholders, the influence of each shareholder on corporate policy is directly proportional to the fraction of the total equity that he owns. We may describe this as the *ownership model.* This model illustrates in a rather vivid manner the difference between decision-making by majority vote of the shareholders and decision-making through the market which takes account of all shareholders in proportion to their stake in the company.

In general the value of α_i will be a function of the shareholder's wealth, his attitude towards risk, and the technological relationship between the value of the firm's policy variable and its profits in each state of the world. However, *ceteris paribus*, there is one additional factor which leads to an interesting difference between shareholders. This is their differential access to, and possession of, information about the potential profitability of the firm's activities. The major differential access to information is likely to arise between managers and shareholders, but within the class of shareholders there are likely to be significant differences, and the better informed a shareholder is the more sensitive he is likely to be to the firm's choice of policy. Consequently, well informed shareholders will have larger than average values of α_i, and hence, *ceteris paribus*, more influence on the choice of policy, whereas ill-informed shareholders will have small values of α_i, and hence little impact on corporate policy. In the limit a shareholder whose demand for shares is independent of the firm's choice of policy has no influence at all on that choice of policy. For example, a widow who had inherited her shares from her husband but took no interest in the company's activities would exert no influence on the firm even if her shareholding were substantial, while an institution might exert an influence out of all proportion to the size of its holding. For this reason we may call this model the *influence model.*

The influence which a shareholder has depends not only on the size of his shareholding, but also on the value of his coefficient of sensitivity.

The assumption that an individual's demand for shares can be expressed in the form of equation (5.45) is of course highly restrictive, and we have used it purely for illustrative purposes. It imposes a symmetry on the demand response to changes in the policy variable in either direction from the optimum which may be quite unrealistic, and we may identify two reasons for expecting to find difficulty in generating demand functions of a simple analytical form. Firstly, an individual's demand for the shares of a firm will be a function of his expectations about which policy the firm will in fact pursue. In the model we have just considered, the problem can be overcome provided the firm knows which policy will maximize the share price. It then announces this policy and shareholders act on the certain belief that this policy will be adopted. However, this arrangement imposes quite stringent informational requirements on the firm because it has to know the demand function for its shares for *each* of the policy alternatives open to it, and if it tries to learn about these demand functions by trial and error then, at each iteration in the process, shareholders (provided they realize the firm may be experimenting) will not assume that the currently announced policy will be maintained and hence will undermine the basis for the experiments.

Secondly, the direct utility function of each individual is defined on the quantities of contingent commodities in his consumption bundle. In order to facilitate the derivation of demand functions we may consider his indirect utility function which is defined on the prices of the contingent commodities (the use of indirect utility functions is discussed further in the next chapter). Since the (implicit) prices of contingent commodities are a function of the firm's policy, to construct an analytical form for the consumer's demand curve for the firm's shares we have to make some assumption about the functional form both of the consumer's utility function *and* of the mapping from the firm's policy to the set of contingent commodity prices.

These two reasons make it unlikely, even in the straight-forward two-period model that we have examined, that we could derive simple functional forms for the demand curve for a firm's shares, the complications would become even greater in a multi-period model. It will still be true, however, that the optimal policy for the firm u^* will be a function of the desired policies of the shareholders, the u_i^*, although the function will be a complex one.

In this chapter we have seen that there are some real theoretical problems with the pure neoclassical theory of the firm, that the axiom of share price maximization (the dynamic equivalent of static profit maximization) is not obviously acceptable, and that there is no unique answer to the question of what constitutes the objective function of the firm. This enables institutional factors to be introduced into the theory of the firm, and in particular, creates room for management to play a special role. The divorce between rigidly neoclassical and rigidly managerial theories of the firm is artificial. It is the existence of differences between shareholders which allows management to hold the ring and it would be wrong to characterize the effects of uncertainty in terms of a simple management–shareholder confrontation. In the last section we have tried to show that the link between ownership and control of a company may be a complex and subtle relationship, but it would be an exaggeration to describe this situation as exemplifying complete separation of ownership and control, a stylization which is commonplace in current discussion. In a situation in which market opportunities are limited, as, for example, in a world of uncertainty with an incomplete set of markets, the utility of wealth cannot be measured simply by its market value because it also confers 'power', in the technical sense used in this chapter of being able to influence investment decisions in the economy.

Chapter 6

ECONOMETRIC MODELS OF DIVIDEND BEHAVIOUR

> Economics is a science of thinking in terms of models joined to the art of choosing models which are relevant to the contemporary world (John Maynard Keynes, in a letter to Roy Harrod, 1938).

In previous chapters we have looked at corporate behaviour from the theoretical point of view, and it is now time to examine the empirical evidence. An empirical analysis is important because some knowledge of the quantitative response of companies to changes in their environment is essential to the correct formulation of public policy, such as the design of an 'optimal' company tax system. We shall concentrate on the U.K. experience because there has been sufficient variation in the corporate environment, both fiscal and otherwise, in the U.K. to provide an opportunity for econometric estimation and to point out lessons for the future.

In Chapter 4 we analysed the optimal financial policy under different personal and corporate tax regimes, and Chapter 5 demonstrated that considerable complications are created by the introduction of uncertainty into the analysis. We shall try to bring together the rather different approaches of these two chapters within the framework of an econometric study of corporate financial behaviour. In this chapter we examine the determinants of corporate dividend behaviour, and the subsequent chapter deals with the testing of the hypotheses about the effect of taxation on financial policy developed in Chapter 4, and also with a model of the debt–equity ratio.

Why do we single out dividend behaviour for special treatment? There are several reasons for wishing to explore the behaviour of corporate dividends in some detail. Firstly, one of the principal aims of past reforms of the corporate tax system has been to alter the incentive to distribute earnings by changing the relative tax costs of dividends and retentions, and it is clearly important to know how effective these reforms have been. Secondly, and related to the first point, is the fact that, as we saw in Chapter 2, ordinary shares are one of the most highly concentrated forms of wealth-holding and measures of the distribution of income conventionally exclude capital gains from the definition of income while including dividends. Hence a shift from dividends to retentions, induced perhaps by a change in the tax system, may lead to an apparent change in the distribution of income even though post-tax profits and the underlying real distribution have remained unchanged. This is likely to be particularly true for those measures which concentrate on the share of total income received by the top 1% or the top 5%.

Thirdly, there appear to be two interesting empirical phenomena to explain as illustrated by Figures 6.1 and 6.2. In the first diagram the level of dividends paid by U.K. companies in aggregate in the period 1950–71 appears to have grown along a relatively stable and smooth path without large fluctuations either up or down, although with some levelling out towards the end of the period. In the second diagram it can be seen that the aggregate payout ratio of the same companies has neither remained constant nor fluctuated in a totally

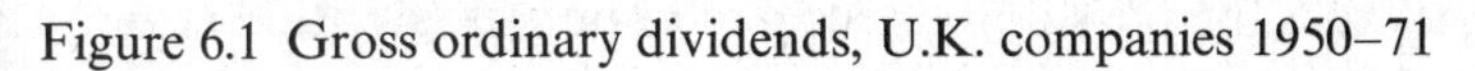
Figure 6.1 Gross ordinary dividends, U.K. companies 1950–71

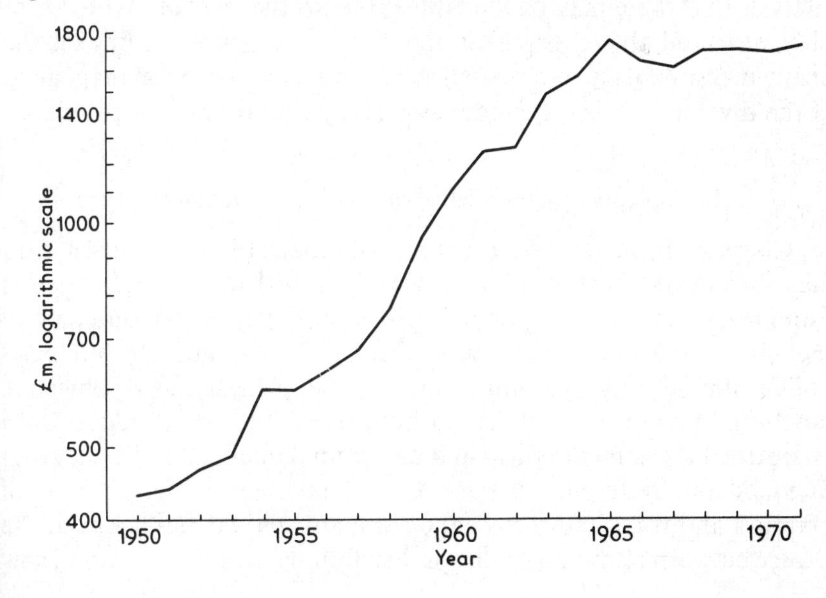

Figure 6.2 Payout ratio, U.K. companies 1950–71

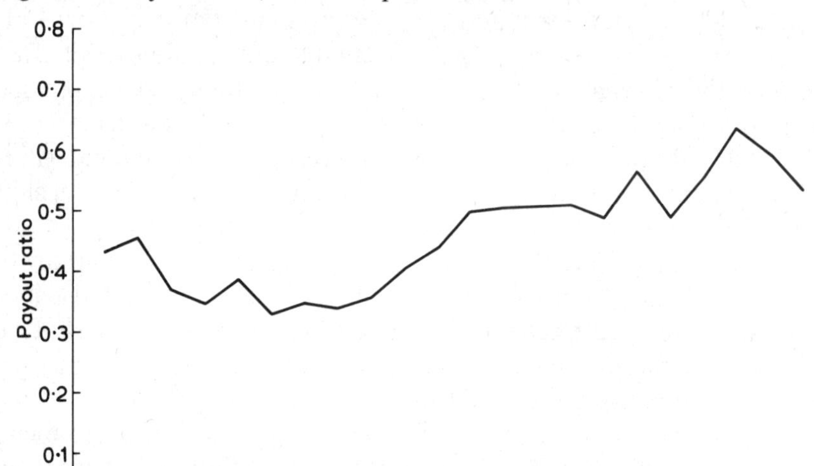

Note: The payout ratio is defined as the ratio of gross dividends to the sum of dividends and retentions net of capital consumption and stock appreciation.

random manner. The more systematic changes in the payout ratio clearly require further investigation.

Finally, there is the possibility once uncertainty is admitted into the analysis that there may be a positive role for the level of dividends to play, over and above its part in the flow of funds used to finance the firm's investment: a role related perhaps to the use by management of the dividend decision to convey information to the shareholders.

6.1 *Specifying models of dividend behaviour*

In Chapter 4 we derived the optimal financial policy for a firm maximizing its share price in a world of perfect certainty. In this framework the dividend policy is given implicitly by the outcome of the joint determination of both the investment and the financial policy implied by maximization of the shareholders' objective function. Maximization of the market value of the firm produces both an optimal investment policy and an optimal financial policy, leaving dividend policy to play a passive residual role. In the absence of taxation and transaction costs the company will be indifferent to the choice between retaining profits or distributing profits and issuing new shares, and we might expect to find that it is the introduction of taxation which yields an optimum dividend policy. One of the aims of this chapter is to investigate the relationship between taxation and payout ratios.

Nevertheless, the model of Chapter 4 cannot be regarded as a sufficient basis in itself for the development of an estimating equation for the level of dividends. It would predict that the payout ratio would be either unity, when external finance was the cheapest source of finance, or lie between zero and unity, when retentions were the optimal source of finance, or zero when retentions were inadequate to finance the desired level of investment. From Figures 6.1 and 6.2 we can see that the level of dividends seems to show more stability than would be implied by this model and by the swings in investment expenditure from year to year. A satisfactory estimating equation requires that dividends be regarded as something more than a mere residual.

It is by no means obvious that the introduction of uncertainty into the model provides a solution to the problem, since in Chapter 4 we saw also that uncertainty about future profits, while giving rise to the concept of an optimal debt–equity ratio, does not in itself lead to any preference for dividends over retentions, on the part of the shareholders. Uncertainty about the potential profitability of an investment project will affect the shareholders' desired level of investment (and hence indirectly the optimum level of dividends), but it does not create any relevant distinction between the two sources of equity funds, retentions and new share issues.

It is only a positive role for the level of dividends itself, the possibility of which depends crucially on the existence of uncertainty, which can justify a model of dividend behaviour where the level of dividends is the active decision variable. Such a role might derive from the use of dividends by management to convey information to shareholders, and the acceptance of this process by shareholders, in a world in which management and shareholders enjoy differential access to information about the firm's prospects.

To reconcile the attempts to evolve an estimating equation for the level of dividend payments with the theoretical considerations outlined above, we may identify three approaches to the problem.

(1) The *ad hoc* empirical approach, in which the factors alleged to influence dividend behaviour are listed, and a convenient estimating equation (usually linear) is specified. The advantage of this approach is that the functional form of the equation can be chosen for convenience

of estimation, but its weakness is that it takes no account of the constraints on either the form of the equation or on the parameters which are implied by theoretical considerations. A good deal of the empirical work on dividend behaviour can be seen as a combination of the *ad hoc* approach and approach (2) discussed below. In this category, for example, we might put the work of Brittain (1964, 1966) and Fama and Babiak (1968), and the *ad hoc* introduction of taxation into the model can be seen in Brittain (1964), Feldstein (1970), Fisher (1970) and King (1971).

(2) The second approach we might describe as the 'income model'. In this model dividends are assumed to be a stable function of corporate income, and early proponents of the model were Tinbergen (1939), Modigliani (1949) and Dobrovolsky (1951). The idea was formalized by Lintner (1953, 1956) who, on the basis of interviews with 28 U.S. companies over the period 1947–53, concluded that companies had in mind some target payout ratio relating the level of dividends to current profits. Subsequent developments consisted of testing the model for several different definitions of income, the inclusion of other variables as determinants of the target payout ratio, and an interesting application of the permanent income hypothesis to corporate saving and distribution behaviour by Fisher (1957).

Lintner found also that management desired stability in the time path of dividends. There was evidence of only partial adjustment of dividends to changes in profits, and the dependent variable as seen by companies was not so much the *level* of dividends as the *change* in dividends from the previous year's level. Most companies had rather definite ideas about their target payout ratio and the speed with which they would normally adjust towards a new level of dividends. Moreover investment requirements appeared to have little direct effect on dividend policy. This suggests the following two-equation model. The first equation states that the optimum level of dividends in year t, G_t^*, is related to the current level of profits, Y_t, by the target payout ratio, q, which is assumed to be constant over time.

$$G_t^* = qY_t + \varepsilon_t. \tag{6.1}$$

ε_t denotes the error term, the distribution of which we shall discuss later when we turn to estimation. The second equation describes the partial adjustment of actual dividends to the optimum level as given by equation (6.1).

$$G_t - G_{t-1} = a_0 + a_1(G_t^* - G_{t-1}) + u_t. \tag{6.2}$$

The error term is denoted by u_t, the speed of adjustment coefficient by a_1, and a constant term, a_0, is used to represent the greater reluctance to reduce than to raise dividends which Lintner claimed to have found. The reduced form of the model is

$$G_t - G_{t-1} = \alpha_0 + \alpha_1 Y_t + \alpha_2 G_{t-1} + V_t \tag{6.3}$$

where
$$\alpha_0 = a_0,$$
$$\alpha_1 = q a_1,$$
$$\alpha_2 = - a_1,$$
$$V_t = u_t + a_1 \varepsilon_t.$$

Two points about this formulation may be noted. First, the model was proposed by Lintner as an empirical generalization of the results of interviews, and not as a deduction from a theory of corporate behaviour. Thus we cannot rule out the existence of other factors influencing dividend behaviour which were not mentioned in the interviews, but which might be important in other time periods and in other countries. Secondly, we have explicitly introduced error terms into both equations (6.1) and (6.2). This practice was not followed by Lintner nor by many of the subsequent studies in which the equation determining the optimum level of dividends is often assumed to be non-stochastic. Much of the discussion of the income model in the literature has turned on the question of how best to measure company income, whether to use profits before or after tax, before or after some estimate of depreciation, or to use some measure of cash flow. We shall explore the questions of error structure and the definition of income when we come to discuss the econometric estimates of a somewhat different model. The income model represents something more than mere 'ad hoccery', although it is not based on a model of optimizing behaviour.

(3) The final approach that we might distinguish is to assume that dividend behaviour is the outcome of an explicit optimization process but one in which the objective function is more complicated than that examined in Chapter 4.

The model we shall propose is the following. When making its dividend decision the firm is assumed to have a well-defined objective function defined on the current levels of dividends, G, and retentions, R.

$$U = U(G, R). \tag{6.4}$$

The firm maximizes this function subject to the constraint that dividends plus retentions plus taxes equal pre-tax profits, which are assumed to be exogenous. The essential characteristic of this approach is that the division of profits between corporate distributions and corporate saving, although influenced by the relative tax costs of dividends and retentions, is not determined solely by tax considerations.

We suggested above that the existence of uncertainty about future profits did not, *per se*, provide a justification for defining a utility function which distinguished between dividends and retentions (apart from the obvious tax differences), except in so far as uncertainty affected the level of investment or created a positive role for the level of dividends. We shall now argue that the effect of uncertainty as modelled in Chapter 5 is to create a positive role for dividend behaviour, and leads to a model in which the level of dividends is given by the maximization of a managerial utility function of the form shown in equation (6.4) subject to the following constraints:

(a) the firm's budget constraint
(b) a constraint on the rate at which dividends can be adjusted over time.

In Chapter 5 we saw that even in the case where shareholders have perfect information about the effects of different policies on the firm's profits in any given state of the world, they will agree on the choice of policy only under very restrictive conditions about the range of policies from which the firm can choose. It is not permissible, therefore, to speak of the interests of the shareholders as if they implied a unique optimal policy. In this situation the role of management is to take the initiative and adopt a policy for the firm, accepting that the risk it takes is of pursuing a policy which results in its replacement by an alternative management team, a phenomenon we may loosely describe as 'take-over'. This view of management actively deciding on policy while shareholders either passively accept the policy or replace the current management team corresponds to the legal position according to which, as was described in Chapter 2, shareholders are not allowed to vote on company policy but only to elect the Board of Directors. Clearly, there are many factors in the actual behaviour of managers and shareholders which are not captured by this simple characterization, but it will prove a useful way to represent the decision-making process of the firm. Management will have a set of preferences, which we may represent by a utility function, which will include the desire to remain in control of the firm and so will reflect the perceived risk of take-over. We shall discuss the influence of this threat on the form of the utility function below.

Shareholders, of course, do not have perfect information about the consequences of different policies. For instance, they may be uncertain about the firm's technology, as given, for example, by the parameters of the production function. In itself, this creates no new theoretical difficulties because the problem may be modelled by a finer partition of the states of the world. The definition of a state of the world can be extended to include an assumption about the value taken by a particular parameter of the production function. This enables us to use the model of Chapter 5 as before, although increasing the extent of uncertainty exacerbates the problems of defining 'shareholders' interests'. More interesting is the case of differential access to information which is explicitly recognized by the participants. Shareholders may disagree with each other but they will recognize that management probably has access to better information about those factors likely to affect the firm's profits than do they as shareholders. This has two consequences. Firstly, shareholders have a collective interest in receiving some of this information from management in order to improve their portfolio decisions. Secondly, knowing that shareholders act on the basis of this information, management may have an incentive to convey false information in order to further its own aims; for example, when faced by a take-over bid from a rival management team it might be tempted to convey excessively optimistic information to the shareholders to enhance its chances of staying in control of the company.

The problem, then, is to find a way for management to signal to shareholders that there has been a change in the firm's prospects by means of a signal in which shareholders will place some confidence. The need for a signal is illustrated by considering what might happen in the stock market if there were no signal. In the previous chapter we assumed that the demand curve for a firm's shares could be written as a function of the policy pursued by the firm and its share price. If, however, investors are uncertain about the effects of the policy and if they further believe that others in the market have access to better or to 'inside' information, then their demand for shares may be a function also of the demand by others as reflected in the share price. The share price is used as a signal of the 'quality' of the share. Such behaviour means that an equilibrium in the stock market may not be possible. Suppose that at the existing price of a firm's shares there is excess supply. A fall in the share price might be expected to increase demand until the firm's shares were absorbed into investors' portfolios, but if investors interpret the fall in price as a sign of a deterioration in the firm's prospects then there may be no share price at which an equilibrium between supply and demand can exist. The simplest example is that of a new company trying to float its first share issue. The better the apparent terms of the issue, the bigger may be the perceived risk of being taken for a ride by an unscrupulous entrepreneur or management team. This phenomenon is an example of the behaviour studied by Akerlof (1970) in his paper on information and the market in second-hand cars. Being unsure of the quality of their prospective purchase buyers are afraid of being sold a defective car (a 'lemon').

Even if a signalling mechanism exists, an equilibrium may not exist if shareholders have little confidence in the signal which they receive. In this case 'bad management drives out good', a situation which could be said to have characterized the activities of some company promoters in the nineteenth century and is not unknown today.

In order to resolve the problem, the signalling mechanism must satisfy certain conditions. Firstly, since the aim of the signal is to convey from management to shareholders information about the consequences of the company's policy, the signal cannot itself be a part of that policy. In more formal terms, and using the notation of Chapter 5, if the firm's policy vector is $\mathbf{u}$ then the variable which comprises the signal, s, cannot be an element of $\mathbf{u}$. It is likely that the management will wish to convey information about the effects of its policies concerning 'real' variables, such as investment, output and pricing policies, in which case the signal must consist of a variable different from these. Secondly, the signal must be well-defined, not too costly to make, and its value must be capable of being measured so that there is no disagreement as to what the signal is, or what it was in the past. Finally, given that differential access to information on the part of shareholders and management gives rise to the possibility of the non-existence of an equilibrium, management will have to agree to some constraint on its use of the signal in order to convince shareholders that the signal is being used to convey genuine information. The nature of the problem suggests that an arbitrary convention would be adopted, adherence to which would help to prevent abuse of the signal by management.

Since the 'game' being played between management and shareholders is a multiperiod game, this fact can be exploited in the construction of a suitable convention. In order to prevent temporary abuse of the signal, by for example, an increase in the value of the signal which management plans to reverse later, the sort of convention which is likely to emerge is one which limits the rate at which the signal can be changed. This might be formalized into a rule limiting the rate at which management may adjust the value of the signal towards a new desired level, and constraining the process of adjustment to be made over a number of periods. In this way management is under pressure to relate the signal to long-run expectations and not to use it as a temporary expedient, and, if shareholders observe that management behaviour appears to conform to the convention, then they will feel able to place more confidence in the signals being made. We shall assume that management believes that it is in its own long-term interests to make only a fraction λ of the proportionate adjustment towards what would otherwise be the new optimal level of the signal.

Having described the main characteristics of a suitable signal, we must now ask the question of which variable management is likely to select for the role of the signal? In terms of its ability to satisfy the above criteria, the level of dividends seems an obvious candidate for the role of the signal. The level of dividends can be changed independently of any of the real variables comprising the firm's policy, and the payment of the dividend is the principal direct line of communication from management to shareholder. The only cost incurred is the extra tax involved in pursuing a financial policy which may not be the cost-minimizing policy as analysed in Chapter 4. This suggests that we might represent the dividend decision in terms of a model in which management maximizes an objective function of dividends and retentions subject to a budget constraint, which takes account of the tax costs of dividends and retentions, and the further constraint that dividends can be adjusted only partially towards a new optimal level. We shall assume that the optimal level of dividends is given by the maximization of the objective function (6.4) and that the adjustment of actual dividends to this level is described by a simple partial adjustment model. The rationale for expressing the objective function in terms of current dividends and retentions is that the firm is operating in a world of incomplete markets, and so it will follow a time path which is a sequence of temporary equilibria. The game-theoretic nature of the relationship between management and shareholders which recurs in a succession of temporary equilibria raises the possibility of dynamic inconsistency in the firm's choice of policy (as discussed by Strotz (1956) and Hammond (1976)). As has been shown by Hammond (1976) there is no way out of this dilemma which provides a satisfactory solution strategy, and so for empirical work we assume that the objective function is restricted to current values of the arguments. We may thus describe it as a partial temporary equilibrium managerial utility function.

The model of dividend behaviour we have just described will be tested in the next section for a particular representation of the objective function. Its main weakness is that it assumes a stable set of preferences between dividends and retentions and does not allow for sudden changes in the desired level of the signal. This assumption may not be too implausible in aggregate because rapid short-run adjustments are ruled out by the convention of partial adjustment. The difficulty here is that we are trying to develop a predictable relationship between dividends and other variables for the purposes of econometric estimation. However, if the model could be used to successfully predict the level of dividends conditional on the values taken by the explanatory variables, then it is not unreasonable to suppose that, at least in principle, the shareholders would learn about this predictable relationship. Hence as a signal the level of dividends would convey little new information, although it may still be an efficient route by which to transmit information about the other variables.

We shall, however, try to examine one particular systematic use of the level of dividends as a signal in connection with the influence of take-overs. We argued above that the preferences of management will reflect its desire to remain in control of the company, and hence its fear of being taken-over. When threatened by take-over management may either accede to the bid or resist by signalling to shareholders that they would be advised to vote against the bidder. It can do this by raising the level of dividends, and so we shall test below the hypothesis that the weight given to dividends in the managerial utility function is greater, the higher is the perceived risk of being taken-over.

6.2 *An application of duality theory*

We shall proceed in this section on the assumption that the optimal level of gross dividends is determined by the maximization of the managerial utility function given by equation (6.4) subject to the following budget constraint.

$$p_G G + p_R R = Y. \tag{6.5}$$

Y is the level of pre-tax income which is necessary in order to finance the combination (G, R) and the 'tax prices' of dividends and retentions are given (from Chapter 3) by

$$p_G = (\hat{\theta}\pi)^{-1}$$
$$p_R = \pi^{-1} \tag{6.6}$$

where π is defined as unity minus the corporate tax rate on undistributed profits, that is, using previous notation, $\pi = 1 - \tau$. The tax prices are defined to be those facing the company directly and we shall postpone until Section 6.4 a discussion of the influence of the distribution of personal tax rates of the shareholders. The actual level of dividends will be assumed to adjust to the optimal level by a partial adjustment mechanism dictated by the convention that the value of the signal must not adjust too rapidly.

To facilitate empirical work it will prove helpful to apply duality theory rather than use the direct utility function expressed in equation (6.4). This will enable us to handle in a tractable manner more complex specifications than can be managed with the direct utility function, and the approach is well suited to extending the model to include additional variables as we shall see later. We define the 'normalized tax prices' of dividends and retentions, v_G and v_R, as

$$v_G = (\hat{\theta}\pi Y)^{-1}$$
$$v_R = (\pi Y)^{-1}. \tag{6.7}$$

We may denote the indirect managerial utility function by $g(v_G, v_R)$ which measures the maximum utility that can be attained given the levels of pre-tax profits and tax rates. If we assume that the function g is continuous, non-increasing and quasi-convex then it completely determines the underlying direct utility function which can be shown to be continuous, non-decreasing and quasi-concave (Diewert, 1974). When considering specific functional forms as a first step to deriving estimating equations, it will prove helpful to consider a quasi-concave function in order to exploit existing results on functional forms for production functions. To this end we may define the reciprocal indirect utility function

$$h(v_G, v_R) = [g(v_G, v_R)]^{-1}. \tag{6.8}$$

The advantage of using duality theory is that the demand functions for dividends and retentions can be derived directly from the indirect utility functions rather than as the solution to an optimization problem. By the modified form of Roy's Identity (see Diewert, 1974) we know that the optimal level of dividends is given by

$$G = \frac{\partial h/\partial v_G}{\sum_j v_j \partial h/\partial v_j} \qquad j = G, R. \tag{6.9}$$

A similar expression holds for the optimal level of retentions.

For the purposes of estimation it is necessary to specify a particular functional form for the reciprocal indirect utility function equation (6.8). A number of functional forms for reciprocal indirect utility functions have been considered in the literature, most of them being second order numerical approximations to an arbitary function. For example, there is the Generalized Leontief form suggested by Diewert (1971), and the Translog form proposed by Lau and Mitchell (1970) and by Christenson, Jorgenson and Lau (1973). Since all such approximations are equivalent in principle, we can choose that particular form which is most suited to the problem in question.

We shall be interested in measuring the response of the ratio of dividends to retentions to changes in their relative tax prices, that is, to changes in the tax discrimination variable $\hat{\theta}$. This suggests that we choose a functional form which allows us to focus on the elasticity of substitution between dividends and retentions. To simplify matters we shall assume homothetic preferences and assume that the income elasticities of demand for both dividends and retentions are unity. We shall use the following generalized homothetic approximation for the reciprocal indirect utility function which is adapted from the form proposed by Denny (1974) in the context of production theory

$$h(v_G, v_R) = \left(\sum_i \sum_j a_{ij} v_i^{\beta\gamma} v_j^{\beta(1-\gamma)} \right)^{1/\beta} \qquad i,j = G, R. \tag{6.10}$$

To ensure concavity of the function we impose the following constraints on the parameters

$$a_{ij} \geqslant 0 \text{ for all } i,j$$

$$\beta \leqslant 1$$

$$0 \leqslant \gamma \leqslant 1.$$

A number of special cases are of interest,

(a) $a_{ij} = 0, i \neq j$. When the cross-product terms disappear the generalized homothetic approximation reduces to the constant elasticity of substitution (CES) form, with an elasticity of substitution, σ say, equal to $1 - \beta$.

(b) In case (a) as $\beta \to 0$, the function tends towards the Cobb–Douglas form.

(c) $\beta = 1$ and $\gamma = \frac{1}{2}$. This is equivalent to Diewert's (1971) homothetic Generalised Leontief form.

In the general case it follows from equation (6.9) that

$$\frac{G}{R} = \frac{\partial h / \partial v_G}{\partial h / \partial v_R}. \qquad (6.11)$$

Since h is homogeneous this expression can be written as some function of the ratio of the tax prices, v_R/v_G, which equals $\hat{\theta}$. Hence we may write

$$\frac{G}{R} = f(\hat{\theta}). \qquad (6.12)$$

Combining this equation with the budget constraint we have

$$\frac{G}{\pi Y} = \frac{\hat{\theta} f(\hat{\theta})}{\hat{\theta} + f(\hat{\theta})} = q(\hat{\theta}) \qquad (6.13)$$

This equation determines the optimal level of the signal, G^*, and the convention on adjusting the value of the signal yields the partial adjustment model

$$\frac{G_t}{G_{t-1}} = \left(\frac{G_t^*}{G_{t-1}} \right)^{\lambda}. \qquad (6.14)$$

These two equations lead to the following estimating equation for the level of dividends

$$\log G_t = \lambda \log P_t + \lambda \log q(\hat{\theta}) + (1 - \lambda) \log G_{t-1} + u_t \qquad (6.15)$$
$$\text{where} \quad P_t = \pi_t Y_t.$$

This is a nonlinear estimation problem. The error term u_t is the reduced form of the error structure associated with both equations (6.13) and (6.14).

We may examine the form of the function $q(\hat{\theta})$ in two simple cases

(i) CES reciprocal indirect utility function

$$q(\hat{\theta}) = \frac{\hat{\theta}}{1 + c\hat{\theta}^{\beta}} \qquad (6.16)$$

$$\text{where} \quad c = \frac{a_{RR}}{a_{GG}}.$$

Even in the CES case the estimating equation is nonlinear.

(ii) Cobb–Douglas reciprocal indirect utility function

$$q(\hat{\theta}) = k\hat{\theta} \tag{6.17}$$

$$\text{where} \quad k = \frac{a_{GG}}{a_{GG} + a_{RR}}.$$

This produces the linear estimating equation

$$\log G_t = \lambda \log k + \lambda \log P_t + \lambda \log \hat{\theta}_t + (1 - \lambda) \log G_{t-1}. \tag{6.18}$$

It is striking that only a Cobb–Douglas reciprocal indirect utility function leads to a linear estimating equation (in logarithms) and that all other forms produce a nonlinear estimation problem. The loglinear form was used by Feldstein (1970) in his study of dividend behaviour in the U.K., but as we can see its disadvantage is that it constrains the elasticity of substitution to a value of unity when in fact one of the aims of the exercise is to measure the size of the elasticity. We shall estimate the loglinear form both to test the hypothesis that the Cobb–Douglas form is acceptable and to experiment with a variety of assumptions about the error structure while working with a linear estimating equation, but to obtain a direct estimate of the elasticity of substitution between dividends and retentions it will be necessary to estimate a nonlinear model.

We shall estimate both the Cobb–Douglas and the CES forms on aggregate annual data for U.K. companies during the period 1950–71, by assuming that income is exogenous and is defined by equation (6.5).

6.3 *Data and estimation*

There are two basic sources of data on U.K. companies. The first data set derives from the national income accounts and is based on information obtained from tax returns to the Inland Revenue. The second set is based on the analysis of the annual accounts of quoted companies published by the Department of Industry. Appendix B describes these sources of data in detail, and constructs income and appropriation accounts for five samples of companies. The first three are from the national accounts source and are for (a) all companies,

(b) 'non-nationalized companies', which includes all companies which remained in private hands throughout the period 1938–71, and (c) industrial and commercial companies, which exclude financial companies. The remaining two samples are based on quoted company data and cover (d) manufacturing, distribution, construction and certain other industries, and (e) manufacturing only. There are a number of important differences between these samples and for a discussion of these the reader is referred to Appendix B.

The income and appropriation accounts of the five samples of companies are shown in Tables B.1–B.5. For samples (a) and (b) series can be constructed annually for the period 1950–71, for sample (c) for the period 1956–71, and for samples (d) and (e), for the period 1949–71. The figures for any given year refer to profits earned in that year, dividends paid out of profits earned in that year, and taxes paid on profits earned in that year. In other words, all the figures are for accruals and not actual payments in a year.

For each sample an attempt was made to construct series for two definitions of income. The first definition, income definition A, is nearer to 'gross cash flow' in that no allowance is made for either capital consumption or stock appreciation. The second definition, income definition B, measures income net of capital consumption at current replacement cost and stock appreciation for samples based on national accounts data (except for non-nationalized companies for which no data for these items were available), and in this way is nearer to an estimate of real income at current prices. However, it is measured after deduction of nominal interest payments and so excludes capital gains arising out of the fall in the real value of corporate debt in times of inflation. For the two quoted company samples, income definition B is gross profit net only of companies' own depreciation provisions. Because, as explained in Appendix B, most companies in the sample period calculated depreciation on an historic cost basis, income definition B measures the concept of net income which companies themselves published, and may well have used as the basis for their dividend decisions, and not 'real' income. Unfortunately, there were no reliable data to enable estimates of capital consumption and stock appreciation for quoted companies to be made, and so it was not possible to obtain estimates of the real income of quoted companies.

The calculation of the various series for tax rates has been discussed in Chapter 3, and the details are given in Appendix A. Of particular importance is the need to decide what tax rates were applied to profits earned in a given period because the relationship between accruals and payments of tax varied over the sample period as the tax system changed; and for a full discussion of the construction of the tax variables the reader is again referred to the Appendix. The use of annual data offers several advantages. The dividend decision is an annual decision, and quarterly data are distorted by the differing number of companies whose accounting periods end in each quarter, and by changes in the timing of dividend payments induced by changes in the tax system (see Figure A.2).

All the results which are reported in this chapter were estimated on data ending in 1971, although the final year's dividend figure refers to dividends paid out of profits earned in 1971 which would have been distributed mainly in 1972. There were two reasons for ending the series in 1971. First the definition of dividends in the national accounts data was changed after 1971 and no series on the new basis was available for the postwar period. Secondly, 1971 was the last year for which it was possible, at the time of writing, to calculate estimates for the distribution of personal tax rates charged on dividends paid out of profits earned in the year.

Of course, the use of aggregate data, especially in the estimation of a nonlinear equation, raises the standard problem of aggregation bias. Grunfeld and Griliches (1960) have argued that, on the contrary, aggregation might result in a gain in efficiency because it would reduce the specification errors involved in postulating a functional form for each micro decision-making unit such as the firm. Chateau (1975) while casting doubt on the empirical validity of the aggregation gain concept when applied to dividend behaviour, found that the aggregation biases were small. Much depends on the particular relationship to be estimated. We have argued above that the exact specification of a model of dividend behaviour for an individual firm would depend upon the preferences of the management, the impact of uncertainty on the firm's prospects and, perhaps, the distribution of tax rates of its shareholders (on which there are no data for individual firms). This suggests that there is scope for a compensating efficiency gain in using aggregate data which might, at least to some extent, offset simple aggregation bias.

Moreover, the use of aggregate data does offer some distinct advantages. Firstly, the estimate of depreciation in the data drawn from the national accounts is the only estimate we have of depreciation on a current replacement cost basis, and this can be obtained only for the company sector in aggregate until such time as companies publish their accounts on a replacement cost basis. These data enable us to test the hypothesis that companies base their dividend decision on a measure of income calculated on a replacement cost basis as opposed to an historic cost basis. Secondly, using aggregate data enables us to examine the effect of the composition of share ownership on distribution policy because we can assume that the distribution of income (and hence tax rates) is given exogenously when looking at shareholders in aggregate. For an individual firm there is a severe problem of simultaneity because the distribution of tax rates of its shareholders will affect its dividend policy, and in turn its dividend policy will affect the identity of its shareholders via the clientele effect. At the aggregate level it is more reasonable to suppose that the tax rates of investors as a whole are exogenous, and so we might hope to identify the effect of ownership on corporate policy.

Before turning to the results obtained by estimating the models we have described above, it remains only to discuss the assumptions about the error term in the reduced form of the estimating equation. Since the equation includes a lagged dependent variable then, even in the absence of autocorrelated errors, ordinary least squares (OLS) estimates will be biased although consistent. However, the error term in the reduced form may well be autocorrelated because of misspecification of the equation (6.13) determining the optimum level of dividends, and if this is the case then OLS will yield both biased and inconsistent estimates with misleading estimates of the standard errors of the regression coefficients. A number of linear methods for dealing with this problem have been proposed (see, for example, Feldstein (1970)), but the approach we shall adopt is the following. We shall assume that the error term can be specified in one of the four following ways.

(i) OLS, $u_t = \varepsilon_t$ (6.19)

(ii) a first-order autoregressive error term (AR)

$$u_t = \rho u_{t-1} + \varepsilon_t \qquad (6.20)$$

(iii) a first-order moving average error term (MA)

$$u_t = \varepsilon_t - \gamma \varepsilon_{t-1} \qquad (6.21)$$

(iv) a mixed first-order autoregressive and moving average error term (AR-MA)

$$u_t = \rho u_{t-1} + \varepsilon_t - \gamma \varepsilon_{t-1}. \tag{6.22}$$

In each case the error term ε_t is assumed to be a normally and independently distributed random variable. With this assumption we may estimate each model for the four different specifications of the error structure by searching over the ρ and γ space for values which maximize the likelihood function. The resulting maximum likelihood estimates have the desirable large sample properties of being consistent and asymptotically efficient. However, our results derive from a relatively small sample, at most 22 observations on postwar data, and it is not clear that an estimation method which possesses nice large sample properties necessarily has the lowest mean squared error when using small samples. A Monte-Carlo study by Hendry and Trivedi (1972) of the small sample properties of the maximum likelihood estimates of the error schemes (i)–(iii) found that although the estimates of the autocorrelation parameters themselves were poor, it was apparent that,

> One may therefore safely conclude that taking some account of autocorrelation, even if the form is misspecified, is a superior policy to ignoring it completely (*op. cit.* p. 127).

The first model we shall estimate is the loglinear form

$$\log G_t = \alpha_0 + \alpha_1 \log \hat{\theta}_t + \alpha_2 \log P_t + \alpha_3 \log G_{t-1} + u_t. \tag{6.23}$$

We shall denote this by Model I. If the reciprocal indirect utility function were Cobb–Douglas we would expect to find that the values of both $\alpha_2/(1-\alpha_3)$, (equals α, say) and $\alpha_1/(1-\alpha_3)$, (equals β, say), would be unity, implying values of unity for the income and substitution elasticities respectively.

The results of estimating Model I on data for each of the five samples of companies are shown in Tables 6.1–6.9. In all cases the goodness of fit is very satisfactory and in almost all cases the independent variables are highly significant. The point estimates given by α and β, however, do not coincide with the values implied by the Cobb–Douglas assumption, and it is clear that the model as it stands is inadequate. For the samples based on national accounts data the values of α and β are well above unity, and for quoted companies either the value of α is above unity or the value of β is below unity. It would have been companies, 1951–71: income definition A (standard errors in brackets)

Model	Error specification	Constant	Log $\hat{\theta}$	Log P	Log TK	Time trend	Log G_{t-1}	α	β	ρ	γ	χ^2	$\bar{R}^2$	DW
I	OLS	−1.092	0.361	0.367			0.725	1.33	1.31				0.990	2.66
		(0.439)	(0.075)	(0.124)			(0.091)							
I	AR	−0.913	0.341	0.311			0.766	1.33	1.46	−0.438		3.99	0.992	1.91
		(0.319)	(0.051)	(0.091)			(0.065)							
I	MA	−0.852	0.324	0.294			0.777	1.32	1.45		0.948	11.18	0.993	1.46
		(0.218)	(0.027)	(0.061)			(0.041)							
I	AR–MA	−0.852	0.324	0.294			0.777	1.32	1.45	0.029	0.952	11.20	0.993	1.49
		(0.224)	(0.028)	(0.062)			(0.042)							
II	OLS	−0.518	0.329	0.284	0.068		0.711	0.98	1.14				0.992	3.14
		(0.471)	(0.069)	(0.118)	(0.031)		(0.082)							
II	AR	−0.324	0.313	0.221	0.068		0.757	0.91	1.29	−0.610		9.70	0.995	2.12
		(0.277)	(0.037)	(0.069)	(0.019)		(0.047)							
II	MA	−0.273	0.299	0.200	0.065		0.776	0.89	1.33		0.951	15.49	0.997	2.44
		(0.258)	(0.024)	(0.058)	(0.021)		(0.034)							
II	AR–MA	−0.251	0.297	0.193	0.065		0.780	0.88	1.36	−0.237	0.951	16.70	0.997	1.96
		(0.218)	(0.019)	(0.049)	(0.018)		(0.027)							
III	OLS	−0.095	0.378	0.267		0.011	0.678	0.83	1.18				0.990	2.65
		(1.359)	(0.078)	(0.177)		(0.013)	(0.109)							
III	AR	−0.135	0.355	0.231		0.008	0.731	0.86	1.32	−0.448		4.14	0.992	1.91
		(0.964)	(0.053)	(0.128)		(0.010)	(0.077)							
III	MA	−0.201	0.336	0.226		0.007	0.750	0.91	1.35		0.949	11.44	0.993	1.42
		(0.744)	(0.031)	(0.096)		(0.008)	(0.051)							
III	AR–MA	−0.201	0.336	0.226		0.007	0.750	0.90	1.35	−0.005	0.952	11.45	0.993	1.39
		(0.744)	(0.031)	(0.095)		(0.008)	(0.051)							

Note: The χ^2 statistic is for the likelihood ratio test of the assumed error structure relative to OLS.

Table 6.2 Dividend equations for all U.K. companies, 1951–71 : income definition B (standard errors in brackets)

Model	Error specification	Constant	Log $\hat{\theta}$	Log P	Log TK	Time trend	Log G_{t-1}	α	β	ρ	γ	χ^2	$\bar{R}^2$	DW
I	OLS	−0.687	0.272	0.238			0.835	1.44	1.65				0.989	2.76
		(0.347)	(0.065)	(0.090)			(0.062)							
I	AR	−0.616	0.269	0.211			0.855	1.45	1.85	−0.382		3.35	0.991	2.08
		(0.275)	(0.045)	(0.072)			(0.047)							
I	MA	−0.571	0.255	0.203			0.858	1.43	1.79		0.875	6.52	0.993	1.67
		(0.212)	(0.024)	(0.056)			(0.033)							
I	AR–MA	−0.594	0.255	0.208			0.855	1.43	1.75	0.212	0.952	7.85	0.993	2.04
		(0.253)	(0.028)	(0.065)			(0.038)							
II	OLS	−0.152	0.258	0.168	0.068		0.806	0.87	1.33				0.991	3.00
		(0.411)	(0.060)	(0.090)	(0.033)		(0.058)							
II	AR	−0.051	0.259	0.133	0.069		0.830	0.78	1.52	−0.550		7.41	0.994	2.10
		(0.283)	(0.034)	(0.061)	(0.023)		(0.037)							
II	MA	0.004	0.251	0.125	0.075		0.827	0.72	1.45		0.949	13.39	0.995	2.03
		(0.200)	(0.018)	(0.049)	(0.022)		(0.027)							
II	AR–MA	0.024	0.252	0.121	0.076		0.829	0.71	1.47	−0.136	0.951	13.73	0.995	1.80
		(0.218)	(0.016)	(0.044)	(0.021)		(0.024)							
III	OLS	0.680	0.355	0.184		0.019	0.662	0.55	1.05				0.991	2.91
		(0.756)	(0.073)	(0.087)		(0.010)	(0.104)							
III	AR	0.537	0.343	0.169		0.016	0.704	0.57	1.16	−0.053		6.05	0.993	2.22
		(0.484)	(0.046)	(0.061)		(0.006)	(0.069)							
III	MA	0.552	0.326	0.152		0.016	0.723	0.55	1.18		0.951	13.83	0.995	2.31
		(0.368)	(0.027)	(0.046)		(0.005)	(0.047)							
III	AR–MA	0.569	0.325	0.149		0.016	0.724	0.54	1.18	−0.152	0.952	14.29	0.995	2.09
		(0.327)	(0.024)	(0.040)		(0.004)	(0.041)							

Model	Error specification	Constant	Log $\hat{\theta}$	Log P	Log TK	Time trend	Log G_{t-1}	α	β	ρ	γ	χ^2	$\bar{R}^2$	DW
I	OLS	−1.163 (0.434)	0.374 (0.075)	0.389 (0.124)			0.710 (0.090)	1.34	1.29				0.991	2.59
I	AR	−0.948 (0.331)	0.350 (0.054)	0.320 (0.096)			0.761 (0.069)	1.33	1.46	−0.409		3.34	0.992	1.94
I	MA	−0.881 (0.229)	0.332 (0.030)	0.299 (0.065)			0.776 (0.045)	1.33	1.48		0.946	10.03	0.994	1.62
I	AR–MA	−0.886 (0.241)	0.333 (0.032)	0.300 (0.068)			0.775 (0.047)	1.33	1.48	0.063	0.952	10.12	0.994	1.71
II	OLS	−0.619 (0.469)	0.339 (0.070)	0.309 (0.118)	0.063 (0.029)		0.698 (0.083)	1.02	1.12				0.993	3.07
II	AR	−0.366 (0.293)	0.315 (0.040)	0.228 (0.074)	0.065 (0.019)		0.756 (0.051)	0.93	1.29	−0.583		8.54	0.995	2.16
II	MA	−0.300 (0.270)	0.299 (0.027)	0.200 (0.063)	0.062 (0.021)		0.781 (0.037)	0.91	1.36		0.950	14.20	0.997	2.41
II	AR–MA	−0.270 (0.239)	0.296 (0.023)	0.192 (0.055)	0.062 (0.018)		0.786 (0.031)	0.90	1.38	−0.191	0.951	14.95	0.997	2.07
III	OLS	−0.688 (1.496)	0.377 (0.077)	0.338 (0.198)		0.005 (0.015)	0.692 (0.108)	1.10	1.22				0.990	2.60
III	AR	−0.414 (1.119)	0.351 (0.054)	0.260 (0.154)		0.005 (0.010)	0.744 (0.079)	1.01	1.37	−0.419		3.51	0.992	1.95
III	MA	−0.333 (0.900)	0.334 (0.031)	0.236 (0.119)		0.006 (0.009)	0.761 (0.052)	0.98	1.40		0.947	10.41	0.994	1.64
III	AR–MA	−0.347 (0.913)	0.334 (0.031)	0.238 (0.121)		0.005 (0.008)	0.761 (0.053)	0.99	1.40	0.029	0.952	10.43	0.994	1.67

Note: The χ^2 statistic is for the likelihood ratio test of the assumed error structure relative to OLS.

Table 6.4 Dividend equations for U.K. industrial and commercial companies 1957–71 : income definition A (standard errors in brackets)

Model	Error specification	Constant	Log $\hat{\theta}$	Log P	Log TK	Time trend	Log G_{t-1}	α	β	ρ	γ	χ^2	$\bar{R}^2$	DW
I	OLS	−1.384 (0.695)	0.378 (0.082)	0.429 (0.138)			0.697 (0.080)	1.41	1.25				0.983	2.53
I	AR	−0.995 (0.575)	0.338 (0.065)	0.342 (0.115)			0.743 (0.063)	1.33	1.32	−0.454		2.80	0.986	1.89
I	MA	−0.780 (0.586)	0.308 (0.064)	0.307 (0.115)			0.755 (0.057)	1.25	1.26		0.907	7.34	0.989	1.75
I	AR–MA	−0.740 (0.569)	0.303 (0.061)	0.299 (0.113)			0.759 (0.055)	1.24	1.26	−0.086	0.933	7.50	0.988	1.53
II	OLS	−1.107 (0.696)	0.367 (0.079)	0.395 (0.135)	0.043 (0.030)		0.677 (0.078)	1.22	1.14				0.984	2.99
II	AR	−0.700 (0.467)	0.331 (0.051)	0.304 (0.091)	0.048 (0.019)		0.724 (0.050)	1.10	1.20	−0.615		6.81	0.990	2.11
II	MA	−0.683 (0.529)	0.323 (0.058)	0.295 (0.104)	0.042 (0.022)		0.735 (0.052)	1.11	1.22		0.912	9.28	0.992	2.32
II	AR–MA	−0.619 (0.476)	0.314 (0.051)	0.282 (0.094)	0.040 (0.018)		0.743 (0.047)	1.09	1.22	−0.245	0.930	10.10	0.993	1.84
III	OLS	−3.123 (1.627)	0.369 (0.081)	0.621 (0.212)		−0.015 (0.013)	0.737 (0.086)	2.37	1.40				0.983	2.47
III	AR	−2.168 (1.253)	0.336 (0.065)	0.481 (0.174)		−0.010 (0.010)	0.760 (0.065)	2.00	1.40	−0.441		2.39	0.986	1.90
III	MA	−1.780 (1.127)	0.313 (0.063)	0.436 (0.169)		−0.008 (0.008)	0.756 (0.057)	1.79	1.28		0.902	6.91	0.988	1.53
III	AR–MA	−1.740 (1.108)	0.311 (0.063)	0.430 (0.167)		−0.008 (0.008)	0.757 (0.056)	1.77	1.28	−0.022	0.933	7.00	0.987	1.37

[illegible] the likelihood ratio test of the assumed error structure relative to OLS.

(standard errors in brackets)

Model	Error specification	Constant	Log $\hat{\theta}$	Log P	Log TK	Time trend	Log G_{t-1}	α	β	ρ	γ	χ^2	$\bar{R}^2$	DW
I	OLS	−0.899	0.258	0.284			0.819	1.57	1.43				0.977	2.42
		(0.775)	(0.072)	(0.135)			(0.063)							
I	AR	−0.384	0.230	0.190			0.850	1.26	1.53	−0.354		1.38	0.979	1.98
		(0.662)	(0.057)	(0.116)			(0.052)							
I	MA	0.220	0.176	0.103			0.861	0.74	1.26		0.875	5.58	0.982	1.59
		(0.500)	(0.037)	(0.095)			(0.041)							
I	AR–MA	−0.575	0.247	0.217			0.846	1.41	1.61	−0.738	−0.512	1.53	0.979	2.04
		(0.693)	(0.062)	(0.121)			(0.055)							
II	OLS	−0.703	0.262	0.277	0.057		0.773	1.22	1.15				0.980	2.78
		(0.731)	(0.067)	(0.125)	(0.034)		(0.064)							
II	AR	−0.189	0.240	0.182	0.060		0.803	0.92	1.21	−0.534		4.24	0.986	2.02
		(0.511)	(0.044)	(0.090)	(0.024)		(0.045)							
II	MA	−0.004	0.220	0.159	0.060		0.802	0.80	1.11		0.913	8.32	0.989	2.02
		(0.400)	(0.037)	(0.084)	(0.026)		(0.044)							
II	AR–MA	0.057	0.217	0.146	0.060		0.807	0.76	1.13	−0.171	0.932	8.73	0.989	1.72
		(0.407)	(0.033)	(0.076)	0.024		(0.040)							
III	OLS	−0.129	0.366	0.312		0.016	0.658	0.91	1.07				0.981	2.75
		(0.806)	(0.087)	(0.123)		(0.009)	(0.103)							
III	AR	0.101	0.353	0.259		0.016	0.684	0.82	1.12	−0.471		3.44	0.985	2.10
		(0.561)	(0.071)	(0.100)		(0.007)	(0.083)							
III	MA	0.234	0.337	0.250		0.016	0.675	0.77	1.03		0.917	8.87	0.989	1.90
		(0.405)	(0.070)	(0.096)		(0.006)	(0.080)							
III	AR–MA	0.276	0.335	0.242		0.016	0.678	0.75	1.04	−0.126	0.933	9.09	0.989	1.67
		(0.373)	(0.068)	(0.092)		(0.006)	(0.078)							

Note: The χ^2 statistic is for the likelihood ratio test of the assumed error structure relative to OLS.

Table 6.6 Dividend equations for U.K. quoted companies in manufacturing and distribution 1950–71 : income definition A (standard errors in brackets)

Model	Error specification	Constant	Log $\hat{\theta}$	Log P	Log *TK*	Time trend	Log G_{t-1}	α	β	ρ	γ	χ^2	$\bar{R}^2$	DW
I	OLS	−1.056	0.418	0.637			0.419	1.10	0.72				0.992	2.33
		(0.282)	(0.072)	(0.119)			(0.103)							
I	AR	−0.990	0.412	0.602			0.449	1.09	0.75	−0.233		1.06	0.992	1.97
		(0.251)	(0.063)	(0.109)			(0.095)							
I	MA	−0.815	0.387	0.538			0.498	1.07	0.77		0.709	3.03	0.992	1.34
		(0.212)	(0.050)	(0.097)			(0.082)							
I	AR–MA	−0.862	0.397	0.568			0.469	1.07	0.75	0.321	0.956	7.54	0.990	1.06
		(0.222)	(0.052)	(0.101)			(0.086)							
II	OLS	−0.761	0.392	0.567	0.033		0.439	1.01	0.70				0.992	2.31
		(0.403)	(0.076)	(0.137)	(0.032)		(0.105)							
II	AR	−0.716	0.389	0.539	0.031		0.466	1.01	0.73	−0.253		1.19	0.992	1.92
		(0.351)	(0.065)	(0.122)	(0.029)		(0.094)							
II	MA	−0.585	0.370	0.486	0.028		0.510	0.99	0.75		0.666	2.65	0.992	1.44
		(0.323)	(0.054)	(0.113)	(0.028)		(0.085)							
II	AR–MA	−0.635	0.378	0.515	0.026		0.485	1.00	0.73	0.317	0.956	7.20	0.991	1.18
		(0.340)	(0.057)	(0.118)	(0.029)		(0.088)							
III	OLS	−0.808	0.423	0.605		0.003	0.411	1.03	0.72				0.991	2.31
		(0.888)	(0.075)	(0.163)		(0.010)	(0.110)							
III	AR	−0.857	0.414	0.584		0.002	0.446	1.05	0.75	−0.229		0.99	0.992	1.97
		(0.801)	(0.065)	(0.152)		(0.011)	(0.099)							
III	MA	−0.993	0.384	0.563		−0.002	0.501	1.13	0.77		0.719	3.12	0.992	1.36
		(0.653)	(0.051)	(0.133)		(0.007)	(0.084)							
III	AR–MA	−0.884	0.397	0.571		−0.000	0.470	1.08	0.75	0.319	0.956	7.43	0.989	1.07
		(0.713)	(0.055)	(0.140)		(0.009)	(0.090)							

Model	Error specification	Constant	Log $\hat{\theta}$	Log P	Log TK	Time trend	Log G_{t-1}	α	β	ρ	γ	χ^2	$\bar{R}^2$	DW
I	OLS	−1.109	0.368	0.498			0.627	1.33	0.99				0.989	2.22
		(0.382)	(0.081)	(0.126)			(0.088)							
I	AR	−1.076	0.368	0.483			0.637	1.33	1.02	−0.214		0.88	0.989	1.91
		(0.353)	(0.072)	(0.118)			(0.082)							
I	MA	−0.970	0.358	0.462			0.644	1.30	1.01		0.891	5.73	0.990	1.28
		(0.300)	(0.053)	(0.104)			(0.069)							
I	AR–MA	−1.000	0.358	0.475			0.636	1.30	0.98	0.258	0.955	7.37	0.990	1.41
		(0.325)	(0.058)	(0.112)			(0.075)							
II	OLS	−0.674	0.334	0.412	0.044		0.633	1.12	0.91				0.989	2.12
		(0.539)	(0.086)	(0.145)	(0.038)		(0.087)							
II	AR	−0.687	0.341	0.408	0.040		0.641	1.14	0.95	−0.225		0.87	0.989	1.82
		(0.487)	(0.075)	(0.134)	(0.035)		(0.081)							
II	MA	−0.583	0.330	0.385	0.038		0.651	1.10	0.95		0.908	6.17	0.991	1.35
		(0.429)	(0.056)	(0.120)	(0.031)		(0.068)							
II	AR–MA	−0.624	0.332	0.399	0.037		0.642	1.12	0.93	0.228	0.955	7.27	0.991	1.48
		(0.462)	(0.062)	(0.129)	(0.034)		(0.073)							
III	OLS	0.330	0.454	0.421		0.020	0.443	0.76	0.81				0.991	2.39
		(0.660)	(0.079)	(0.114)		(0.008)	(0.105)							
III	AR	0.205	0.445	0.410		0.018	0.480	0.79	0.86	−0.280		1.51	0.992	1.97
		(0.554)	(0.067)	(0.104)		(0.007)	(0.091)							
III	MA	−0.067	0.427	0.421		0.013	0.520	0.88	0.89		0.873	5.49	0.991	1.07
		(0.447)	(0.054)	(0.093)		(0.005)	(0.078)							
III	AR–MA	0.099	0.439	0.419		0.016	0.491	0.82	0.86	0.295	0.956	7.90	0.989	1.01
		(0.495)	(0.059)	(0.100)		(0.006)	(0.085)							

Note: The χ^2 statistic is for the likelihood ratio test of the assumed error structure relative to OLS.

Table 6.8 Dividend equations for U.K. quoted companies in manufacturing only 1950–71 : income definition A (standard errors in brackets)

Model	Error specification	Constant	Log $\hat{\theta}$	Log P	Log TK	Time trend	Log G_{t-1}	α	β	ρ	γ	χ^2	$\bar{R}^2$	DW
I	OLS	−1.033 (0.283)	0.420 (0.072)	0.614 (0.116)			0.440 (0.100)	1.10	0.75				0.991	2.38
I	AR	−0.954 (0.246)	0.411 (0.061)	0.574 (0.104)			0.475 (0.089)	1.09	0.78	−0.257		1.31	0.991	2.01
I	MA	−0.711 (0.191)	0.366 (0.043)	0.480 (0.085)			0.547 (0.071)	1.06	0.81		0.903	6.13	0.991	1.16
I	AR–MA	−0.788 (0.212)	0.381 (0.049)	0.518 (0.094)			0.515 (0.079)	1.07	0.79	0.261	0.955	7.79	0.991	1.26
II	OLS	−0.711 (0.411)	0.392 (0.076)	0.539 (0.135)	0.036 (0.033)		0.460 (0.101)	1.00	0.72				0.991	2.35
II	AR	−0.666 (0.352)	0.388 (0.064)	0.508 (0.118)	0.033 (0.029)		0.491 (0.089)	1.00	0.76	−0.271		1.39	0.991	1.96
II	MA	−0.498 (0.315)	0.349 (0.048)	0.431 (0.104)	0.025 (0.028)		0.558 (0.074)	0.98	0.79		0.859	5.19	0.992	1.35
II	AR–MA	−0.563 (0.339)	0.363 (0.054)	0.466 (0.113)	0.027 (0.030)		0.527 (0.081)	0.99	0.77	0.269	0.955	7.29	0.991	1.39
III	OLS	−0.695 (0.858)	0.428 (0.076)	0.572 (0.156)		0.004 (0.010)	0.426 (0.107)	0.99	0.75				0.990	2.36
III	AR	−0.744 (0.759)	0.415 (0.064)	0.547 (0.142)		0.003 (0.009)	0.467 (0.095)	1.03	0.78	−0.250		1.19	0.991	2.01
III	MA	−0.771 (0.571)	0.365 (0.046)	0.489 (0.112)		0.001 (0.006)	0.549 (0.076)	1.08	0.81		0.891	5.79	0.991	1.22
III	AR–MA	−0.771 (0.707)	0.384 (0.053)	0.509 (0.126)		0.001 (0.007)	0.511 (0.084)	1.04	0.78	0.269	0.955	7.58	0.990	1.24

Note: The χ^2 statistic is for the likelihood ratio test of the assumed error structure relative to OLS.

Table 6.9 Dividend equations for U.K. quoted companies in manufacturing only 1950–71 : income definition B (standard errors in brackets)

Model	Error specification	Constant	Log $\hat{\theta}$	Log P	Log TK	Time trend	Log G_{t-1}	α	β	ρ	γ	χ^2	$\bar{R}^2$	DW
I	OLS	−1.064	0.372	0.468			0.654	1.35	1.07				0.987	2.27
		(0.384)	(0.083)	(0.122)			(0.083)							
I	AR	−1.022	0.371	0.450			0.667	1.35	1.11	−0.249		1.19	0.988	1.93
		(0.344)	(0.072)	(0.111)			(0.075)							
I	MA	−0.881	0.350	0.417			0.682	1.31	1.10		0.936	7.39	0.990	1.33
		(0.282)	(0.051)	(0.095)			(0.061)							
I	AR-MA	−0.914	0.352	0.428			0.674	1.31	1.08	0.195	0.955	8.12	0.990	1.51
		(0.307)	(0.056)	(0.102)			(0.066)							
II	OLS	−0.581	0.334	0.374	0.048		0.656	1.09	0.97				0.987	2.15
		(0.553)	(0.088)	(0.143)	(0.040)		(0.082)							
II	AR	−0.611	0.341	0.372	0.042		0.667	1.12	1.02	−0.250		1.07	0.988	1.84
		(0.493)	(0.076)	(0.130)	(0.036)		(0.074)							
II	MA	−0.516	0.323	0.345	0.036		0.684	1.09	1.02		0.933	7.20	0.990	1.43
		(0.430)	(0.055)	(0.113)	(0.032)		(0.060)							
II	AR-MA	−0.538	0.324	0.354	0.037		0.677	1.10	1.00	0.181	0.955	7.80	0.991	1.59
		(0.460)	(0.060)	(0.122)	(0.034)		(0.065)							
III	OLS	0.366	0.463	0.396		0.021	0.456	0.73	0.85				0.990	2.43
		(0.642)	(0.080)	(0.109)		(0.008)	(0.104)							
III	AR	0.226	0.451	0.383		0.018	0.499	0.76	0.90	−0.303		1.77	0.991	1.99
		(0.538)	(0.067)	(0.096)		(0.007)	(0.088)							
III	MA	−0.017	0.419	0.379		0.013	0.554	0.85	0.94		0.921	6.77	0.989	1.02
		(0.425)	(0.052)	(0.085)		(0.005)	(0.074)							
III	AR-MA	0.118	0.434	0.382		0.015	0.524	0.80	0.91	0.254	0.955	8.17	0.989	1.10
		(0.472)	(0.058)	(0.093)		(0.006)	(0.081)							

Note: The χ^2 statistic is for the likelihood ratio test of the assumed error structure relative to OLS.

possible to test the joint hypothesis that both α and β equal unity by re-estimating the equations constraining the values of α and β to unity, and using the residuals to compute the log-likelihood ratio test statistic. However, in the next section we shall estimate the elasticity of substitution directly using a nonlinear model and so a discussion of the confidence interval for the substitution effect is deferred until then.

The results for the five different samples of companies are fairly similar, although those for quoted companies show lower values of α and β, a smaller coefficient of the lagged dependent variable, and less evidence of autocorrelated errors. In all cases the use of income definition B leads to a deterioration in the goodness of fit and an increase in the estimates of α and β. This suggests that allowing for depreciation and stock appreciation when defining income does not necessarily lead to a better prediction of dividend behaviour.

As far as the error structure is concerned, there is support for the conclusions of the simulation study by Hendry and Trivedi (1972) in that making some allowance for autocorrelated errors seems to be more important than the precise specification of the form of the autocorrelation. There is strong evidence of negative autocorrelation and in most of the results the first-order error structure is a significant (at the 5% level) improvement on the OLS estimates, although the MA scheme may have induced a degree of positive autocorrelation in the residuals to judge by the Durbin–Watson (DW) statistic, especially when it is remembered that it is biased towards the value 2 because of the presence in the estimating equation of the lagged dependent variable. There are some interesting differences between the samples of companies in the way in which making some allowance for autocorrelation affects the estimates. For both all and non-nationalized companies the first-order error schemes have little effect on the value of α but lead to an increase in β, whereas for industrial and commercial companies the value of α is reduced and β unchanged. The introduction of an autocorrelated error scheme into the equations for quoted companies changes neither α nor β, although it does slightly raise the coefficient of the lagged dependent variable.

It was argued earlier that there were strong *a priori* reasons for expecting the threat of take-over to influence the level of dividends paid out by a firm, and we have seen that the simple Cobb–Douglas specification (Model I) is inadequate. We shall first retain the basic Cobb–Douglas framework and let the distributive parameters of the indirect utility function depend upon a variable measuring the perceived risk of take-over. If management relates the general aggressiveness of raiders to the level of take-over activity in the economy, then we may represent the subjective risk of take-over by a variable measuring the amount of take-over activity in the economy, denoted by TK, defined as the total expenditure by quoted companies on the acquisition of subsidiaries deflated by the value of total net assets of all quoted companies. This series for take-over activity is shown in Table 6.10, and it shows clearly the boom in take-overs in the 1960s reaching a peak in 1968.

If we assume that the distributive parameters of the reciprocal indirect utility function are related to the amount of take-over activity by the equation

Table 6.10 Take-over activity, U.K. 1950–71

1950	0.64
1951	0.52
1952	0.53
1953	1.13
1954	1.47
1955	1.15
1956	1.29
1957	1.28
1958	1.12
1959	2.42
1960	2.72
1961	2.84
1962	2.17
1963	2.05
1964	3.00
1965	2.76
1966	2.05
1967	3.64
1968	8.18
1969	3.89
1970	3.52
1971	2.69

Note: Take-over activity is defined as the expenditure on the acquisition of subsidiaries by quoted companies expressed as a percentage of the value of quoted companies' total net assets.

Source: *Economic Trends* April 1962, *Annual Abstract of Statistics* 1970, and *Business Monitor M3*, various issues.

$$\frac{a_{GG}}{a_{GG} + a_{RR}} = \beta_0(TK)^{\beta_1} \tag{6.24}$$

then the estimating equation for Model II, which incorporates the take-over hypothesis, is the same as for Model I except that the logarithm of take-over activity is included as an additional independent variable. The results of estimating Model II are shown in the second panel of Tables 6.1–6.9. In every case the inclusion of the take-over variable reduces the values of both α and β and implies estimates for α much closer to its theoretical value of unity than were obtained with Model I. The take-over variable itself is significantly different from zero at the 5% level in all the results based on national accounts data, and has the correct sign and t-values of about unity in the results based on quoted company data. It might be that the take-over variable is simply acting as a time trend, and to examine this hypothesis Model III was estimated by replacing the take-over variable by a linear time trend. The results, which are given in the third panel of the tables, show clearly that the time trend is an inadequate explanatory variable, and its performance is inferior to that of the take-over variable.

Of course, a simple time trend may be a very poor proxy for the other influences on dividend behaviour. A number of other hypotheses were examined but none proved successful. The existence of dividend control might be thought to have exercised a depressing effect on dividends, but apart from a 'freeze' on dividend payments between July 1966 and July 1967, statutory control was not in force during the estimation period and such control began seriously only in November 1972. There were voluntary controls during the periods 1948–50 and 1967–9, but attempts to pick up the effect of these controls by dummy variables proved unsuccessful. This reinforces the findings of Fane (1975) who also found no significant effect for dividend controls in the U.K. Another influence on dividend payments might have been the control on issues of new shares exercised in the postwar period by the Capital Issues Committee. These controls were gradually relaxed and abolished in 1958. However, the effect of these controls, whether measured by a dummy variable of constant value until 1958 or a dummy variable whose value declined linearly to a value of zero in 1959, proved insignificant.

There is thus some econometric evidence that take-over activity does affect corporate dividend policy, and it is interesting that statutory dividend control in the U.K. introduced after the end of the estimation period recognized this possibility by providing that one of the grounds on which a company could claim exemption from control was if it needed to raise its dividend level to ward off a take-over bid. Paragraph 13 of the White Paper outlining the principles of statutory dividend control which began in November 1972 reads as follows,

> When the Treasury are satisfied that an actual takeover bid situation exists ... companies wishing to defend themselves from the bidder by increasing their dividends will normally be allowed to do so (Cmnd. 5444).

Unfortunately no rationale for this criterion for exemption from dividend control was provided, but it is certainly consistent with our view of dividends as a signalling device.

6.4 *A CES model*

A better estimate of the elasticity of substitution between dividends and retentions can be obtained by direct nonlinear estimation of the demand function for dividends derived from a CES form of the reciprocal indirect utility function. The estimating equation for the CES version of Model II is

$$\log G_t = \lambda \log P_t + \lambda \log\left[\frac{\hat{\theta}_t}{1 + c_t \hat{\theta}_t^{\,1-\sigma}}\right] + (1-\lambda)\log G_{t-1} + u_t \qquad (6.25)$$

$$\text{where} \quad c_t = [A(TK_t)^\eta]^{-1}.$$

The estimation of a nonlinear model is relatively expensive in its use of computing time, and so we shall only estimate Model II, (that is, including the take-over activity variable), and only the AR error structure. This restriction is not serious because making some allowance for autocorrelated errors is more important than the precise form of structure estimated. We shall, however, expand estimation in another dimension by examining the effect of different assumptions about the influence of shareholders' personal tax rates. In an early study of dividend behaviour in the U.S., Lintner (1959) concluded that

> Of all areas of corporate financial behaviour, the response of cash dividends to changed earnings should have been most sensitive to changes in the relation of management to ownership, as urged by Berle and Means; the stability actually found in dividend policies is hardly consonant with the expectation.

Although we may concur with Lintner's finding that there are stable patterns to corporate dividend policy, it is possible to interpret this as evidence in favour of the signalling model of dividend behaviour described above which is based on a distinct role for management. This view is supported by the significance of the take-over activity variable found in the previous section. A further aspect of the same question is the impact of changes in the personal tax rates of shareholders on the dividend decision. In the models we have examined so far the reciprocal indirect utility function was assumed to have been defined on the levels of gross dividends and retentions with the relative tax price given by the variable $\hat{\theta}$. But an alternative hypothesis is that the arguments of the managerial utility function are net dividends (denoted by D) and retentions, and in this case the relative tax price is θ. As we saw in Chapter 3 there is no unique value for either net dividends or the variable θ because shareholders face different marginal rates of income tax. Hence to estimate this model we have to make some assumption about the 'representative' tax rate. We shall examine two alternative assumptions, the first is that the relevant tax rate is the average marginal income tax rate, and the second is that the relevant rate is the median marginal income tax rate. The appropriate values for the relative price θ, (θ_a and θ_m for the mean and median shareholders respectively) can be found in Table A.6. The estimating equation is as shown in equation (6.25) with G replaced by D and $\hat{\theta}$ replaced by θ_a or θ_m. To facilitate comparison each equation was estimated with log G as the dependent variable by using the transformation $D = (1 - m)G$, and so in those models which define the relative price to be θ_a or θ_m the appropriate income tax rates are included as additional explanatory variables. This should be borne in mind when comparing the $\bar{R}^2$ of the different equations in Tables 6.11–6.15. The assumption that the utility function is defined in terms of gross dividends is equivalent to the assumption that it is defined in terms of net dividends with the representative income tax rate taken to be zero. This means that we may compare the different models in terms of their assumptions about the representative tax rate which enters the managerial decision process, a zero tax rate, the mean tax rate, or the median tax rate.

The results of estimating the CES model on data for the five samples of companies are shown in Tables 6.11–6.15. The performance of the model is, on the whole, very satisfactory and the parameter estimates are well determined. In every case the estimate of the elasticity of

Table 6.11 Nonlinear dividend equations, all U.K. companies 1951–71 (standard errors in brackets)

Income tax rate	A	σ	η	λ	ρ	$\bar{R}^2$
Income definition a						
Zero	0.159	0.844	0.202	0.259	–0.618	0.9958
	(0.015)	(0.144)	(0.028)	(0.038)	(0.172)	
Mean	0.404	0.631	0.162	0.276	–0.407	0.9936
	(0.158)	(0.180)	(0.056)	(0.055)	(0.207)	
Median	0.311	0.620	0.181	0.265	–0.521	0.9948
	(0.076)	(0.132)	(0.041)	(0.045)	(0.189)	
Income definition b						
Zero	0.225	0.788	0.245	0.179	–0.538	0.9945
	(0.034)	(0.224)	(0.045)	(0.033)	(0.187)	
Mean	0.553	0.454	0.276	0.186	–0.499	0.9940
	(0.278)	(0.271)	(0.089)	(0.035)	(0.191)	
Median	0.432	0.459	0.265	0.181	–0.499	0.9940
	(0.158)	(0.216)	(0.072)	(0.035)	(0.191)	

Table 6.12 Nonlinear dividend equations, U.K. non-nationalized companies, 1951–71 (standard errors in brackets)

Income tax rate	A	σ	η	λ	ρ	$\bar{R}^2$
Income definition a						
Zero	0.160	0.845	0.203	0.257	– 0.592	0.9959
	(0.015)	(0.148)	(0.028)	(0.040)	(0.177)	
Mean	0.399	0.606	0.164	0.283	– 0.360	0.9937
	(0.158)	(0.176)	(0.056)	(0.058)	(0.216)	
Median	0.312	0.612	0.182	0.267	– 0.490	0.9950
	(0.078)	(0.131)	(0.041)	(0.048)	(0.195)	

Table 6.13 Nonlinear dividend equations, U.K. industrial and commercial companies 1957–71 (standard errors in brackets)

Income tax rate	A	σ	η	λ	ρ	$\bar{R}^2$
Income definition a						
Zero	0.182	0.739	0.179	0.267	–0.667	0.9928
	(0.028)	(0.122)	(0.043)	(0.034)	(0.196)	
Mean	0.349	0.547	0.206	0.291	– 0.346	0.9863
	(0.144)	(0.190)	(0.088)	(0.058)	(0.268)	
Median	0.288	0.545	0.209	0.276	– 0.598	0.9914
	(0.071)	(0.114)	(0.059)	(0.039)	(0.217)	
Income definition b						
Zero	0.247	0.502	0.253	0.206	– 0.554	0.9893
	(0.061)	(0.188)	(0.069)	(0.036)	(0.223)	
Mean	0.262	– 0.072	0.456	0.230	– 0.565	0.9905
	(0.103)	(0.193)	(0.104)	(0.033)	(0.217)	
Median	0.284	0.074	0.380	0.218	– 0.552	0.9899
	(0.105)	(0.158)	(0.094)	(0.035)	(0.220)	

Table 6.14 Nonlinear dividend equations, U.K. quoted companies in manufacturing and distribution 1950–71 (standard errors in brackets)

Income tax rate	A	σ	η	λ	ρ	$\bar{R}^2$
Income definition a						
Zero	0.280	0.370	0.059	0.538	– 0.262	0.9939
	(0.017)	(0.071)	(0.017)	(0.075)	(0.217)	
Mean	0.489	0.046	0.021	0.627	0.003	0.9926
	(0.097)	(0.102)	(0.033)	(0.084)	(0.216)	
Median	0.431	0.126	0.034	0.565	– 0.238	0.9941
	(0.061)	(0.067)	(0.024)	(0.072)	(0.211)	
Income definition b						
Zero	0.347	0.298	0.152	0.346	– 0.208	0.9914
	(0.038)	(0.125)	(0.031)	(0.064)	(0.253)	
Mean	0.519	– 0.348	0.196	0.379	– 0.201	0.9927
	(0.135)	(0.221)	(0.053)	(0.057)	(0.232)	
Median	0.487	– 0.154	0.181	0.362	– 0.222	0.9922
	(0.105)	(0.151)	(0.044)	(0.059)	(0.242)	

subsitution, σ, is less than unity and in some cases well below unity. This suggests that a serious mis-specification is implied by estimating a loglinear dividend equation which may have consequences for the significance of other variables. For example, the coefficient of the take-over activity variable is significantly different from zero at the 5% level in 23 out of the 27 estimated equations, whereas in the loglinear model it was not significant in the case of quoted companies. The samples drawn from national accounts data produce larger estimates of the elasticity of substitution and of the coefficient of the take-over activity variable than do the samples of quoted companies.

The introduction of information about the distribution of shareholders' marginal tax rates, at least in so far as it can be represented by the mean or the median, does not lead to any uniform improvement in the results. This is not perhaps very surprising because the previous chapter demonstrated the difficulty in formulating a precise hypothesis about the influence of any one group of shareholders. Nevertheless, the issue is important because the results show clearly that allowing for changes in the distribution of tax rates over time

Table 6.15 Nonlinear dividend equations, U.K. quoted companies in manufacturing only 1950–71 (standard errors in brackets)

Income tax rate	A	σ	η	λ	ρ	$\bar{R}^2$
Income definition a						
Zero	0.270	0.411	0.058	0.518	– 0.275	0.9932
	(0.017)	(0.076)	(0.018)	(0.072)	(0.215)	
Mean	0.475	0.086	0.020	0.624	0.055	0.9911
	(0.097)	(0.110)	(0.035)	(0.085)	(0.218)	
Median	0.422	0.169	0.031	0.552	– 0.211	0.9931
	(0.062)	(0.072)	(0.026)	(0.072)	(0.212)	
Income definition b						
Zero	0.330	0.373	0.154	0.329	– 0.234	0.9904
	(0.038)	(0.134)	(0.033)	(0.061)	(0.248)	
Mean	0.543	– 0.215	0.184	0.365	– 0.188	0.9913
	(0.157)	(0.217)	(0.058)	(0.056)	(0.231)	
Median	0.490	– 0.054	0.176	0.349	– 0.230	0.9911
	(0.112)	(0.150)	(0.047)	(0.057)	(0.239)	

reduces the point estimate of the elasticity of substitution quite substantially, and in some cases the estimate is insignificantly different from zero. Compared to the results for gross dividends, those derived from the mean or median tax rates produce estimates of the elasticity which are smaller by an amount ranging from 0.2 to 0.4. In most cases there is evidence of negatively autocorrelated errors, but this tendency is less pronounced in the results using the mean tax rate and, to a lesser extent, the median tax rate.

In this chapter we have tried to show that a positive role for the level of dividends can be explained in terms of a signalling model of dividend behaviour, in which management conveys information to shareholders by means of a signal which has to satisfy certain criteria and conventions for it to be useful to both parties. We argued that the level of dividends could provide a satisfactory signalling mechanism. The distribution of ownership of the company is also important because the estimates of the elasticity of substitution between dividends and retentions, knowledge of which is crucial for policy prescription, seem to be sensitive to the choice of the 'representative' tax rate of the shareholders which management is assumed to use in its decision-making process. Ownership will also be a determinant of the nature and extent of take-over activity, a phenomenon which appears to influence dividend behaviour. Clearly, the relationship between the structure of ownership and corporate behaviour is a subject which requires further research.

Chapter 7

AN ECONOMETRIC ANALYSIS OF CORPORATE FINANCIAL POLICY

A thing may look specious in theory, and yet be ruinous in practice; a thing may look evil in theory, and yet be in practice excellent (Edmund Burke, 1788).

Chapter 4 demonstrated the potential importance of taxation in determining the financial policy which would be chosen by a firm maximizing its market value, and in the previous chapter we looked at its effects on one aspect of this, dividend policy. It is the purpose of this chapter to examine the empirical evidence on the pattern of corporate financing to see whether taxation has had any quantitative impact in practice.

One factor which emerged clearly from the theoretical discussion was the importance of the personal tax position of the shareholder as a determinant of the firm's optimal financial policy. So in our empirical investigation we shall have to bear in mind both (i) changes over time in the taxation of corporate profits, and (ii) changes over time in personal tax rates and in the composition of share ownership.

7.1 *Tax incentives in the UK*

The following conclusions about the effects of taxation emerged from the analysis of Chapter 4 (assuming that interest payments are tax deductible).

(1) For a given amount of debt, investment will be financed by issuing new shares rather than out of retained earnings if the variable $(\theta + z - 1)$ is positive.

(2) For a given amount of retentions, new share issues will be preferred to debt finance if the variable $[\theta(1 - \tau) - (1 - m)]$ is positive.

(3) For a given volume of new share issues, investment will be

financed by borrowing rather than from retained earnings if the variable $[(1-m)-(1-z)(1-\tau)]$ is positive.

We shall try to investigate the relationship between the values of these tax incentive variables and the actual pattern of corporate financing in the U.K. For ease of notation we shall denote the three tax incentive variables mentioned above by V_A, V_B, and V_C respectively. Their values in the U.K. over the period 1947–71 are shown in Table 7.1, which shows the values of the tax incentive variables for both the *mean* marginal income tax rate of shareholders, (V_A^a, V_B^a, V_C^a)

Table 7.1 Tax incentives to corporate financing, U.K. 1947–71.

Year	$\theta + z - 1$		$\theta(1-\tau)-(1-m)$		$(1-m)-(1-z)(1-\tau)$	
	V_A^a	V_A^m	V_B^a	V_B^m	V_C^a	V_C^m
1947	−0.447	−0.130	−0.076	−0.119	−0.145	0.055
1948	−0.319	−0.130	−0.094	−0.119	−0.064	0.055
1949	−0.312	−0.136	−0.097	−0.122	−0.057	0.055
1950	−0.330	−0.168	−0.115	−0.143	−0.041	0.064
1951	−0.422	−0.285	−0.152	−0.187	−0.048	0.052
1952	−0.403	−0.272	−0.147	−0.180	−0.050	0.047
1953	−0.394	−0.262	−0.161	−0.192	−0.030	0.065
1954	−0.384	−0.263	−0.131	−0.157	−0.080	0.012
1955	−0.384	−0.266	−0.143	−0.171	−0.068	0.025
1956	−0.424	−0.316	−0.170	−0.202	−0.062	0.029
1957	−0.426	−0.320	−0.172	−0.204	−0.060	0.030
1958	−0.236	−0.097	−0.097	−0.115	−0.028	0.064
1959	−0.157	0.0	−0.084	−0.100	0.004	0.100
1960	−0.161	0.0	−0.099	−0.118	0.020	0.118
1961	−0.159	0.0	−0.121	−0.143	0.046	0.143
1962	−0.156	0.0	−0.126	−0.149	0.054	0.149
1963	−0.156	0.0	−0.126	−0.149	0.054	0.149
1964	−0.107	0.0	−0.130	−0.162	0.044	0.162
1965	−0.103	0.123	−0.039	−0.049	−0.023	0.123
1966	−0.318	−0.190	−0.204	−0.235	0.014	0.121
1967	−0.314	−0.189	−0.215	−0.246	0.032	0.137
1968	−0.314	−0.195	−0.230	−0.261	0.056	0.153
1969	−0.315	−0.206	−0.229	−0.253	0.050	0.136
1970	−0.301	−0.196	−0.222	−0.244	0.044	0.127
1971	−0.292	−0.182	−0.224	−0.245	0.048	0.136

Source: Tables A1, A5, A6 and A8.

and also for the *median* marginal tax rate (V_A^m, V_B^m, V_C^m). Both series were constructed using the estimates of the effective tax rates on capital gains derived in Chapter 3 as a measure of the value of z in the expressions for V_A and V_C.

A number of points stand out from Table 7.1. As can be seen from the first and third columns, there was no year between 1947 and 1971 when new share issues were the optimal source of finance in the U.K. for the 'average' shareholder, and only in 1965 would the *median* shareholder have preferred to raise finance by issuing new shares. Even this rare preference for new equity finance can be seen as an aberration, in that the 1965 values of the relevant tax incentive variables (V_A and V_B) were abnormally high because of the transitional arrangements for the introduction of corporation tax, and it was known with virtual certainty that their value would fall in 1966. It is clear, therefore, that a profit-maximizing firm would have issued new shares only when constrained by non-tax factors to follow such a policy. For example, a firm wishing to expand rapidly might have found that its desired investment expenditure exceeded its available retained earnings. In itself, however, this would not have led to new share issues because, as can be seen from the values of V_B in Table 7.1, debt finance would have been preferred to new issues in every year by both mean and median shareholders. The incentive to issue new shares derived from the interaction between the constraint on the debt–equity ratio and the inadequacy of retained earnings. As a source of funds new share issues have been in the U.K. a 'source of last resort', and they would properly have been regarded as such by a profit-maximizing firm. It would be quite wrong, therefore, to construe the observation that share issues have in fact been a minor source of funds (see below) as evidence that the stock market has produced an inefficient allocation of resources to investment. A paucity of new issues would be predicted by the theory that the stock market is a highly competitive market which successfully disciplines firms into adopting profit-maximizing behaviour. Conversely, the fact that new issues are quantitatively small does not prove that the stock market leads to an efficient allocation of resources.

The tax incentives to the use of debt finance increased in the postwar period in the U.K. in two ways. Firstly, after 1958 the value of V_C increased which indicates a reduction in the cost of debt relative to that of retained earnings. Secondly, the value of V_B fell after the introduction of corporation tax in 1965 which made borrowing even more attractive in comparison to new share issues than it had been before. Although corporation tax has often been accused of providing a bias towards debt finance, it is interesting to note that its introduction in 1965 affected only the trade-off between debt and new issues, leaving the relative costs of debt and retentions unchanged.

An alternative way to present these changes in the tax incentives for different methods of finance is to look at the critical values of the income tax rate at which a shareholder would be indifferent to choosing between the different sources of finance. These are given by the income tax rates which are the solutions to the equations obtained by setting each of the tax incentive variables to zero. We have seen already in Chapter 4 that when interest payments are deductible for tax purposes debt finance is cheaper than new share issues for all shareholders, no matter what their tax rate, because of the restriction that the ACID Test Statistic is less than unity. Consequently, we shall look only at the critical values of the income tax rate at which (a) the shareholder is indifferent to choosing between retained earnings and new share issues ($V_A = 0$), and (b) the shareholder is indifferent to choosing between retained earnings and debt finance ($V_C = 0$). The values of these critical rates for 1947–75 in the U.K. are shown in Table 7.2; shareholders facing income tax rates higher than the critical rate would have preferred the firm to use retained earnings. The critical rates were calculated using the expression for the effective tax rate on capital gains given by equation (3.37) and employing the same assumptions as were used to construct Table 3.10.

The final column of Table 7.2 shows the actual average marginal income tax rate of U.K. shareholders. Again it is not difficult to see why in the past new share issues have been relatively infrequent. The critical rate for the choice between retentions and debt has tended to be fairly close to the actual average tax rate, although the actual rate fell over the period, from a level somewhat above the critical rate to a level somewhat below, indicating a tendency that debt finance has become more attractive over time.

Examination of the tax incentives in the U.K. leads to three predictions. Firstly, that retained earnings would have been the major source of finance in the postwar period; secondly, that new share issues would have been very small; and, finally, that borrowing would have grown in importance as a source of funds over time. These expectations are borne out by the figures of the actual pattern of financing of U.K. quoted companies shown in Table 7.3. Retained

Table 7.2 Critical and actual values of the income tax rate, U.K. 1947–75 (per cent).

Year	Critical values		Actual mean marginal tax rate of shareholders
	Retentions/New issues	Retentions/Debt	
1947	36.7	50.5	65.0
1948	36.7	50.5	56.9
1949	36.3	50.5	56.2
1950	35.5	52.8	56.8
1951	26.5	52.8	57.5
1952	26.2	51.0	56.0
1953	25.0	51.5	54.5
1954	23.7	45.0	53.0
1955	21.7	45.0	51.8
1956	16.0	45.4	51.6
1957	15.5	45.5	51.5
1958	34.3	47.0	49.8
1959	38.8	48.8	48.4
1960	38.8	50.6	48.6
1961	38.8	53.1	48.5
1962	38.8	53.8	48.3
1963	38.8	53.8	48.3
1964	40.0	56.3	51.8
1965	46.0	52.3	53.3
1966	0.0	52.2	48.9
1967	0.0	54.4	48.8
1968	0.0	56.6	48.1
1969	0.0	54.6	46.9
1970	0.0	51.7	45.2
1971	0.0	51.2	44.1
1972	27.2	51.2	n.a.
1973	40.5	60.2	n.a.
1974	42.2	62.1	n.a.
1975	43.4	62.2	n.a.

Source: Table A5 and own calculations.
n.a. = not available

earnings accounted for around 75% of the total sources of funds, and new share issues for only a small proportion of total funds. On average new share issues for cash (excluding issues made in exchange for companies acquired) provided only 7.3% of the total sources of funds

Table 7.3 Sources of finance, U.K. quoted companies 1950–72 (per cent).

Year	Retentions	Long term debt	Bank borrowing	Total borrowing	Ordinary share issues	Total sources of funds
1950	77.8	12.1	4.9	17.0	5.3	100
1951	75.3	7.6	10.9	18.5	6.2	100
1952	83.7	7.7	– 4.6	3.1	13.3	100
1953	90.9	9.3	– 5.0	4.3	5.0	100
1954	82.2	11.3	3.1	14.4	3.5	100
1955	74.8	9.3	5.7	15.0	10.1	100
1956	73.6	9.8	6.4	16.2	10.3	100
1957	68.3	13.3	4.1	17.4	14.3	100
1958	81.5	8.0	1.7	9.7	8.9	100
1959	80.9	5.8	4.9	10.7	8.3	100
1960	74.8	2.4	8.8	13.2	14.2	100
1961	65.3	6.3	11.0	17.3	17.6	100
1962	66.8	20.7	5.4	26.1	7.1	100
1963	77.5	8.9	7.1	16.0	6.3	100
1964	76.8	9.0	8.6	17.6	5.5	100
1965	69.3	14.0	14.5	28.5	2.2	100
1966	68.8	18.7	9.5	28.2	3.0	100
1967	74.5	19.8	2.8	22.6	2.9	100
1968	75.7	7.2	8.5	15.7	8.6	100
1969	69.9	6.1	17.8	23.9	6.2	100
1970	70.2	8.4	19.3	27.7	2.2	100
1971	85.6	14.6	– 4.0	10.6	3.9	100
1972	82.9	6.1	7.1	13.2	3.9	100

Source: HMSO (1975; Table P4).
The data cover quoted companies in manufacturing, distribution and other services.

Note: Row totals may not come to 100 because of rounding errors.
Issues of long term debt include issues of preference shares (which were negligible), and issues of ordinary shares exclude shares issued in exchange for companies acquired.

of quoted companies in the period 1950–72, and this proportion fell towards the end of the period. In contrast, borrowing grew in importance over the period accounting for about 15–25% of funds in the 1960s. Such an impressionistic interpretation of the evidence cannot, however, substantiate the claims made above for the effects of taxation on corporate financial policy. A more formal econometric test of the relationship is required.

7.2 *Estimation of financing ratio equations*

To test for the effects of taxation on financial behaviour we may look at either flows or stocks. The former consists of the relationships summarized in Table 7.3 for the flow of funds of the company sector, and the latter is measured by the value of balance sheet items such as the debt–equity ratio. The change in the value of the items in the balance sheet between two dates is given by the flows in the intervening period plus revaluations. We shall look first at the flow of funds data contained in Table 7.3. At this stage we are concerned solely with the method by which investment is financed and not with the determinants of the level of investment expenditure. Hence we shall be concerned with the proportions of total funds which are raised from the three sources, and since these proportions must sum to unity there are only two independent ratios. Let p_{SR} be the ratio of the value of new share issues to retained earnings, and p_{SD} the ratio of the value of new share issues to borrowing, then p_{DR}, the ratio of new debt to retained earnings, is equal to p_{SR}/p_{SD}.

From our previous theoretical discussion we would expect that the values of these financing ratios would depend upon the relevant tax incentive variables, and we would expect the following relationships to hold

$$p_{SR} = f_1(V_A), \tag{7.1}$$

$$p_{SD} = f_2(V_B), \tag{7.2}$$

$$p_{DR} = f_3(V_C). \tag{7.3}$$

In each case we would expect the financing ratios to be positively related to the tax incentive variables. Although the three ratios are multiplicatively dependent, we shall estimate the relationships separately because the three tax incentive variables are independent of each other, being functions of the four basic corporate and personal tax variables θ, τ, m and z. A major problem in estimating equations (7.1) to (7.3) is that it is likely that the functional forms are highly nonlinear. In the simplest model considered above, the financing ratios took the values zero or unity, and the use of more than one source of finance could be seen as the result of introducing additional binding constraints on the firm's financial policy, such as, for example, constraints on the debt–equity ratio and the inadequacy of current retained earnings.

A good illustration of this is afforded by the determinants of new share issues. We have seen (from Table 4.1) that with the interest-deductibility provision for debt finance, it would never be optimal to issue new shares in a world of certainty. Only if the firm cares about its debt–equity ratio will it consider issuing new shares, in which case the influence of the tax incentive variable will be greater the higher the debt–equity ratio. It may be the case, therefore, that the tax cost of new share issues relative to other forms of finance is a relevant consideration at the margin only when the debt–equity ratio is a matter of concern to the firm. In other circumstances the firm may choose extreme policies of the form $p_{SR} = p_{SD} = 0$. Where non-tax factors constrain the firm's choice of policy, the trade-off at the margin between the different sources of finance will be a function of the tax incentive variables, and this suggests that the tax variables and the debt–equity ratio may interact multiplicatively, with the tax variable having a larger influence the higher is the debt–equity ratio above some acceptable level.

The general linear form of equations (7.1)–(7.3) is (omitting subscripts)

$$p = \alpha_0 + \alpha_1 v. \tag{7.4}$$

We would expect the sign of α_1 to be positive for all three financing ratio equations. If we add the hypothesis that the size of the coefficient of the tax incentive variable is itself a function of the difference between the current debt–equity ratio, d, and an 'acceptable' level, $\bar{d}$, then we have

$$\alpha_1 = \beta_0 + \beta_1 (d - \bar{d}). \tag{7.5}$$

The equation to be estimated is then

$$p = \alpha_0^1 + \alpha_1^1 v + \alpha_2^1 (vd), \tag{7.6}$$

where

$$\alpha_0^1 = \alpha_0$$

$$\alpha_1^1 = \beta_0 - \beta_1 \bar{d}$$

$$\alpha_2^1 = \beta_1$$

The constant term in equation (7.6) is the same as that in equation (7.4), but the sign of the coefficient of the tax incentive variable is indeterminate. The coefficient of the multiplicative term we would expect to be positive.

It should be stressed that these equations are linear forms of what are likely to be highly nonlinear relationships. In the case of new share issues, for example, we have seen that in every year between 1947 and

1971 new issues were the most expensive source of funds (for both average and median shareholders) and, in the absence of additional constraints, would have been made only when retained earnings were exhausted *and* debt issues were constrained by the size of the debt–equity ratio. In this situation we would expect that the aggregate volume of new share issues would not only be small but would also depend critically on the distribution of financial surpluses among firms. If the economy were growing steadily at a constant rate each firm might have adequate retentions for its desired investment, but if the economy were experiencing either rapid expansion or structural change in the pattern of demand then some firms would wish to grow very rapidly relative to their existing resources and others might wish to decline. In aggregate the volume of new issues might be substantial. Consequently, an econometric model of the aggregate volume of new share issues will fail to capture much of the richness of the process of the rise, expansion and fall of new firms. We shall, however, attempt to allow for this in a very rough and ready fashion by including as an additional independent variable the rate of growth of the corporate sector capital stock, (denoted by g and measured by net fixed capital formation divided by the net capital stock of companies at current replacement cost).

Ideally, these factors would be examined by using pooled cross-section and time series data, but such data were not available for the U.K. for this study, and in order to test the effects of taxation we shall restrict our attention to aggregate time series data, (a major problem with using the existing data for individual companies since the war is that they are based on accounting conventions which do not allow for inflation and hence, for example, allow the debt–equity ratio to be calculated only at book value and not at the more appropriate market value).

Equations for the financing ratios were estimated on aggregate annual data covering both U.K. quoted companies for the period 1950–71 (as shown in Table 7.3), and also for another independent sample of industrial and commercial companies based on national accounting data over the period 1954–71. Details of the data used are given in Appendix B. One problem which arises with the data for industrial and commercial companies is that they include a number of unquoted companies which by definition did not have access to issues of easily marketable securities. This suggests that for this sample of companies the results for the financing ratios involving share issues may be less reliable, and for the ratio p_{SD} we have taken the ratio of share issues to issues of long-term debt whereas for p_{DR} we have taken debt to include bank borrowing as well as issues of debentures. For both data samples issues of shares have been taken to be issues for cash. Issues of shares in exchange for subsidiaries are really only a paper book-keeping transaction and do not result in a change in the company's requirements for new funds. Hence we do not regard such issues as a source of finance, and we look only at new share issues for cash.

The two samples were used to estimate equations (7.4) and (7.6) using the tax incentive variables shown in Table 7.1 (except for the 1965 values which as argued above were known to be abnormally high and so were set to their 1966 values), and a series for the debt–equity ratio at market value which is described later in this chapter. The estimated equations for the three financing ratios, p_{SR}, p_{SD}, and p_{DR}, for the two data samples are shown in Tables 7.4–7.9. Each equation was estimated assuming a first-order autoregressive error specification (by the method described in the previous chapter).

From theoretical considerations we would expect that the coefficients of the tax incentive variables in equation (7.4) would be positive, and that the coefficients of the multiplicative tax term in equation (7.6) would also be positive. In addition, the coefficients of the growth rate of the corporate sector would be expected to be positive if significant.

In general, these predictions are confirmed by the empirical results. The tables show estimates based on 36 specifications and in only one case is the sign of the coefficient of the tax variable negative when we would expect it to be positive, although the standard errors are too large to be confident about the quantitative importance of the impact of tax incentives on financial policy. The first two rows of each table show the estimates of equation (7.4) using, first, the average tax rate and, second, the median tax rate. Of the twelve coefficients of the tax variables eleven are positive and the results for the ratios p_{SD} and p_{DR} are much superior to those for p_{SR}. The next two equations in each table are for estimates of the specification shown in equation (7.6) for both tax rates, and in every case the coefficient of the multiplicative tax term is positive. The sign of the coefficient of the tax incentive variable in this specification is indeterminate on *a priori* grounds, and, although in every case the coefficient turned out to be negative, in only two cases was it significantly different from zero at the 5% level. The

Table 7.4 Estimated equations for financing ratio p_{SR}, U.K. quoted companies 1950–71 (standard errors in brackets).

Constant	V_A^a	V_A^m	$(V_A^a \times d)$	$(V_A^m \times d)$	g	ρ	$\bar{R}^2$	DW
0.092 (0.069)	−0.018 (0.231)					0.480[1]	0.177	1.81
0.098 (0.037)		0.007 (0.164)				0.467	0.176	1.81
0.081 (0.069)	−0.371 (0.442)		1.232 (1.269)			0.445	0.171	1.84
0.099 (0.038)		−0.289 (0.567)		1.142 (0.902)		0.466	0.138	1.81
−0.151 (0.129)	−0.536 (0.401)		1.394 (1.134)		4.108 (2.075)	0.557[1]	0.304	2.04
−0.117 (0.113)		−0.545 (0.519)		1.734 (1.865)	4.222 (2.154)	0.581[1]	0.272	2.01

[1]First-order autoregressive process significant according to the χ^2 likelihood-ratio test.

Table 7.5 Estimated equations for financing ratio p_{SR}, U.K. industrial and commercial companies 1954–71 (standard errors in brackets).

Constant	V_A^a	V_A^m	$(V_A^a \times d)$	$(V_A^m \times d)$	g	ρ	$\bar{R}^2$	DW
0.092 (0.030)	0.089 (0.102)					0.107	0.011	1.89
0.078 (0.016)		0.075 (0.083)				0.115	0.015	1.89
0.070 (0.029)	−0.331 (0.260)		1.343 (0.776)			0.003	0.110	1.94
0.079 (0.015)		−0.348 (0.367)		1.603 (1.359)		0.073	0.036	1.92
−0.026 (0.079)	−0.448 (0.272)		1.515 (0.773)		1.549 (1.145)	0.022	0.150	1.99
−0.005 (0.071)		−0.487 (0.378)		1.936 (1.364)	1.582 (1.266)	0.106	0.071	1.98

Table 7.6 Estimated equations for financing ratio p_{SD}, U.K. quoted companies, 1950–71 (standard errors in brackets).

Constant	V_B^a	V_B^m	$(V_B^a \times d)$	$(V_B^m \times d)$	g	ρ	$\bar{R}^2$	DW
0.999 (0.284)	3.215 (1.640)					0.365	0.423	1.84
1.045 (0.303)		3.029 (1.530)				0.351	0.419	1.83
0.844 (0.315)	−0.134 (2.691)		9.644 (7.534)			0.471	0.444	1.93
0.864 (0.336)		−0.067 (2.248)		8.613 (6.677)		0.465	0.440	1.93
0.482 (0.507)	−0.102 (2.547)		9.914 (7.511)		7.948 (9.136)	0.507[1]	0.435	2.00
0.502 (0.518)		−0.033 (3.312)		8.823 (6.684)	7.950 (9.138)	0.504	0.431	2.00
0.491 (0.451)			9.721 (4.629)		7.946 (8.829)	0.504[1]	0.473	1.99
0.506 (0.456)				8.763 (4.233)	7.950 (8.833)	0.502[1]	0.469	1.99

[1]First-order autoregressive process significant according to the χ^2 likelihood-ratio test.

Table 7.7 Estimated equations for financing ratio p_{SD}, U.K. industrial and commercial companies 1954–71 (standard errors in brackets).

Constant	V^a_B	V^m_B	$(V^a_B \times d)$	$(V^m_B \times d)$	g	ρ	$\bar{R}^2$	DW
2.015 (0.803)	6.053 (4.692)					0.260	0.195	1.68
2.089 (0.863)		5.627 (4.396)				0.254	0.191	1.69
1.688 (0.848)	− 2.934 (9.465)		27.809 (25.053)			0.263	0.207	1.74
1.726 (0.913)		− 2.605 (8.403)		25.217 (22.121)		0.256	0.206	1.74
0.410 (1.465)	− 2.136 (9.286)		26.016 (24.777)		27.684 (26.878)	0.318	0.209	1.74
0.461 (1.489)		− 1.891 (8.595)		23.473 (21.937)	27.304 (26.509)	0.314	0.207	1.75
0.551 (1.844)			21.303 (12.531)		27.979 (25.669)	0.306	0.259	1.73
0.616 (1.318)				19.495 (11.468)	27.585 (25.542)	0.301	0.257	1.73

Note: The definition of debt used in this table does not include bank borrowing.

Table 7.8 Estimated equations for financing ratio p_{DR}, U.K. quoted companies 1950–71 (standard errors in brackets).

Constant	V_C^a	V_C^m	$(V_C^a \times d)$	$(V_C^m \times d)$	g	ρ	$\bar{R}^2$	DW
0.246 (0.027)	0.583 (0.549)					0.136	0.061	1.70
0.189 (0.059)		0.600 (0.508)				0.107	0.067	1.73
0.252 (0.029)	– 2.879 (3.310)		13.998 (13.331)			0.206	0.064	1.55
0.174 (0.056)		– 0.718 (0.932)		6.178 (3.700)		0.066	0.159	1.65
– 0.135 (0.166)	– 5.401 (3.158)		19.757 (12.665)		8.218 (3.482)	0.421	0.270	1.60
– 0.085 (0.144)		– 1.926 (1.035)		6.609 (3.777)	7.684 (3.493)	0.356	0.303	1.74

Table 7.9 Estimated equations for financing ratio p_{DR}, U.K. industrial and commercial companies 1954–71 (standard errors in brackets).

Constant	V_C^a	V_C^m	$(V_C^a \times d)$	$(V_C^m \times d)$	g	ρ	$\bar{R}^2$	DW
0.247 (0.036)	1.543 (0.665)					0.497[1]	0.603	1.53
0.119 (0.079)		1.359 (0.663)				0.534[1]	0.594	1.48
0.259 (0.019)	−6.781 (2.030)		35.228 (8.231)			0.275	0.795	1.42
0.070 (0.053)		−0.286 (0.817)		8.813 (3.182)		0.286	0.686	1.53
0.153 (0.114)	−7.146 (2.127)		35.630 (8.524)		2.240 (2.383)	0.344	0.793	1.40
0.035 (0.127)		−0.369 (0.923)		8.602 (3.321)	1.016 (3.079)	0.321	0.666	1.51

[1]First-order autoregressive process significant according to the χ^2 likelihood-ratio test.

Note: The definition of debt used in this table includes bank borrowing.

remaining equations include the growth rate of the corporate sector capital stock as an additional independent variable. The coefficient of the growth rate is positive in every estimated equation, and significantly so at the 5% level for the two ratios p_{SR} and p_{DR} in the case of quoted companies. This result is in line with the expectation that the growth rate acts, at least to some extent, as a proxy variable for the need to resort to external finance, and so would be expected to influence the financing ratios involving retained earnings.

For the two financing ratios involving new share issues the goodness of fit of the estimated equations is better for quoted companies than for industrial and commercial companies which substantiates the point made earlier that the results for these two ratios may be less reliable for the sample of industrial and commercial companies because it includes some unquoted companies which are unable to issue easily marketable securities.

Although the equations were estimated separately thus ignoring the cross-equation constraint that the three ratios must be multiplicatively dependent, the size of the standard errors suggests that the hypothesis that the constraint holds would be accepted at any reasonable level of significance for all the estimates.

It is interesting to note that the average tax rate seems to give better results than does the median tax rate. If we look at the specification which produces the highest $\bar{R}^2$ in each of the six tables, then in five of the six cases this corresponds to the use of the mean marginal tax rate in the construction of the tax incentive variables.

Two other hypotheses were tested and rejected, and we report only the conclusions of the tests. The first hypothesis was that there is a positive relationship between new share issues and the share price index because companies like to issue shares when the price of those shares is high relative to recent experience. Such a relationship was inferred from diagrammatic evidence by the Royal Commission on the Distribution of Income and Wealth (HMSO (1975, para. 227)). In fact no relationship between the financing ratios and share prices could be detected and the share price index was never significant. This is not surprising, however, because there is no obvious theoretical reason for the degree of optimism about the future, as reflected in share prices, to affect financial policy directly, although there may be an indirect effect either through changes in the debt–equity ratio, which our specification already captures, or through a revision in the desired level of investment. An independent effect of the level of share prices would require not only that the intra-marginal shareholders (who are presumed to control the company's policy) valued the shares more highly than the marginal purchasers to whom the new issue would be made, but also that (a) this differential in valuation was itself a function of the level of share prices, which might be the case when there was a large change in expectations, and (b) retentions were not available as an alternative to new share issues. If retentions were available the decision to issue new shares would be simply a decision about the nominal division of a given total of equity into an arbitrary number of shares, and would depend on the relevant tax and transactions costs involved. Uncertainty will affect shareholders' valuation of the total equity of the company but the way in which the equity is divided into individual shares will not, apart from the tax factor, alter this valuation. The evidence supports this view in that there seems to be no independent effect of share prices on the method by which investment is financed, although there may well be other effects operating through the debt–equity ratio, or through the total level of investment itself.

A second factor affecting the volume of new share issues in the sample period might have been the existence of controls on capital issues which were in force from the end of the Second World War until 1958. During this period all capital issues in any twelve month period in excess of a certain amount (£50 000 until 1956 and thereafter £10 000) required the permission of the Capital Issues Committee of the Treasury which had to decide whether the issue was 'in the public interest'. Attempts to represent the activity of the Capital Issues Committee by dummy variables, whether constant in value or declining representing an easing of the control, were unsuccessful and the results are not reported (the *t*-values of the dummy variables were less than 0.5). There appears little evidence for a major impact of the controls on new issues.

These results based on aggregate time series data may be compared with the results of a cross-section study of U.K. quoted companies by Meeks and Whittington (1976) covering two periods, 1948–64 and 1964–71. They were not concerned with taxation but with the influence of growth and size on the pattern of financing. They found that new share issues were associated predominantly with rapidly growing companies which had exhausted their retained earnings, and, more interestingly, that companies with the largest volume of issues were not those companies with the largest amount of retentions. These results are consistent with the theoretical considerations discussed in Chapter 4, in which the various sources of finance were regarded as competing alternatives, but cast doubt on the thesis suggested by by Kaldor (1971) that financial policy is dictated by the need to complement new share issues by internally generated funds, and not by tax or other cost factors. The existence of uncertainty may impose a constraint on the firm's desired debt–equity ratio but it should not affect the choice between new share issues and retained earnings for a large public company.

7.3 *A model of the debt–equity ratio*

In the equations which we estimated for the financing ratios the underlying model was specified in terms of the optimal flow of funds year by year without any direct reference to the optimum portfolio of assets and liabilities held by the company. The debt–equity ratio was seen to be a significant factor in determining the response of the flows to changes in the tax incentive variables, but the flows were not given by a desired adjustment towards a target portfolio describing the firm's optimal capital structure. If we look at the company's balance sheet then, on the financial liabilities side there are two main items, debt and equity. By looking at the flow of funds it is possible to distinguish between retentions and new share issues, but on the balance sheet both sources contribute to total equity. Hence it would be impossible to use a portfolio adjustment model to explain the proportion of new funds raised by new issues as opposed to retentions. A portfolio adjustment model is appropriate, however, for explaining the behaviour of the debt–equity ratio (denoted by d).

The 'optimal' debt–equity ratio is the outcome of a complex interaction between the impact of uncertainty on the firm and the effects of the tax system. We saw in Chapter 5 that the very factors which lead management and shareholders to care about the firm's debt–equity ratio are the same factors which undermine the assumption that the firm will aim to maximize its share price, and in these circumstances a broader view of the firm's objective function may be appropriate, if indeed a unique decision-taker with a well-defined objective function can be postulated. Since the concept of an 'optimal' debt–equity ratio depends upon those ramifications of uncertainty which themselves lead one to doubt the validity of assuming profit-maximizing behaviour, it is unlikely that we shall be able to derive a single estimating equation based on optimizing behaviour, nor to encapsulate the influence of uncertainty in only one or two independent variables. So we shall concentrate on estimating simple relationships which emphasize the effect of taxation.

The target debt–equity ratio will be a function of the tax incentive variables and from our earlier discussion we would expect it to be negatively related to V_B and positively related to V_C. We shall assume a linear relationship between the target debt–equity ratio and the tax incentive variables V_B and V_C, and if we further assume that the firm adjusts only partially towards its target debt–equity ratio in each period, we obtain the following estimating equation:

$$d_t = \alpha_0 + \alpha_1 V_B + \alpha_2 V_C + \alpha_3 d_{t-1}. \tag{7.7}$$

This model was estimated using U.K. data for industrial and commercial companies over the period 1955–71. The value of the debt–equity ratio d_t was defined to be the ratio of the sum of bank advances and the market value of debentures to the sum of the market values of ordinary and preference shares at the end of year t. Data for industrial and commercial companies were used in preference to data for quoted companies, because in the latter case no data on market valuations were available, and from the theoretical point of view the market value debt–equity ratio is of more interest than the nominal debt–equity ratio. On this basis a series for the debt–equity ratio since 1960 was constructed from data published in the *Bank of England Quarterly Bulletin* (June 1976; Table B, p. 196). Additional estimates were made for the period 1954–61 by assuming that the interest rate on bank advances was the same as that on debentures (debenture interest was not distinguished from other interest in the data for the period

Table 7.10 Debt–Equity ratio, U.K. industrial and commercial companies, 1954–71 (End-year).

1954	0.239	1963	0.184
1955	0.249	1964	0.215
1956	0.279	1965	0.222
1957	0.267	1966	0.325
1958	0.264	1967	0.265
1959	0.198	1968	0.211
1960	0.166	1969	0.252
1961	0.188	1970	0.352
1962	0.190	1971	0.283

Sources: *National Income and Expenditure 1964*
Annual Abstract of Statistics, 1964
Bank of England Quarterly Bulletin, June 1976

before 1960). The estimates common to both series, for the years 1960 and 1961, were used to link the earlier series to that obtained from the *Bank of England Quarterly Bulletin*, and the resulting series is shown in Table 7.10. Although the debt–equity ratio certainly changed over the period there is no obvious trend in the figures shown in the table.

The results of estimating equation (7.7) are shown in Table 7.11. In each case the model was estimated assuming a mixed autoregressive and moving average error structure of the form discussed in the previous chapter. The first two equations show that when the basic model is estimated the coefficient of the tax incentive variable V_B has the correct sign and is significantly different from zero at the 5% level for both specifications of the marginal tax rate on shareholders, the mean and the median. However, the coefficient of the tax incentive variable V_C has the wrong sign, is insignificantly different from zero for the median tax rate and only just significant for the average tax rate.

To capture one of the features of uncertainty we might extend the model to incorporate a hypothesis suggested in the previous chapter where we examined the effect on the target payout ratio of the threat of being taken-over as measured by the amount of take-over activity taking place. Since it is necessary to buy only the equity of a company to obtain control, we might expect that the higher the debt–equity ratio, *ceteris paribus*, the bigger the risk of being taken-over. Hence the target debt–equity ratio may be a negative function of the take-over activity variable. As in the previous chapter we shall ignore the simultaneity involved in this relationship and use single-equation estimation methods. The results of including the take-over activity variable (as defined in Chapter 6) are shown in the third and fourth rows of Table 7.11. The coefficient of the variable is negative and highly significant, and its inclusion not only improves the goodness of fit markedly but produces a positive sign for the coefficient of the tax incentive variable V_C. The coefficients of V_C are, however, still insignificant and so in the remaining estimates the variable V_C is omitted. The last pair of estimated equations test the hypothesis that changes in the debt–equity ratio can better be explained by a time trend than by the extent of take-over activity. The results show clearly that this hypothesis may be rejected.

The evidence implies that quite a reasonable picture of the determinants of the debt–equity ratio of U.K. industrial and commercial companies can be obtained from a simple model relating the target debt–equity ratio to the tax incentives to the use of debt finance, and

Table 7.11 Determinants of debt–equity ratio, U.K. industrial and commercial companies 1955–71 (standard errors in brackets).

Constant	V_B^a	V_B^m	V_C^a	V_C^m	TK	Time trend	d_{t-1}	ρ	γ	χ^2	$\bar{R}^2$	DW
0.078 (0.027)	−0.596 (0.114)		−0.375 (0.174)				0.296 (0.166)	0.023	0.942	8.43	0.686	1.98
0.165 (0.078)		−0.519 (0.211)		−0.473 (0.282)			0.161 (0.227)	0.886	0.885	0.33	0.388	2.19
0.034 (0.018)	−0.745 (0.069)		0.094 (0.125)		−0.019 (0.004)		0.575 (0.109)	−0.525	0.938	15.68	0.848	2.29
0.030 (0.036)		−0.652 (0.084)		0.003 (0.146)	−0.015 (0.005)		0.535 (0.149)	−0.282	0.939	11.54	0.785	2.17
0.045 (0.012)	−0.746 (0.072)				−0.017 (0.003)		0.503 (0.063)	−0.431	0.939	15.38	0.847	2.17
0.031 (0.014)		−0.652 (0.084)			−0.015 (0.003)		0.532 (0.077)	−0.280	0.939	11.79	0.801	2.16
0.053 (0.026)	−0.687 (0.206)					−0.003 (0.002)	0.448 (0.158)	0.057	0.942	7.61	0.624	2.03
0.037 (0.025)		−0.576 (0.181)				−0.003 (0.002)	0.501 (0.152)	0.059	0.942	7.35	0.604	2.01

Note: The χ^2 statistic is for the likelihood ratio test of the mixed AR–MA error structure relative to OLS.

to the amount of take-over activity going on in the economy. The tax incentive variable which has the larger effect is that pertaining to the choice between debt and new share issues, whereas that relating to the cost of debt versus retained earnings turned out to be insignificant in the estimated equations. These results suggest that the neoclassical theory of the firm can be used to derive fruitful hypotheses about the influence of taxation on financial policy, but that in itself it is inadequate as a guide to corporate behaviour under uncertainty, as shown by the theoretical arguments of Chapter 5 and the econometric estimates of the last two chapters on the importance of the take-over activity variable.

We may use the estimates in Table 7.11 to analyse the change in the debt–equity ratio which might result from a reform of the corporate tax system. In 1973 the U.K. moved from the classical system of corporation tax to the imputation system, and if we use the equations given in the fifth and sixth rows of Table 7.11 we obtain the following estimates of the predicted change in the debt–equity ratio which such a change would bring about, both in the short-run and in the long-run, corresponding to the equations employing the average marginal tax rate and the median marginal tax rate in the construction of the tax incentive variables.

Estimate based on	Impact change	Long-run change
Average tax rate	– 0.053	– 0.107
Median tax rate	– 0.051	– 0.108

Both equations yield very similar predictions of an initial fall in the debt–equity ratio of just over 5 percentage points, and a long-run fall of over 10%. This would reduce the debt–equity ratio from its level in 1971 of 28.3% to the levels of around 18% obtained in the period 1959–68 when the profits tax system was in force. These predictions assume, of course, that the marginal tax rates on shareholders' investment income and the level of take-over activity would not change. Data on the independent variables were not available for the period after 1971 and so it was not possible to derive formal predictions for years outside the estimation period. The implied changes in the debt–equity ratio do not seem unreasonable in the context of the sample period, and yet after 1971 it is very likely that the debt–equity ratio rose in a manner not captured by the estimated equations. One explanation for this is that a sudden change of expectations about potential future profits might have led to a reduction in share prices, and thus to a large unanticipated rise in the debt–equity ratio. The equations in Table 7.11 might still be a correct representation of the target debt–equity ratio, but the unexpected rise in the actual debt–equity ratio would take a long time to undo (unless share prices recovered) because of the costs involved in making very large share issues to redeem debt, which would in any event be unnecessary if share prices did rise, and would necessitate a major change in the lag structure implied by our econometric estimates. Hence it may be that the recent high levels of the debt–equity ratio reflect factors which in turn produced a change in the lag structure of companies' financial behaviour but not in its underlying determinants as given by the model estimated here.

Chapter 8

THE INVESTMENT DECISION

Negative Capability, that is, when a man is capable of being in uncertainties, mysteries, doubts, without any irritable reaching after fact and reason (John Keats, in a letter, 1817).

In recent years economic policy-makers in several countries have tried to stimulate domestic investment by a variety of 'investment incentives' which have varied from additional tax allowances or cash subsidies to cheap loans. No advanced country has experimented with more schemes of this kind than the U.K., where a bewildering variety of policies have been deployed (for a description of these see King (1972) and Melliss and Richardson (1976)). Although the ratio of investment to net output in U.K. manufacturing industry has risen to levels which exceed those in either West Germany or the U.S. (Matthews and King, 1977), widespread doubts have been expressed about the ability of fiscal incentives to influence the investment decisions of firms on the grounds that this most important decision is dominated by the impact of uncertainty.

The importance of long-term expectations about an uncertain future as a determinant of the level of investment expenditure was stressed by Keynes, who was sceptical about the relevance of a model in which individuals were assumed to optimize in the face of uncertainty by, for example, maximizing their expected utility,

> Most, probably, of our decisions to do something positive, the full consequences of which will be drawn out over many days to come, can only be taken as a result of animal spirits – of a spontaneous urge to action rather than inaction, and not as the outcome of a weighted average of quantitative benefits multiplied by quantitative probabilities. Enterprise only pretends to itself to be mainly actuated by the statements in its own prospectus, however candid and sincere (Keynes, 1936, p. 161).

Keynes, however, believed that corporate decisions were neither random nor immune to the influence of public policy,

> Thus after giving full weight to the importance of the influence of short-period changes in the state of long-term expectations as distinct from changes in the rate of interest, we are still entitled to return to the latter as exercising, at any rate, in normal circumstances, a great, though not a decisive, influence on the rate of investment (*op. cit.* p. 164).

Although economists have sometimes played down the role of *the* rate of interest as either a desirable or feasible target for economic policy, we shall see that the crucial feature of the tax system is that the government can, by manipulating taxes, alter the opportunity cost of funds to a firm corresponding to any given market rate of interest. In this way the government may give incentives or disincentives to invest in certain types of assets. We shall analyse the effect of taxation assuming the degree of 'animal spirits' to be given. To say that we do not have a complete theory of investment is not the same thing as saying that we know nothing about the determinants of investment expenditure.

Although uncertainty raises fundamental and searching questions about the way we model the behaviour of firms and, in particular, its decisions about future production levels, we shall leave aside the problems discussed in Chapter 5 in order to analyse the relationship between the tax system and a firm's investment decision. Once this has been done we may return to the question of whether our conclusions would be radically altered by the relaxation of some of the assumptions.

8.1 *A simple model*

Despite the complexities involved in assessing the likely impact of a tax change on the level of investment, some of the basic results about the nature of the corporate profits tax may be illustrated by a very simple model. To analyse the investment decision of a 'typical' firm we shall make the following assumptions.

(1) There is no uncertainty about the firm's profits, and the firm faces a determinate profit function which we may write as

$$\pi_t = \pi_t(K_t, \tau_t). \tag{8.1}$$

The level of pre-tax profits in period t, π_t, is expressed as a function of the level of productive capacity, or 'capital stock', in period t denoted by K_t, and the tax rate on corporate profits τ_t. The definition of the tax rate was described in more detail in Chapter 3. The profit function is assumed to be continuous in K. In general the level of profits will be a function of the vectors of both prices and quantities of the firm's inputs and outputs, and the reason for representing the profit function by equation (8.1) is simply to emphasize two points. Firstly, the assumption we shall need is that for a given change in the level of capital input, there is a determinate change in the firm's profits. We may call the partial derivative of the profit function with respect to the level of productive capacity the marginal rate of return, denoted by MRR. A different marginal rate of return may be defined for each kind of input. Although we shall speak as if there were only one capital input the results hold also for the case of many inputs. The second reason for writing the profit function as equation (8.1) is to clarify the fact that the marginal rate of return will depend upon the tax rate because, in general, a change in the tax rate will affect the equilibrium price and output vectors, and hence both the demand curve for the firm's output and the supply curve for its inputs.

(2) Investment made in period $t - 1$ is assumed to add to productive capacity, and hence profits, only in period t. In each period a proportion δ of the capital stock wears out due to physical depreciation.

(3) There are no transactions costs and the firm may costlessly adjust its capital stock either upwards or downwards by as much or as little as it desires.

(4) There is a perfect capital market and the firm may borrow or lend at the market rate of interest r.

(5) There is no constraint on the firm's financial policy. In Chapter 4 we saw that the existence of differential tax rates on different legal forms of income necessitated a set of legal constraints on corporate financial policy. The effects of these will be explored in the next section.

(6) Tax rates and the interest rate are constant over time. We shall also ignore differences in tax rates between shareholders.

(7) There is no inflation and the price of capital goods in every period is defined to be unity. Inflation raises some interesting questions about the effects of the tax system in an inflationary era, and we shall deal with these separately in Section 8.3.

(8) The firm is assumed to maximize profits. As we saw in Chapter 5 this requires that the firm act as a price-taker in every market and is adopted here as a simplifying assumption.

We shall first analyse the optimal investment decision in the absence of taxation. Imagine that the firm is following an optimal policy and consider the following deviation from that path in which the firm's capital stock is increased by one unit in period t, holding the size of the capital stock at all other dates unchanged. From assumption (2) such a deviation requires an increase in gross investment in period $t-1$ of one unit, and a decrease in gross investment in period t of an amount $1-\delta$, from the levels implied by the optimal policy. Because there is no constraint on the firm's financial policy we know that it is feasible for the firm to finance the required expenditure in period $t-1$ by borrowing one unit in money terms and repaying both principal and interest in period t. The extra profits before tax arising from this operation are MRR, the interest payments are r, and the repayment of the principal of the loan is unity. Of this figure $(1-\delta)$ is provided by a reduction in investment expenditure and the remaining amount must come out of the profits of the operation. Hence the net profits of the deviation policy are

$$MRR - r - \delta. \tag{8.2}$$

By assumption this operation could not have been profitable (since the original path was optimal) and so the above expression must be nonpositive. Equally, we could have considered the alternative deviation of decreasing the capital stock in period t by one unit, holding the capital stock at all other dates constant. By a completely analogous argument the profits of this operation are given by

$$r + \delta - \text{MRR}. \tag{8.3}$$

This expression too must be nonpositive, and so we have that on the optimal path the following condition must hold

$$\text{MRR} = r + \delta. \tag{8.4}$$

This equation shows that the basic condition for optimality is that the return from employing an extra unit of capital must equal the marginal cost of capital services, or 'cost of capital' for short. The cost of capital comprises both a financial cost, because the firm's financial resources are locked up in fixed investment for a period, and a physical cost, because part of the capital stock deteriorates during the period.

When we introduce taxation we shall see that the crux of the matter is the set of assumptions made about two aspects of the tax system relating, firstly, to depreciation allowances and, secondly, to the tax-deductibility of debt interest payments. On the question of depreciation allowances we shall analyse the general case in which three kinds of allowance or subsidy are given for investment expenditure.

(1) A fraction f_1 of investment expenditure qualifies for an annual depreciation allowance at a rate of a per cent per annum on the written-down value of the asset. For investment in period $t-1$ the first allowance may be claimed in period t.

(2) A fraction f_2 of investment expenditure may be deducted against income for tax purposes in the year in which the expenditure is made. This is the case of immediate or 'free' depreciation in which the firm writes off its investment expenditure against tax as fast as it wishes.

(3) A fraction f_3 $(=1-f_1-f_2)$ of investment expenditure qualifies for a cash subsidy at a rate of g per cent.

We shall proceed on the assumption that profits are always adequate to enable tax allowances to be claimed, or that the tax system provides for 'complete loss offset' so that when allowances exceed income firms receive a refund. The same result can be achieved by allowing firms to carry losses forward provided the money value of these losses is increased each period by the net of tax interest rate.

As far as interest payments are concerned, we shall assume that a fraction γ of these payments are deductible against corporate profits tax, and that the rest are non-deductible.

We may consider the same perturbation policy as before, namely a unit increase in K_t leaving the capital stock at all other dates unchanged. Given the investment incentives described above the effective price of one unit of investment in period $t-1$ is given by

$$f_1+f_2(1-\tau)+f_3(1-g)=1-f_2\tau-f_3g. \tag{8.5}$$

Free depreciation reduces the cost of a fraction f_2 of the investment project by an amount equal to the rate of corporate profits tax, and the cash grant reduces the cost of a fraction f_3 of the project by the rate of grant. Because of these subsidies the firm may purchase an extra unit of investment by borrowing in period $(t-1)$ an amount equal to

$$(1-f_2\tau-f_3g).$$

In period t the extra profits are MRR, the interest payments on the loan are $r(1-f_2\tau-f_3g)$, and the taxable profits are gross profits minus deductible interest payments, and minus annual depreciation allowances. Hence the extra tax is

$$\tau[\mathrm{MRR} - \gamma r(1 - f_2\tau - f_3 g) - af_1]. \tag{8.6}$$

The reduction in investment of $1 - \delta$ in period t helps to repay the principal of the loan, but an additional amount is required equal to δ multiplied by the effective price of investment goods. The net profits of the perturbation policy are therefore given by

$$\mathrm{MRR} - r(1 - f_2\tau - f_3 g) - \tau[\mathrm{MRR} - \gamma r(1 - f_2\tau - f_3 g) - af_1] \\ - \delta(1 - f_2\tau - f_3 g). \tag{8.7}$$

As before, we may argue that at equilibrium this expression must be zero, and so along the optimal path we have

$$\mathrm{MRR} = r\left(\frac{1 - \gamma\tau}{1 - \tau}\right)(1 - f_2\tau - f_3 g) - \tau a\left(\frac{1 - f_2 - f_3}{1 - \tau}\right) \\ + \delta\left(\frac{1 - f_2\tau - f_3 g}{1 - \tau}\right). \tag{8.8}$$

In general the cost of capital is a function of the rate of corporate profits tax, the system of investment incentives, and the tax treatment of debt interest payments. We may examine the three systems of investment incentives in turn.

(1) *annual depreciation allowances* ($f_1 = 1$)

$$\mathrm{MRR} = r\left(\frac{1 - \gamma\tau}{1 - \tau}\right) + \left(\frac{\delta - a\tau}{1 - \tau}\right). \tag{8.9}$$

We shall define the corporate profits tax to be *nondistortionary* if the cost of capital is not an *explicit* function of the rate of tax, and if the optimal path is given by equation (8.4). For this to be the case in equation (8.9) the rate of annual depreciation allowance must be

$$a = \delta + r(1 - \gamma). \tag{8.10}$$

If interest payments are fully deductible for tax purposes then the rate of depreciation allowance must be equal to the rate of physical depreciation, in other words the tax system gives an allowance equal to 'true economic depreciation' which is the value at current replacement cost of physical wear and tear. Given the assumption of constant prices this is also equal to depreciation at historic or original cost. The definition of true economic depreciation in times of inflation will be discussed below in Section 8.3.

If interest payments are not deductible then the nondistortionary allowance is equal to the rate of physical depreciation plus the rate of interest, but since this is equivalent to granting tax-deductibility of interest payments and true economic depreciation, we may ignore this case.

A nondistortionary tax system merely means that the decision rule which firms use for choosing investment projects is independent of the rate of tax. It does not mean that changing the tax rate would have no effect on investment because, in general, both the marginal rate of return function (of the capital stock) and the rate of interest will themselves be functions of the tax rate. The theory of tax incidence is concerned with these general equilibrium effects of the corporate profits tax, but it is useful to distinguish between those cases in which the tax is distortionary from those in which it does not affect the analytical expression for the cost of capital. This point will be taken up again in the final section.

(2) *free depreciation* ($f_2 = 1$)

$$\text{MRR} = r(1 - \gamma\tau) + \delta. \tag{8.11}$$

With free depreciation the tax system is nondistortionary if and only if interest payments are *not* deductible for tax purposes. If interest payments are deductible then the result of free depreciation is that the cost of capital is *negatively* related to the rate of corporate profits tax. For a given rate of interest and a given marginal rate of return function, an increase in the rate of corporate profits tax would actually lead to an increase in the desired capital stock. This is because the effects of the tax are more than offset by the two subsidies, free depreciation and interest deductibility, the values of both of which depend on the tax rate.

(3) *investment grants* ($f_3 = 1$)

$$\text{MRR} = \left(\frac{1 - g}{1 - \tau}\right)[r(1 - \gamma\tau) + \delta]. \tag{8.12}$$

Clearly if the rate of investment grant equals the rate of tax then the system is equivalent to free depreciation. A rate of grant which is higher or lower than the rate of tax multiplies the free depreciation cost of capital by a factor of $(1 - g)/(1 - \tau)$. If the tax system does not provide for complete loss offset, a system of investment grants may offer a more effective incentive to invest because the receipt of the grant is not conditional on the firm having sufficient profits from other projects without which the free depreciation allowance would be less valuable. Cash grants might be particularly helpful in this respect to new firms. Nevertheless, when looking at nondistortionary tax systems we shall regard a cash grant at the rate of tax as equivalent to free depreciation.

In this section we have used a simple model to investigate the cost of capital under different systems of investment incentives. The general expression for the cost of capital is given by equation (8.8). We have identified two special cases in which the corporate profits tax may be described as nondistortionary. The first case is that of true economic depreciation and deductibility of interest payments, and the second case is where there is free depreciation but interest payments are not deductible. Before assessing the merits of these two systems we shall look at the cost of capital in a more complex world where we relax the assumption that there is no constraint on the firm's financial policy.

8.2 *The cost of capital in a more complex world*

The arguments of the previous section were based on the use of debt finance and required the assumption that at the margin an increase or decrease in debt finance was *feasible*. We have already analysed in Chapter 4 the conditions under which the use of debt finance would be optimal, and one of our conclusions was that if there were differences between the costs of various sources of finance, there would be a need for legal constraints on the financial policy which the firm could pursue. For example, when either retained earnings or new share issues were cheaper sources of funds than borrowing, a constraint on the firm's ability to lend would be necessary, and we represented this by a non-negativity constraint on the level of the firm's debt. Dividends were also constrained to be less than profits and greater than zero, and share issues to be non-negative. Uncertainty raises the possibility that the firm might be unwilling to exceed some acceptable debt–equity ratio, and so the existence of constraints on financial policy means that it is necessary to examine the cost of capital under alternative financial policies.

Using the same model as before, we may examine the consequences of financing the marginal project by equity finance. Suppose that in period $t-1$ the firm raises the necessary funds (the effective price of investment goods) from its shareholders. In period t it has two choices: it may either distribute the profits as dividends and repay the original capital (or make a rights issue), or retain the profits and reduce other sources of funds by a corresponding amount. The former policy allows shareholders to receive the profits as dividends, and the latter as capital gains because the shareholder may sell off some of his shares.

In the first case, which corresponds to financing by new share issues, the shareholders receive net dividends equal to

$$d(t) = \theta[\mathrm{MRR} - \tau(\mathrm{MRR} - af_1) - \delta(1 - f_2\tau - f_3g)] \qquad (8.13)$$

where θ is the tax discrimination variable defined in Chapter 3.

However, in order to induce the shareholders to subscribe to the company the dividend must, from the condition for equilibrium in the capital market (equation 4.1), be given by

$$d(t) = (1-m)r(1 - f_2\tau - f_3g) \qquad (8.14)$$

where m is the shareholders' marginal rate of income tax.

There is no capital gain to be taken into account because all profits are distributed and prices are constant. Combining the above two equations yields the equilibrium condition for investment financed by new share issues

$$\mathrm{MRR} = \left[\left(\frac{1-m}{\theta}\right)r + \delta\right]\left(\frac{1 - f_2\tau - f_3g}{1-\tau}\right) - \tau a\left(\frac{1 - f_2 - f_3}{1-\tau}\right). \qquad (8.15)$$

This gives the following expressions for the cost of capital in the two special cases which we distinguished above:

(i) True economic depreciation ($a = \delta$)

$$\mathrm{MRR} = \left(\frac{1-m}{\theta(1-\tau)}\right)r + \delta. \qquad (8.16)$$

(ii) Free depreciation ($f_2 = 1$)

$$\mathrm{MRR} = \left(\frac{1-m}{\theta}\right)r + \delta. \qquad (8.17)$$

The expressions for the variable θ under different systems of corporation tax as given in Chapter 3 were

(1) classical system, $\theta = 1 - m$.

(2) imputation or two-rate system, $\theta = \dfrac{1-m}{1-s}$

(3) integrated system, $\theta = 1$, and $\tau = m$.

This information is sufficient to enable the reader to work out the cost of capital for new share issues in a wide variety of cases with different assumptions about the system of corporation tax and the investment incentives available to the firm. We may note that when investment is financed by new share issues the tax system will be nondistortionary only in the following cases.

(i) True economic depreciation and an integrated tax system
(ii) True economic depreciation and an imputation system with the rate of imputation equal to the rate of corporation tax. This is effectively an integrated system.
(iii) Free depreciation and a classical system of corporation tax.

When investment is financed by retained earnings the shareholders receive the net profits of the investment project in the form of capital gains. The amount of the post-tax capital gain which will result from the marginal investment project which we have considered above is

$$(1-z)[\mathrm{MRR} - \tau(\mathrm{MRR} - af_1) - \delta(1 - f_2\tau - f_3 g)] \qquad (8.18)$$

where z is the rate of capital gains tax.

By the same argument as before this must be equal to the right-hand side of equation (8.14) for the shareholders to have invested in the project. Thus the cost of capital in the case of internal finance is

$$\mathrm{MRR} = \left[\left(\frac{1-m}{1-z}\right)r + \delta\right]\left(\frac{1 - f_2\tau - f_3 g}{1-\tau}\right) - \tau a\left(\frac{1 - f_2 - f_3}{1-\tau}\right). \qquad (8.19)$$

From this equation we can see that the tax system will be nondistortionary if the rates of income tax and capital gains tax are equal, and the system provides for free depreciation. In all other circumstances a nondistortionary outcome could arise only from a fortuitous constellation of tax rates and allowances.

Table 8.1 summarizes some of the main results about the cost of capital under different tax and allowance systems. Each entry in the table is the expression for the 'financial cost of capital' which is the

Table 8.1 The financial cost of capital under different tax systems

	Source of funds				
	Retentions	Debt		New issues	
		Interest deductible	Interest not deductible	Classical system	Imputation system
True economic depreciation	$\left[\frac{(1-m)}{(1-z)(1-\tau)}\right]r$	r	$\frac{r}{1-\tau}$	$\frac{r}{1-\tau}$	$\left(\frac{1-s}{1-\tau}\right)r$
Free depreciation	$\left(\frac{1-m}{1-z}\right)r$	$r(1-\tau)$	r	r	$(1-s)r$

marginal rate of return (pre-tax) net of depreciation, MRR $-\delta$. We shall defer evaluation of the merits of these different outcomes until Section 8.4.

Although in the cases we have examined the cost of capital has depended in a rather complex way on the detailed provisions of the tax system, in each case the optimal investment decision could be described as 'myopic' in that the cost of capital was a function only of variables in periods $t-1$ and t. Even this, however, holds out the possibility of complications because if in period $t-1$ the firm knows or thinks that the tax rate may be different in period t from its current value, then the effective price of investment goods will be expected to change, and the previous results will not hold unless $f_2 = f_3 = 0$, in which case the effective price is independent of the tax rate. However, in the case of free depreciation an anticipated rise in the tax rate will act as a disincentive to investment because it will produce an expected capital loss on fixed assets.

Any investment project to which the firm is committed for more than one period will raise the same problem. Changes in tax rates can therefore undermine the nondistortionary effect of free depreciation. A more fundamental objection to the myopic view of investment decisions derives from the existence of adjustment costs. Such costs make it necessary to consider both immediate and future needs when deciding on how much capacity to install, and in these circumstances the cost of capital will be a good deal more complicated than the simple expressions derived above. Moreover the existence of adjustment costs can undermine the nondistortionary nature of the other special scheme which we examined, namely true economic depreciation and deductibility of interest payments. The reason for this is that each investment plan will have associated with it a time path of adjustment costs (for example, additional labour costs) which have to be taken into account. In order to choose the optimal investment plan the firm will have to consider the alternative time paths of these adjustment costs and to do this requires a discount rate. If interest payments are tax-deductible then the appropriate discount rate is the net of tax interest rate which is obviously a function of the tax rate. Hence the optimal investment plan will not be independent of the tax rate. This will not apply to the free depreciation case because interest payments are not tax-deductible, and so the discount rate is independent of the tax rate.

There is one further reason for believing that the investment decision is not myopic. The cost of capital will differ according to the sources of funds and, subject to the legal and other constraints on its financial policy, the firm will choose the cheapest source, but the precise nature of the constraints (for example, the adequacy of retained earnings) will depend upon policy in the past. A high level of investment during this period will increase earnings next period thus relaxing the constraint on internal finance in the next period. This will mean that the expression for the cost of capital using retained earnings will be relevant to more investment projects than before. If we introduce these constraints into the firm's optimization problem, the cost of capital will contain the multipliers corresponding to the binding constraints, thus linking present and future investment policies. A formal demonstration of this may be found in King (1974).

If, to all these considerations, we add the fundamental problems of the specification of the firm's objective function and the modelling of an imperfect capital market in a world of uncertainty, we can see that the appropriate specification of the cost of capital is not a straightforward matter. This conclusion poses serious difficulties for the econometric specification of models of investment behaviour and for attempts to make inferences about the effects of tax policy on the level of investment expenditure.

8.3 *Inflation and the tax system*

In this section we shall relax the assumption of constant prices in order to focus on the interaction between inflation and the tax system. As before, we shall analyse a perturbation policy consisting of a unit increase in K_t holding the capital stock at all other dates unchanged. Let the rate of inflation of investment goods' prices be denoted by ρ so that the price of investment goods in period t is equal to $1 + \rho$. In the case with no taxation the firm borrows one unit in period $t - 1$ and repays the loan in period t. The perturbation policy involves a reduction in investment expenditure in period t by an amount $(1 - \delta)(1 + \rho)$. These funds may be used to help repay the loan and the additional sum required for this purpose is therefore

$$\begin{aligned} & 1 - (1 - \delta)(1 + \rho) \\ & = \delta(1 + \rho) - \rho. \end{aligned} \tag{8.20}$$

The net profits of the operation are given by

$$\text{MRR} - r - \delta(1+\rho) + \rho. \tag{8.21}$$

Using the standard argument that this must be zero at equilibrium, the optimal path in times of inflation is described by the following condition

$$\text{MRR} = (r - \rho) + \delta(1+\rho). \tag{8.22}$$

The cost of capital is affected by the rate of inflation in two ways. Firstly, the relevant interest rate is the 'real' rate of interest, the nominal rate minus the rate of inflation, and, secondly, the depreciation cost is valued at current (period t) replacement cost and not at the historic price of investment goods in period $t - 1$.

If we now introduce taxation into the model of debt finance the argument follows along exactly the same lines which led up to equation (8.8) with two modifications. The first is the point expressed in (8.20) that inflation changes the burden of debt repayment. The second is the treatment of interest payments. An 'indexed' company tax system would extend the privilege of tax-deductibility only to real interest payments, whereas an unindexed system would allow deduction of nominal interest payments. We shall assume that a fraction γ_1 of real interest payments is tax-deductible and a fraction γ_2 of the inflationary element of interest payments is tax-deductible. In an indexed tax system with interest-deductibility $\gamma_1 = 1$ and $\gamma_2 = 0$; in an unindexed system $\gamma_1 = \gamma_2 = 1$. Under these assumptions the tax payments in period t would be

$$\tau(\text{MRR} - af_1 - \gamma_1(r-\rho)p_{\text{I}} - \gamma_2\rho p_{\text{I}}) \tag{8.23}$$

where $p_{\text{I}} = 1 - f_2\tau - f_3 g$ denotes the effective price of investment goods in period $t - 1$, and is the sum borrowed by the firm in period $t - 1$. Depreciation allowances are assumed for the moment to be granted on historic cost expenditure, and we shall return to this below.

The net profits obtained by increasing K_t by one unit are

$$\begin{aligned} &\text{MRR} - rp_{\text{I}} - \tau[\text{MRR} - af_1 - \gamma_1(r-\rho)p_{\text{I}} - \gamma_2\rho p_{\text{I}}] \\ &\quad - p_{\text{I}}(\delta(1+\rho) - \rho). \end{aligned} \tag{8.24}$$

The equilibrium condition for the firm is therefore given by the condition

$$\text{MRR} = \frac{p_{\text{I}}}{1-\tau}[(r-\rho)(1-\tau\gamma_1) + \delta(1+\rho) - \tau\gamma_2\rho]$$

$$-\tau a\left(\frac{1-f_2-f_3}{1-\tau}\right). \tag{8.25}$$

In Section 8.1 we saw that with a zero inflation rate there were two special cases in which the tax system was nondistortionary, and we now pose the question of whether this result survives the introduction of inflation into the model. Consider first the case of free depreciation and non-deductibility of interest payments. In this situation $f_2 = 1$, $p_{\mathrm{I}} = 1 - \tau$, and $\gamma_1 = \gamma_2 = 0$. It is then easy to see that with these values equation (8.25) collapses to equation (8.22) and the tax system is nondistortionary. Free depreciation can produce a nondistortionary outcome even in periods of inflation.

The other special case, of 'true economic depreciation' and interest deductibility, deserves more careful attention. For this case we have $p_{\mathrm{I}} = 1, f_2 = f_3 = 0$, and for the moment we shall leave open the question of the value of a, the annual depreciation allowance in period t. We may consider two forms of interest deductibility. First, only real interest payments are deductible which implies that $\gamma_1 = 1$ and $\gamma_2 = 0$. Equation (8.25) becomes

$$\mathrm{MRR} = (r-\rho) + \frac{\delta(1+\rho) - \tau a}{1-\tau}. \tag{8.26}$$

The value of the allowance a which produces a nondistortionary outcome is given by

$$a = \delta(1+\rho). \tag{8.27}$$

This states that depreciation allowances must be based on current replacement cost and not on historic cost. If this is done then restricting deductibility to real interest payments ensures that the tax system is nondistortionary.

The second case is where nominal interest payments are deductible ($\gamma_1 = \gamma_2 = 1$) and in this case the cost of capital is described by

$$\mathrm{MRR} = (r-\rho) + \frac{\delta(1+\rho) - \tau(a+\rho)}{1-\tau}. \tag{8.28}$$

For a nondistortionary system we require

$$a = \delta(1+\rho) - \rho. \tag{8.29}$$

This is just another way of saying that with inflation the allowances which will produce a nondistortionary result comprise replacement cost depreciation plus deductibility of real interest payments, or, equivalently, deduction of nominal interest payments and the inclusion in the tax base of the fall in the real value of the firm's net monetary liabilities. The real value of the firm's debt has been eroded by inflation and fallen by an amount ρ. An alternative way of looking at this result is that in an unindexed company tax system (where nominal interest payments are tax deductible) the appropriate definition of true economic depreciation is replacement cost depreciation minus the nominal capital gain which accrues on fixed assets. In our model we have assumed a single rate of inflation, but suppose we had assumed different rates for capital goods and some overall index. Then if 'real' interest payments are defined in terms of the average rate of inflation and were tax-deductible, the reader will find that the appropriate definition of true economic depreciation is replacement cost depreciation minus the *real* capital gain accruing on the asset (i.e. the excess of the rate of increase of capital good prices over the average rate of inflation). With this definition of true economic depreciation and interest deductibility the tax system will be nondistortionary with respect to debt finance.

We conclude this section by summarizing the cost of capital for alternative sources of funds under two assumptions, (i) an unindexed personal tax system, in which the condition for equilibrium in the capital market is given by equation (4.1), and (ii) an indexed personal tax system, in which both interest income tax and capital gains tax are indexed, and the equilibrium condition is given by equation (4.31). The reader is referred to Chapter 4 for a discussion of these systems and their impact on the firm's optimal financial policy. The derivation of the expression for the cost of capital follows the same lines as the proofs in Section 8.2.

(1) *new share issues*

(i) an unindexed personal tax system:

$$\text{MRR} = \frac{p_{\text{I}}}{1-\tau}\left[\left(\frac{1-m}{\theta}\right)r - \rho + \delta(1+\rho)\right] - \tau a\left(\frac{1-f_2-f_3}{1-\tau}\right) \tag{8.30}$$

Table 8.2 The financial cost of capital with inflation

	Indexed tax system				Unindexed tax system			
	Retained Earnings	Debt finance[2]		New share issues	Retained earnings	Debt finance[2]		New share issues
		Interest deductible	Interest not deductible			Interest deductible	Interest not deductible	
True Economic depreciation[1]	$\frac{1-m}{(1-z)(1-\tau)}(r-\rho)$	$r-\rho$	$\frac{r-\rho}{1-\tau}$	$\left[\frac{1-m}{\theta(1-\tau)}\right](r-\rho)$	$\left[\frac{1-m}{(1-z)(1-\tau)}\right]r-\rho$	$r-\rho$	$\frac{r-\rho}{1-\tau}$	$\left[\frac{1-m}{\theta(1-\tau)}\right]r-\rho$
Free depreciation	$\left(\frac{1-m}{1-z}\right)(r-\rho)$	$(r-\rho)(1-\tau)$	$r-\rho$	$\frac{1-m}{\theta}(r-\rho)$	$\left(\frac{1-m}{1-z}\right)r-\rho$	$r(1-\tau)-\rho$	$r-\rho$	$\left(\frac{1-m}{\theta}\right)r-\rho$

[1]In an indexed tax system, true economic depreciation is defined to be replacement cost depreciation less the real capital gain on assets, whereas in an unindexed tax system it is defined as replacement cost depreciation less the nominal capital gain on assets.

[2]In an indexed tax system only real interest payments are tax-deductible; in an unindexed system all interest payments are deductible.

(ii) an indexed personal tax system

$$\text{MRR} = \frac{p_{\text{I}}}{1-\tau}\left[\left(\frac{1-m}{\theta}\right)(r-\rho) + \delta(1+\rho)\right] - \tau a\frac{(1-f_2-f_3)}{1-\tau} \tag{8.31}$$

(2) *retained earnings* The equilibrium condition for investment financed out of retained earnings is given by substituting $(1-z)$ for θ in equations (8.30) and (8.31).

In order to bring together the results of this section the values of the financial cost of capital in a number of particular cases are summarized in Table 8.2. The opportunity cost of investment which confronts a firm results from a complex interaction between the tax system and the rate of inflation, and only in special cases can we identify this with the real rate of interest.

Although there appear to be two ways of achieving a nondistortionary outcome, at least with debt finance, it is evident that free depreciation is the easier method because the use of true economic depreciation entails the calculation of replacement cost depreciation and capital gains both of which involve problems of valuation. In contrast, the profits tax with free depreciation is a tax on cash flow with purchases of assets being deductible in the same way as other costs and sales of assets being added to the tax base.

One final case of note is the appropriate tax treatment of stocks, a subject which has received a good deal of attention in the business literature on 'inflation accounting'. If the rate of increase in the price of stocks is ρ then stocks purchased in period $t-1$ at a price of unity may be sold in period t at a price of $(1+\rho)$ either directly through the market or indirectly through their embodiment in final output. In terms of our previous notation $\text{MRR} = 1 + \rho$ and $\delta = 1$. When there is no taxation the equilibrium condition becomes

$$\rho = r. \tag{8.32}$$

In a world of certainty, stocks will be an attractive investment if their price rises at a rate at least equal to the market rate of interest. In practice the rate of inflation is uncertain but if, as an example, we consider a firm which is risk neutral (i.e. one which is concerned only with the expected value of profits and not with their variability) then in equilibrium

$$E(\rho) = r \tag{8.33}$$

where $E(\rho)$ is the expected rate of increase of stock prices. The introduction of a nondistortionary tax system will leave this condition unchanged, but in general taxes will alter the incentive to invest in stocks. In 1974 the U.K. adopted a system of 'stock relief' which extended the benefit of both free depreciation and tax-deductibility of nominal interest payments to marginal stock purchases. For investment in stocks financed from borrowing the cost of capital is given by equation (8.25) with $p_I = 1 - \tau$, $f_2 = 1$, $\gamma_1 = \gamma_2 = 1$. Consequently the U.K. reform led to a new equilibrium condition given by

$$E(\rho) = r(1 - \tau). \tag{8.34}$$

Clearly, this scheme offered a much greater incentive to invest in stocks at the margin and for a given rate of interest, this incentive was larger the higher was the tax rate.

8.4 *The optimal corporation tax*

The approach of the previous two sections which discussed the impact of the tax system in terms of the 'cost of capital' tells us something about the incentive effects of various taxes, but it does not tell us very much about two very important issues. The first of these is the quantitative effect of any given tax change on the level of investment expenditure. The second is the question of the ultimate 'incidence' of a corporate profits tax. It should already be apparent that both the incentive effects and the incidence of a corporate profits tax will depend critically on the detailed provisions of the tax system concerning depreciation, investment incentives, alternative methods of financing and institutional and legal constraints. There is no such thing as *the* corporate profits tax.

As a first step we may consider the following equations

$$\text{MRR}_t = \text{MRR}\,(K_t, \tau_t) \tag{8.35}$$

$$\text{MRR}_t = c_t \tag{8.36}$$

where c_t denotes the cost of capital. Solving these equations yields the following expression for the optimal capital stock

$$K_t = k(c_t, \tau_t). \tag{8.37}$$

The shape of the function k will depend upon both the production possibility frontier (or production function) facing the firm, and the prices of all inputs and outputs. For purposes of econometric estimation of equation (8.37) specific assumptions about these factors will have to be made, and the results will be sensitive to the choice of assumption. For example, it is common in econometric studies to assume that the market prices of capital goods are given independently of the demand for capital goods. This means that when estimating equation (8.37) the price of capital goods may be considered as an exogenous variable and no problem of simultaneity arises. However, in practice supply constraints in the capital goods sector may be significant, and Brechling (1975) has pointed to the importance of such constraints for econometric work on investment behaviour.

The demand for capital goods will depend upon the cost of capital and, as we have seen, this may take a rather complicated form. The financial cost of capital will depend upon which source of funds is used to finance the investment, and in turn this will depend upon both the tax system and the nature of the legal constraints imposed on the firm's financial policy. Since the exact nature of the constraints will be determined by the firm's past investment and financial decisions, the cost of capital will be a function of past levels of investment expenditure thus converting equation (8.37) into a difference equation and introducing time lags into the estimating equation. These lags will be complex and, more importantly, endogenous to the investment decision. Similar problems arise when adjustment costs are introduced explicitly into the model (see the study by Nickell (1977)). As far as the depreciation element of the cost of capital is concerned it is common to assume that the value of the rate of depreciation (which was denoted above by δ) is constant over time, although, as has been shown by Feldstein and Rothschild (1974), there is little theoretical support for this notion.

It is clear then that there are major problems in specifying an estimating equation for the level of investment expenditure, even for a single firm, and we cannot feel confident that a single model would provide a satisfactory description of investment behaviour in all countries and in all time periods. The relationship between investment demand and other economic variables is more complex than has often been supposed, and this conclusion is strengthened when we remember that in addition to the factors mentioned above, there are the fundamental problems posed in Chapter 5 of the specification of the firm's objective function and the role of the capital market in a world of uncertainty. On the theoretical level there is a great deal still to be explored in the realm of corporate behaviour. This should not be interpreted, however, as an argument against econometric investigation of these problems. On the contrary, what is required is further study of a variety of different models and specifications to shed light on which factors are quantitatively important. For example, the cost of capital depends on personal as well as corporate tax rates, and this suggests that there may be a link between the structure of ownership and the level of investment. An econometric investigation of these matters must await a later study, but excellent surveys of the existing literature on the econometrics of investment behaviour may be found in Helliwell (1976) and Lund (1976).

To understand the incidence of the corporate profits tax requires a resolution of the issues discussed above, but it also involves an analysis of the response of all the equilibrium prices and quantities in the economy to a change in the tax rate. In terms of our model the tax may have a direct incentive effect through the expression for the cost of capital, and an indirect effect through changes in either the marginal rate of return function or the market rate of interest. The first effect is concerned with the distortionary nature of the corporation tax, and the second deals with the incidence of the tax. The phrase 'shifting of the corporation tax' is sometimes used to refer to the first of these questions, and sometimes to the second. In so far as shifting refers to the effect of the tax on output prices the distinction is clear. The first-order conditions for optimal factor demands also determine the optimal price-cost ratios, and if the first-order conditions contain the tax rate explicitly, then for given input prices the output price will be a function of the tax rate (on this point see Nordhaus (1972)). Hence shifting will certainly occur in any tax system which is distortionary; but even in nondistortionary tax systems indirect shifting may occur via tax-induced changes in the firm's demand function or input prices, such as, for example, the interest rate.

It is clear that to answer questions about incidence we need a general equilibrium model of the economy. There have been several attempts to analyse this question within different frameworks. Harberger (1974) has developed an approach based on the assumption of constant factor supplies, Diamond (1970) and Feldstein (1973) have examined the incidence of taxes on property income in a neoclassical growth model, and Batra (1975) has attempted to incorporate uncertainty into the model. The basic difficulty, however, is to know exactly what assumptions to make. We know little, for example, about the effects of taxation and interest rates on savings incentives, and all of the studies cited assume a closed economy. Yet if any factor is mobile internationally it is capital. This suggests that if the key to the incidence question is the effect of the tax on the rate of interest, it could be extremely misleading to base policy conclusions on the results of a model of a closed economy. Indeed if capital is perfectly mobile then the effects of changing the rate of corporate profits tax in a small country and maintaining the level of aggregate demand, are described quite well by the partial equilibrium models we have analysed. Focussing on the interest rate also brings us back to the problem of analysing financial and capital markets in a world of uncertainty.

For these reasons we may pose the question, is it necessary to solve the incidence question in order to design an 'optimal' corporation tax? In one sense the answer is, unfortunately, yes it is. A government which is constrained to raise revenue by the use of at least one distorting tax will wish in principle to use as many taxes as possible in order to minimize the total distortion or efficiency loss, or to trade off efficiency losses against equity gains. The problem with this argument is that to design the optimal tax system requires knowledge of all the incidence effects of the different taxes. We have argued that in the corporate sphere this is very difficult and hence there is an argument for looking for a system of corporate (and the related personal) taxes which produces a nondistortionary outcome. With this in mind we shall examine a number of alternative tax systems which would qualify under this heading.

One criterion which it seems very reasonable to impose is that the tax system be *neutral* in the sense used in Chapter 4 in that it does not discriminate between different sources of finance. A neutral tax system would mean that taxes would not influence a company's choice of financial policy, and there would be no need for complicated legal constraints on financial policy which are currently necessary to prevent tax avoidance. There would be no incentive for firms to devote real resources to discovering ways of converting income from one legal form into another. Moreover, we saw in Chapter 4 that a neutral tax system would remove the decision to incorporate from the realm of tax considerations.

Two systems of personal and corporate tax are capable of neutrality. The first is the combination of the classical system of corporation tax with the restriction that interest payments are not tax-deductible and a personal tax system in which capital gains are taxed at full personal income tax rates. The other neutral system is one in which the tax on corporate profits is integrated into the personal income tax with tax-deductibility of interest payments being retained. The imputation and two-rate systems can be neutral only if there is a single marginal rate of income tax. If the marginal income tax rate increases with income these systems are non-neutral. If the personal tax system were to be changed from an income tax to a personal expenditure tax the neutral system would be the classical system without interest-deductibility.

Having restricted our attention to tax systems which are neutral with respect to financial policy we may turn our attention to the effects of taxes on investment. At first sight it might seem that a corporate tax system which did not distort the first-order condition for the demand for capital goods would offer an attractive nondistortionary tax, but this is to ignore the interaction between the corporate and personal tax systems. The fundamental condition for an efficient allocation of resources is that the marginal rate of transformation in production between goods this period and goods next period equals the marginal rate of substitution of individuals between present and future consumption. The argument for choosing a corporate tax system which leaves the financial cost of capital equal to the interest rate is that the market rate of interest measures the rate at which individuals may substitute future for present consumption. But this does not hold if individuals are subject to a personal income tax on unearned income. Under an income tax regime the rate at which individuals may substitute future for present consumption is given by the real post-tax interest rate, *i*, which is

(i) an indexed personal tax system

$$i = (1 - m)(r - \rho).$$

(ii) an unindexed personal tax system

$$i = (1 - m)r - \rho.$$

The corporate tax system which is nondistortionary is one which offsets the distortionary effect of the income tax on savings decisions, and has a financial cost of capital equal to the real post-tax interest rate faced by individuals (on this point see also Flemming (1976) and Stiglitz (1976)). From Table 8.2 it is clear that there is only one tax system capable of achieving this result, the integrated system with free depreciation and tax-deductibility of interest payments. It is interesting to note that the nondistortionary outcome can be achieved by either indexing *both* the personal and the corporate tax systems, or by indexing *neither*. In the latter case the market rate of interest would rise to reflect the lack of indexation of property income. If the post-tax real rate of interest were the same in both cases then the nominal rate of interest in the economy without indexation, r_N, would exceed the nominal rate in the economy with indexation, r_I, by

$$r_N - r_I = \left(\frac{m}{1-m}\right)\rho. \tag{8.38}$$

In the economy with indexation an increase in the inflation rate which left the post-tax real interest rate unchanged would increase the nominal interest rate by the same amount as the rise in the inflation rate. In an unindexed economy the equivalent difference in nominal interest rates when the rate of inflation increases from ρ_1 to ρ_2 is

$$r_2 - r_1 = \frac{\rho_2 - \rho_1}{1-m}. \tag{8.39}$$

The integrated tax system characterized by free depreciation and interest deductibility and a personal income tax is, in terms of resource allocation, equivalent to an expenditure tax. If this removal of intertemporal distortion were thought desirable, and if it were feasible, a more satisfactory system would be to introduce a personal expenditure tax itself as a replacement for the income tax. Each individual would then be able to earn a post-tax return on his savings equal to the real rate of interest. The appropriate corporation tax to accompany the expenditure tax would then be what was described above as a nondistortionary tax system in which the financial cost of capital was equal to the real rate of interest. The only neutral (with respect to financial decisions) systems which are nondistortionary are:

(i) an integrated system with true economic depreciation and interest-deductibility
(ii) a classical system with free depreciation and no tax-deductibility for interest payments.

Of these two schemes the second is the more appealing. The calculation of 'true economic depreciation' in times of inflation poses severe valuation problems, and an integrated system as described in Chapter 3 does not fit neatly with a personal tax system based on expenditure. Consequently, if an expenditure tax is the main personal tax, the appropriate company tax is a classical system combined with free depreciation, and the removal of interest-deductibility (this has been suggested by Summer (1975)). With an income tax, however, the nondistortionary corporate tax would be the integrated system with interest-deductibility and free depreciation. Under both personal tax systems it is necessary to grant companies free depreciation to ensure intertemporal efficiency. A further discussion of the incidence of the corporate profits tax with free depreciation may be found in King (1975c).

We have suggested two possible reforms of the corporate tax system to operate in conjunction with alternative personal tax bases which have the aim of eliminating certain distortions which current tax systems impose on savings and investment decisions. We have not taken into account inefficiencies resulting either from the monopoly power of firms or from the distortions imposed by the tax system on other decisions (the work versus leisure choicc, for cxample). In a fully-fledged general equilibrium model we would allow for all these factors and use a model of the incidence of the corporate tax system to design a more complicated 'optimal' corporate tax system. However, in our present state of knowledge a nondistortionary corporate tax system, in the sense defined above, may be the most we can hope to achieve. The final conclusion of this book must be that in a world of uncertainty there is a great deal about the behaviour of companies and their response to public policy which we do not as yet understand.

Appendix A

UNITED KINGDOM PERSONAL AND CORPORATE TAXATION 1947–75

Chapter 3 discussed the different systems of company taxation used in the U.K. since the war, and compared these systems in terms of two fundamental variables, the tax rate on retained profits, and the tax differential between retentions and distributions. The task of this appendix is, firstly, to describe the calculation of the values of these variables for the period 1947–75, and, secondly, to examine the related issue of personal taxation of dividends and capital gains in the same period. This provides the link between changes in statutory tax rates announced in the Budget, and the composite tax variables defined in the text. It is these composite variables, such as the tax differential between retentions and distributions, which enter the equations explaining company behaviour, whereas the true policy variables of government are the statutory rates of tax. The first task, then, is to derive the values of the two basic tax variables used in the text, for the period 1947–75.

The tax rate on retained profits The formulae given in Chapter 3 express the tax rate on retained profits, τ, in terms of the statutory rates of income tax, profits tax, and corporation tax, depending on which system of company taxation was in force at the time. What we have to decide here is what tax rates were applied to profits earned in a given period. That is, we are concerned with the tax accruing in a given period, and not with actual payments of tax in that period. Accruals of tax, and payments of tax, do not coincide. In practice there are lengthy delays between the time when profits are actually earned, and the time when the tax due on these earnings is paid. There is a delay before assessment is made and then a delay between assessment and payment of taxes. The magnitude of the lag depends partly upon the tax concerned, (for·example, the lags for profits tax were quite different from those for income tax), and partly upon the accounting year of the company. These lags introduce great complexity into the system which would obviously be of importance in explaining the liquidity of the company sector. However, in the models examined in this book, company behaviour is assumed to depend upon the rates of tax which would eventually have to be paid on earnings in a certain period, and so accruals are the relevant concept. The data on profits which are available to us refer to profits earned in calendar years whereas tax rates are set for fiscal years, which in the U.K. begin on 6 April. We shall now attempt to determine what tax rates were applied to profits earned in each calendar year from 1947 to 1975.

There is no difficulty in doing this for corporation tax and the old profits tax. For both taxes, if a rate was set for a particular fiscal year then it applied to profits earned in that fiscal year. Where a company's financial year did not coincide with the fiscal year, the profits of the accounting period were allocated between fiscal years in proportion to the fractions of the accounting period falling within each fiscal year, so that the profits bore the appropriate rate of tax where the tax rate was different in the two fiscal years. Thus we simply need to look at the time periods for which different rates of tax were in force, and average them where necessary to obtain the average rate paid on profits earned in a given calendar year.

A different system applied, however, to the application of income tax to profits, under a profits tax system. Income tax was charged on profits earned in companies' own accounting years ending in the fiscal year. The rate of tax charged was set in the Budget at the end of the fiscal year. For example, all profits earned in accounting periods ending in the fiscal year 1955/6 were taxed at the rate of income tax set in the Budget of 1956. The profits liable to this rate of income tax could have been earned in the period 6 April 1954 to 5 April 1955, or between 6 April 1955 and 5 April 1956, or some intermediate period, depending on the company's accounting year. Thus we need some information on the 'typical' company's accounting period. The available evidence suggests that the average company accounting year ends in December. The sources of evidence for this statement are twofold. First, data given in Maurice (1968; p. 218) on the accounting periods of all companies, and, secondly, a survey taken in 1968 by the Board of Trade of 2000 quoted companies. The results of these studies are shown below.

All companies		Quoted companies	
Accounting year ends in	% (of total profits)	Accounting year ends in	% (of number of companies)
Jan.–March	25	January	8
April–June	10	March	19
July–Sep.	15	June	8
Oct.–Dec.	50	September	12
		December	33
		Other	20

These figures have remained roughly constant throughout the postwar period. The average accounting year for all companies, weighted by profits earned, ends in December. Similarly for quoted companies it seems reasonable to assume that the average accounting year ends in December. Thus we may regard profits earned in companies' accounting years ending in the fiscal year 1955/6, (to return to our example), as approximately equal to profits earned in the calendar year 1955. The rate of income tax paid on profits earned in a given calendar year can therefore be taken to be the income tax rate set in the Budget of the following year. Profits earned in 1955, for example, paid income tax at the rate set in the Budget of 1956.

It is now possible to calculate the tax rates paid on profits earned in any calendar year. There are two further points which should be cleared up. The first is that certain tax rates were determined retrospectively. We have seen that the income tax rate charged on profits earned in a given calendar year was not set until the Budget of the following year, and the corporation tax rate payable on the profits earned in a given fiscal year was set at the end of the fiscal year (although several of the changes in the rate of corporation tax were announced well beforehand, in 1965, 1967 and 1970.) For profits tax the problem did not arise because a change in the rate of profits tax became effective from the date of announcement. So it might be argued that to determine τ for a given calendar year requires knowledge of tax rates set in year $t + 1$, and that this knowledge would not be open to firms when making decisions about, for example, the level of dividends to be paid out. However, since the average accounting year ended in December, the typical set of accounts were not made up until around the Budget of the following year when the rates of corporation and income tax were announced. The series for tax rates derived in this appendix are *ex post* rates, and will differ from expected or *ex ante* tax rates especially when changes in tax rates are announced in advance.

The second point to be considered is the effect of the excess profits levy. This was a special, and temporary, charge levied on profits earned between 1 January 1952 and 31 December 1953. It was levied at 30% of profits in excess of a 'standard' rate of profit, subject to a maximum charge of 15% of total profits. For this purpose 'standard profits' were defined as the average level of profits for any two of the three years 1947, 1948, and 1949. Obviously the ratio of excess profits levy to profits varied between companies, but it is possible to make an estimate of the average effective rate of levy. Standard profits may be taken to be the average of profits for 1948 and 1949. Profits in these two years, and in 1952 and 1953 were as follows

Corporate taxable profits (£m)	
1948	2143
1949	2231
1952	2804
1953	2947

Source: Table 50, 97th Report and Table 50, 100th Report of the Commissioners of HM Inland Revenue.

This gives a figure for standard profits of £2187 m.

The total proceeds of the excess profits levy were £216m. (Table 94, 106th Report of Commissioners of HM Inland Revenue.) This figure may be allocated to the years 1952 and 1953 in proportion to the excess of the profits in those years over the estimate of standard profits. The imputed tax charges are £97m for 1952 and £119m for 1953. An estimate of the average effective rate of excess profits levy, may now be formed by dividing the estimated charge in a given year by taxable profits in that year. The effective rates of excess profit levy given by these calculations are

1952	3.5%
1953	4.0%

The excess profits levy did not affect the amount of tax payable on distributed profits, and its effect was therefore to increase the tax rate on retained profits by an amount which may be approximated by the figures given above.

Bearing all these points in mind the tax rates on company profits in the period 1947–75 can now be constructed, and are shown in Table A.1. The final two columns show the tax rate on retained profits: the first being the actual rate applying to current profits, and the second the average rate applying to profits earned in each calendar year.

The tax discrimination variable, θ The formulae for calculating the value of θ under each of the company tax systems are given in Chapter 3.4, and the relevant profits tax rates are shown in Table A.1. In addition to corporate tax rates the expressions for θ contain both the personal income tax rate of the shareholders and the standard rate of income tax. This raises two issues. The first concerns the distribution of tax rates between shareholders and we return to this below. The second question concerns the value of the income tax rate to be applied to dividends paid out of profits earned in year t.

The relevant rate of income tax depends on the time when the dividends payable out of a given year's profits will be paid out in the following fiscal year. Consider dividends paid out of profits earned in a given calendar year. These profits were earned by companies with a variety of accounting years. Almost all of these companies paid an interim dividend before the Budget in the following year, and some of them, those whose accounting year ended early in the financial year, (e.g. June), paid a final dividend before this time also. However, most final dividends were paid after the Budget of the following year, and thus were liable to the rate of income tax set in that Budget. We shall assume that 50% of total dividends were paid before the Budget and 50% after. Thus the average rate of income tax applied to dividends paid out of profits earned in, for example, the year 1966 was the arithmetic average of the rates for the fiscal years 1966/7 and 1967/8. To put this formally, if m_t is the rate of income tax relevant to the determination

Table A1 Company tax rates in the U.K. 1947–75 (percent).

Year	Profits tax[1]		Income tax[2]	Corporation tax	Rate of tax on retained profits		Year
	Retained	Distributed			Actual rate	Calendar-Year Equivalent	
1947					50.5	50.5	1947
1948	10[1]	25[1]	45			50.5	1948
1949		October 1 30[1]				50.5	1949
1950			47.5		52.75	52.75	1950
1951		50[1]				52.75	1951
1952	2.5 + 3.5[3]		45		51.0	51.0	1952
1953	2.5 + 4.0[3]	22.5			51.5	51.5	1953
1954	2.5	November 1			45	45	1954
1955						45	1955
1956		27.5	42.5			45.375	1956
1957	3	30			45.5	45.5	1957
1958					41.75 48.75	47.0	1958
1959	10					48.75	1959
1960						50.625	1960
	12.5		38.75		51.25	53.125	1961

Year	Profits tax[1]		Income tax[2]	Corporation tax	Rate of tax on retained profits		Year
	Retained	Distributed			Actual rate	Calendar-Year Equivalent	
1962			38.75		53.75	53.75	1962
1963	15					53.75	1963
1964			41.25		56.25	56.25	1964
1965						40	1965
1966				40	40	40	1966
1967				42.5	42.5	41.875	1967
1968				45	45	44.375	1968
1969				42.5	42.5	43.125	1969
1970						40.625	1970
1971				40	40	40	1971
1972						40	1972
1973						49	1973
1974				52	52	52	1974
1975						52	1975

Source: see text

Notes: [1]Between 1 January 1947 and 31 December 1951, profits tax was allowable as a deduction for income tax purposes.
[2]This is the rate of income tax on profits payable by the company.
[3]Excess profits levy.

of θ_t for dividends paid out of profits earned in year t, and if $m_{t,t+1}$ is the statutory rate of income tax for the fiscal year $t/t+1$, then

$$m_t = \tfrac{1}{2}m_{t,t+1} + \tfrac{1}{2}m_{t+1,t+2}. \tag{A.1}$$

In order to construct a series for θ corresponding to any particular value of the personal tax rate, there is only one remaining factor to be considered. When there was a major change in the company tax system, as for example in 1958, 1965 and 1973, there were special transitional arrangements and also measures designed to prevent tax avoidance by speeding up or slowing down the timing of dividend payments. In 1958 and 1973 it was to the advantage of firms to delay distribution, whereas in 1965 it was to the advantage of firms to pay out dividends before 6 April 1966, and, although in each case there were special provisions to prevent this, it is possible that firms may have been able to evade these provisions. To test this hypothesis we examine the pattern of quarterly dividend payments. There is a break in the quarterly series on dividends in 1960 (when dividends paid by U.K. subsidiaries to overseas parent companies were reclassified as 'profits

Figure A.1 Quarterly ordinary dividend payments 1956–63 (all companies) (unadjusted series)

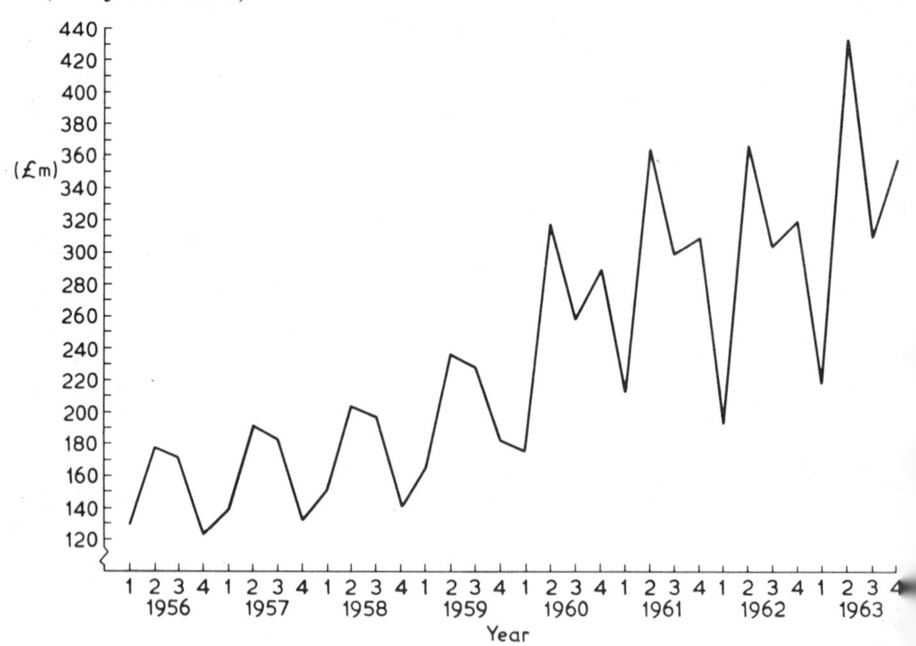

Source: Central Statistical Office.

due abroad'), and so in Figure A.1 we show the series for quarterly dividend payments by all companies over the period 1956–63. From these figures a regular seasonal pattern is apparent, and it seems clear that no exceptional change in the timing of dividend payments took place in 1958.

In 1966, however, the situation was rather different. With the introduction of corporation tax, income tax was payable on the amount of gross dividends distributed, over and above the liability to corporation tax. However, as a transitional arrangement, no income tax was payable on dividends distributed before 6 April 1966. Hence, for dividends paid out of profits earned in 1965, the appropriate value of θ is a weighted average of the values ruling under the old flat-rate profits tax and under the new corporation tax. The weights should be the proportions of dividends paid out before and after 6 April 1966 respectively. We have seen that for profits earned in a given calendar year it is reasonable to assume that normally one half of the dividends paid out of those profits were distributed before 6 April of the following year, and one half after that date. However, in 1966 there was clearly an incentive to alter this pattern and speed

Figure A.2 Quarterly dividend payments (all companies), 1960–75 (seasonally adjusted)

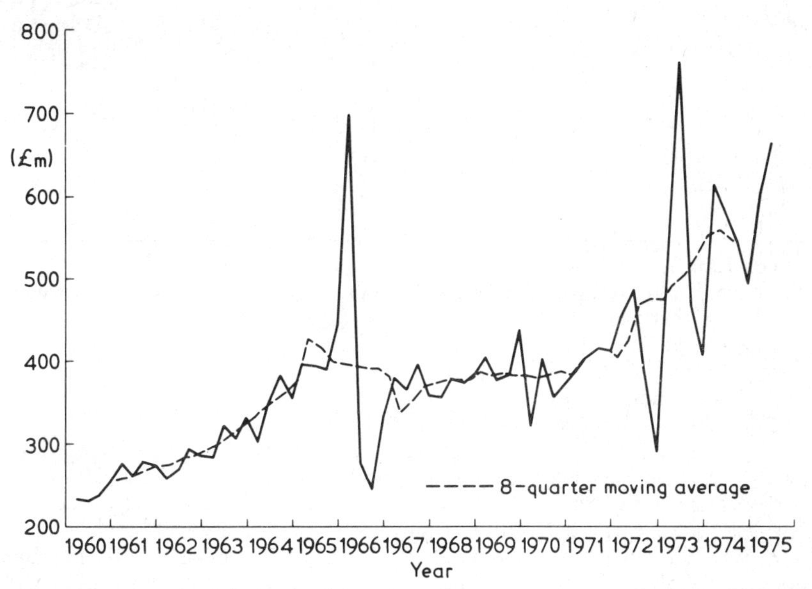

Source: *Economic Trends*: *Annual Supplement* 1975, pp. 122–3 (figures for 1973 II onwards grossed up by the ruling standard rate of income tax).

Table A.2 Calculation of the value of $\hat{\theta}$, U.K. 1947–75.

Year	$p_d - p_u$	m_s		$\hat{\theta}$
1947	0.150	0.45		1.581
1948	0.150	0.45		1.581
1949	0.158	0.45		1.570
1950	0.200	0.4625		1.550
1951	0.400	0.475		1.361
1952	0.200	0.4625		1.356
1953	0.200	0.45		1.333
1954	0.200	0.4375		1.311
1955	0.208	0.425		1.277
1956	0.265	0.425		1.190
1957	0.270	0.425		1.183
1958	0.270	0.425	1.183	1.521
	—	0.3875	1.633	
1959	—	0.3875		1.633
1960	—	0.3875		1.633
1961	—	0.3875		1.633
1962	—	0.3875		1.633
1963	—	0.3875		1.633
1964	—	0.40		1.667
1965	—	0.4125	1.702	1.527
		—	1.0	
1966	—	—		1.0
1967	—	—		1.0
1968	—	—		1.0
1969	—	—		1.0
1970	—	—		1.0
1971	—	—		1.0
1972	—	—	1.0	1.257
		0.3	1.429	
1973	—	0.315		1.460
1974	—	0.34		1.515
1975	—	0.35		1.538

Source: Table A.1 and own calculations.

—signifies that the variable of that column is not relevant to the construction of $\hat{\theta}$ for that year.

p_d = the rate of distributed profits tax.

p_u = the rate of undistributed profits tax.

m_s = the standard rate of income tax.

$\hat{\theta}$ = the tax discrimination variable relating to gross dividends.

The rates are calendar year equivalents and are the average tax rates applying to dividends paid out of profits earned in a particular calendar year. The weights used to construct these averages are, for p_d and p_u, shown in Table A.1, and for m_s are described in the text. The averages of $\hat{\theta}$ for the major transtional years are:

(i) 1958; the value of 1.183 applies for the first quarter, and 1.633 for the remainder of the year (weights, 0.25 : 0.75).

(ii) 1965; the values of 1.702 and 1.0 are weighted by the proportions of dividends paid out before and after 6 April 1966 respectively (see text).

(iii) 1972; the values of 1.0 and 1.429 are weighted by the proportions of dividends paid out before and after 6 April 1973 respectively (see text).

up the payment of dividends. Figure A.2 shows the time-series of quarterly dividend payments seasonally adjusted over the period 1960–75, together with its 8-quarter moving average. It is clear that the timing of dividend payments in 1966 was distorted by the tax change, and comparing the actual payments with the moving average it appears that it is more reasonable to assume that 75% of dividends paid out of profits earned in 1965 were paid before 6 April 1966. Thus the weights (0.75, 0.25) were used to compute the average value of θ for 1965.

A similar distortion in the timing of dividend payments can be observed for 1973, and again, comparing the actual payments with the moving average, it would appear that 60% of dividends paid out of profits earned in 1972 were paid after 6 April 1973, and 40% were paid before that date. The incentive to delay payments in 1973 seems to have been less effective than the incentive to accelerate payments in 1965. These transitional effects had the result of giving to companies a once and for all windfall gain in the years 1965 and 1972.

Because the value of θ is a function of the personal income tax rate of the shareholders we shall calculate its value in two stages. The first is to calculate the value of $\hat{\theta}$, which is the tax discrimination variable in terms of gross dividends and is defined by $\theta = (1 - m)\hat{\theta}$. Table A.2 shows the calculation of $\hat{\theta}$ for the period 1947–75 given the assumptions about tax rates described above and the formulae in Chapter 3.4. The second stage is to look at the personal income tax rates of shareholders.

Personal tax rates of shareholders The distribution of personal tax rates of shareholders is a function of two characteristics of the pattern of shareholding. Firstly, there are the different categories of shareholders, individuals, pension funds and so on, all of whom are taxed in different ways and at different rates. Secondly, within the category of personal shareholdings the distribution of tax rates will depend upon the distribution of income and wealth of the shareholding class.

For the first of these characteristics we have the evidence of Table 2.4 which gives benchmark estimates of the distribution of share ownership between the different institutional categories for the years 1957, 1963, 1969 and 1975. Using these estimates we may consider shareholders as belonging to one of three basic tax categories, (a) 'persons', (b) insurance companies, and (c) pension funds and charities. The first category here includes unit and investment trusts because investment through these intermediaries does not affect the ultimate tax burden borne by the investor. These institutions operate as a tax veil, but offer the investor the opportunity of diversifying his portfolio at low transactions costs and the expertise of the fund managers. The income of life assurance companies is taxed in a special way and so these companies from a second category. Pension funds and charities are lumped together in the third category because they are exempt from tax altogether.

The proportions of total equity owned by the three groups were estimated by linear interpolation and extrapolation from the benchmark estimates of Table 2.4. The holdings of other groups (overseas, banks etc.) were ignored and hence implicitly assumed to be distribut-

Table A.3 Share ownership weights for the basic tax categories, U.K. 1947–75.

Year	Persons	Insurance companies	Pension funds and charities
1947	0.927	0.073	0
1948	0.920	0.076	0.004
1949	0.912	0.078	0.010
1950	0.903	0.081	0.016
1951	0.895	0.083	0.022
1952	0.886	0.086	0.028
1953	0.878	0.088	0.034
1954	0.868	0.091	0.041
1955	0.860	0.093	0.047
1956	0.851	0.096	0.053
1957	0.843	0.098	0.059
1958	0.834	0.101	0.065
1959	0.826	0.103	0.071
1960	0.817	0.106	0.077
1961	0.808	0.108	0.084
1962	0.799	0.111	0.090
1963	0.791	0.113	0.096
1964	0.782	0.117	0.101
1965	0.772	0.122	0.106
1966	0.763	0.126	0.111
1967	0.754	0.130	0.116
1968	0.744	0.135	0.121
1969	0.735	0.139	0.126
1970	0.717	0.143	0.140
1971	0.701	0.146	0.153
1972	0.683	0.150	0.167
1973	0.666	0.153	0.181
1974	0.649	0.157	0.194
1975	0.632	0.160	0.208

Source: derived from Table 2.4: see text.

ed evenly among the three basic tax categories. The shares of the three categories for the period 1947–75 are shown in Table A.3.

The categories are distinguished by their treatment for tax purposes. Pension funds and charities are exempt from tax altogether, and the income of life assurance funds is treated in the following special way. When a fund purchases shares of unit value for its policyholders, the cost to the policyholder is only $1 - \mu m_s$, because tax relief is granted on premiums paid to life assurance companies at a fraction μ of the standard rate of income tax, m_s. From 1947 until 1973, the value of μ was 0.4, and for the remainder of the period it was 0.5. The income of the fund is taxed at a special rate, which in the period considered was 37.5% for dividend income. We may denote this special rate by τ_s; if the fund earns a post-tax return of $1 - \tau_s$ on its unit value shareholding this is equivalent to a post-tax return of $(1 - \mu m_s)(1 - \tau_e)$ on the policy holders' investment, where τ_e is the effective tax rate on the dividend income accruing to the policyholders.

$$\therefore \; (1 - \mu m_s)(1 - \tau_e) = 1 - \tau_s, \tag{A.2}$$

$$\therefore \; \tau_e = \frac{\tau_s - \mu m_s}{1 - \mu m_s}. \tag{A.3}$$

Given a value of 0.375 for τ_s, the appropriate value for μ, and the annual values of the standard rate of income tax from Table A.5, it is possible to calculate the effective tax rates on the dividend income of life assurance companies. These are shown in Table A.4. The tax rates in the Table refer to the income of the life assurance business of insurance companies. A small fraction of the shareholdings of insurance companies relate to ordinary insurance business and to pension business, but these will be ignored because the full income taxation of the former holdings will be offset by the tax exemption of the latter. The tax rates in Table A.4, therefore, are taken to be the rates applying to the total shareholdings of insurance companies.

For insurance companies, pension funds and charities, the tax system is proportional and the marginal tax rate on their dividend income equals the average tax rate. When looking at the personal sector, however, we must distinguish between average and marginal tax rates for each individual shareholder. Since we are concerned primarily with the incentive effects of taxation, we shall focus on marginal tax rates. Individuals, of course, face different marginal tax rates and this raises the question of how we characterize the

Table A.4 Effective dividend income tax rates for insurance companies, U.K. 1947–75 (per cent).

Year	Rate
1947	23.78
1948	23.78
1949	23.78
1950	23.31
1951	22.84
1952	23.31
1953	23.78
1954	24.24
1955	24.70
1956	24.70
1957	24.70
1958	25.37
1959	26.04
1960	26.04
1961	26.04
1962	26.04
1963	26.04
1964	25.60
1965	25.15
1966	25.15
1967	25.15
1968	25.15
1969	25.15
1970	25.60
1971	26.04
1972	27.83
1973	25.82
1974	24.70
1975	24.24

Source: own calculations.

distribution of marginal tax rates between individuals. We shall do this by calculating the mean, median and modal marginal tax rates both for the personal sector, and for all three classes of shareholders together.

The first step is to calculate the marginal tax rates charged on dividends, paid out to the personal sector in each fiscal year. Such a series has been calculated by Orhnial and Foldes (1975) for the period 1919/20 to 1969/70 and this was extracted from data kindly made available by the authors. A method similar to theirs was used to extend the series to 1972/3. Unfortunately no data were available on the distribution of dividends by income range of the recipients. The nearest we could get was a distribution of 'dividends plus interest which is taxed at source' (the interest being mainly that on government bonds) by recipients' 'total net income' (income less allowable interest, superannuation contributions, and capital allowances, but before life assurance relief and personal allowances). Evidence to the Royal Commission on the Distribution of Income and Wealth (HMSO (1975; Appendix J)) suggests that the distribution of dividends by income range is very similar to that for dividends and interest together, and so we can use the latter distribution. The next problem is that the distribution is given by range of total net income, not by range or bands of taxable, or assessed, income. Thus we need a correspondence between levels of assessed income and levels of net income.

To construct this we assume that the ranking of individuals by total net income is the same as that by assessed income. Observations on the two distributions can be obtained from *Inland Revenue Statistics* which provide both the distribution of surtax payers by assessed income and the distribution of 'personal income before tax' (defined to be equal to 'total net income'). The aim of the exercise is to find the level of total income which corresponds to each tax threshold level. In this way the distribution of dividend income can be reclassified as a distribution by bands of taxable income. In each band there is a unique marginal tax rate and the distribution provides weights to calculate the mean, median, or modal marginal tax rate. To construct the correspondence between the two distributions we need continuous distributions, and hence it is necessary to interpolate for values other than the observations obtained from *Inland Revenue Statistics.* Here we follow Orhnial and Foldes (1975) and assume that income is distributed according to a Pareto distribution. If the logarithm of income is plotted against the logarithm of the total number of people with incomes in excess of each level of income the result is approximately a straight line. This yields separate lines for the distribution of assessed income and of total net income which enables the level of total net income, which is equivalent to any level of assessed income, to be read off from the graph. It is now possible to express the thresholds for each rate of tax in terms of total net income, (assuming that all those who fell below the threshold for surtax paid tax at the standard rate), and this enables the distribution of marginal tax rates to be computed. Expressing the tax thresholds in terms of equivalent levels of total net income was preferred to the alternative of defining the correspondence in the opposite direction (as followed by Orhnial and Foldes (1975)) because each range of assessed income corresponds to a unique marginal tax rate.

The final step is to convert the distribution of marginal tax rates for each fiscal year into a distribution of tax rates for calendar years. This was done by assuming that the timing of dividend payments was as described above and that the calendar year tax rates are related to fiscal year rates by equation (A.1) subject to the exceptions described in the notes to Table A.2. In this way it was possible to construct

Table A.5 Marginal income tax rates on dividends, U.K. 1947–71.

Year	Average marginal rate on persons	Average marginal rate on all shareholders	Median and modal marginal rate on all shareholders
1947	0.682	0.650	0.450
1948	0.599	0.569	0.450
1949	0.596	0.562	0.450
1950	0.608	0.568	0.463
1951	0.621	0.575	0.475
1952	0.609	0.560	0.463
1953	0.597	0.545	0.450
1954	0.585	0.530	0.438
1955	0.575	0.518	0.425
1956	0.578	0.516	0.425
1957	0.582	0.515	0.425
1958	0.566	0.498	0.406
1959	0.554	0.484	0.388
1960	0.561	0.486	0.388
1961	0.565	0.485	0.388
1962	0.568	0.483	0.388
1963	0.574	0.483	0.388
1964	0.624	0.518	0.400
1965	0.651	0.533	0.412
1966	0.599	0.489	0.412
1967	0.604	0.488	0.412
1968	0.601	0.481	0.412
1969	0.591	0.469	0.412
1970	0.580	0.452	0.400
1971	0.575	0.441	0.388

Source: Column 1 Orhnial and Foldes (1975), plus own calculations.
Column 2 Tables A.3 and A.4 and column 1.
Column 3 own calculations.

series for personal tax rates on dividend income for the period 1947–71.

Table A.5 shows the mean marginal rate of income tax on dividends of the personal sector over this period, and the mean marginal tax rate of all shareholders together. The latter series is a weighted average of the marginal rates for the personal sector, insurance companies, and for pension funds and charities, the weights being the share ownership weights given in Table A.3. Since our primary aim is to estimate the distribution of marginal tax rates for shareholders as a whole, it will be useful to have estimates of other characteristics of the distribution (see Chapter 3). It turned out that for each year for which data were available, the median and modal marginal tax rates were both equal to the standard rate of income tax, and so in the final column of Table A.5 we show the standard rate of income tax on a calendar year equivalent basis.

The income tax rates shown in Table A.5 may be used to calculate

Table A.6 Values of tax discrimination variables, U.K. 1947–71.

	θ_a	θ_m
1947	0.553	0.870
1948	0.681	0.870
1949	0.688	0.864
1950	0.670	0.832
1951	0.578	0.715
1952	0.597	0.728
1953	0.606	0.738
1954	0.616	0.737
1955	0.616	0.734
1956	0.576	0.684
1957	0.574	0.680
1958	0.764	0.903
1959	0.843	1.0
1960	0.839	1.0
1961	0.841	1.0
1962	0.844	1.0
1963	0.844	1.0
1964	0.803	1.0
1965	0.713	0.898
1966	0.511	0.588
1967	0.512	0.588
1968	0.519	0.588
1969	0.531	0.588
1970	0.548	0.600
1971	0.559	0.612

Source: Tables A.2 and A.5.

values of the tax discrimination variable θ from the values of $\hat{\theta}$ given in Table A.2 and the relationship $\theta = (1 - m)\hat{\theta}$. Two series can be constructed, the first corresponding to the average marginal tax rate on dividends, and the second corresponding to the median (and modal) tax rate. These variables will be denoted by θ_a and θ_m respectively, and their values are shown in Table A.6. These series extend only until 1971 because data on personal income tax rates were not available beyond that year.

Capital gains taxation The conceptual problems of measuring effective tax rates on capital gains have been discussed in Chapter 3. Here we shall simply look at nominal rates on the assumption that shares are held for at least twelve months. This means that we are concerned only with rates of tax on 'long-term gains' which came into force in the U.K. in April 1965. The assumption that shares are held for twelve months is not inconsistent with the hypothesis that some accrued gains are realized immediately, because the gains currently accruing can be realized by selling a small number of shares (in relation to the total portfolio) all of which have been held for at least twelve months. From April 1971 onwards there was no distinction between long- and short-term capital gains, and so this assumption is unnecessary for years after this date.

Capital gains tax was introduced on realized gains in 1965, and originally provided for deemed realization on death. This provision was, however, repealed in 1971. The rate of tax on persons was 30% throughout the period considered except that an individual could elect to be charged on an alternative basis under which one-half of the gains were taxed as income, (but if this basis was used gains in excess of £5000 were taxed as income). We may assume that the marginal rate of capital gains tax was either one-half the income tax rate or 30% whichever was the smaller. Unfortunately no data were available on the distribution of capital gains by income range, and so we could assume that the weights used to calculate average income tax rates on dividends apply equally to the distribution of capital gains. Of course shareholders may specialize in companies to obtain either dividends or capital gains according to their personal tax position, and if this is quantitatively significant then the distribution of capital gains on shares will differ from the distribution of dividends. The only check we can make on this is to look at the relative numbers of individuals who choose to pay capital gains tax at 30% or who elect to pay on the alternative basis. Unfortunately *Inland Revenue Statistics* do not give this breakdown for each type of asset but only for capital gains on all assets. On this basis about 80% of capital gains are taxed at 30% (*Inland Revenue Statistics* (1975); Tables 111–3), compared to around 50% which would be the figure suggested by the use of dividend weights. This indicates that the distribution of capital gains is different from that of dividends, and so we have computed two series for capital gains tax rates, the first using dividend weights, and the second on the assumption that 80% of gains paid tax at 30% and the remainder at one-half the standard rate of income tax. The values for the average marginal capital gains tax rates computed by these two methods are given in Table A.7. The differences between the two series are not large and we shall proceed by taking a simple arithmetic average of the two. The next step is to convert the series into a calendar-year equivalent series relating to capital gains arising out of profits earned in a given year. Here we shall depart from the method used to calculate dividend tax rates in that the capital gains will accrue when earnings become known and dividend announcements are made. We shall assume that the rate relevant to calendar year t is the rate ruling in fiscal year $t/(t+1)$, and the estimated values of the capital gains tax rate charged on persons for the calendar years 1965–72 are shown in the final column of Table A.7.

For the other two categories of shareholders, the taxation of capital

Table A.7 Marginal capital gains tax rates on persons U.K., 1965–72.

	Average capital gains tax rate		Calendar Year rate	
	Method I	Method II		
1965/6	0.270	0.281	1965	0.276
1966/7	0.259	0.281	1966	0.265
1967/8	0.263	0.281	1967	0.272
1968/9	0.263	0.281	1968	0.272
1969/70	0.258	0.281	1969	0.270
1970/1	0.255	0.281	1970	0.268
1971/2	0.251	0.279	1971	0.265
1972/3	0.251	0.279	1972	0.265

Source: own calculations.

Notes: Before 1965 the rate was zero.
Method I employs dividend weights.
Method II assumes that 80% of capital gains paid tax at 30% and the remainder at 0.5 of the standard rate of income tax.

Table A.8 Capital gains tax rates, all U.K. shareholders 1965–72.

	Average rate	Median rate
1965	0.233	0.300
1966	0.223	0.300
1967	0.226	0.300
1968	0.224	0.300
1969	0.218	0.300
1970	0.216	0.300
1971	0.211	0.300
1972	0.210	0.300

Source: Own calculations, and Tables A.3 and A.7.

Note: Before 1965 the rate was zero.

gains is straightforward. For pension funds and charities the tax rate is zero, and for insurance companies capital gains from 1965 onwards were taxed in exactly the same way as dividends except that for capital gains the value of τ_s in equation (A.3) becomes 30%. Given tax rates for all three categories of shareholders we may calculate the average rate of capital gains tax for all shareholders together using the share ownership weights in Table A.3. The average capital gains tax rate on U.K. shareholders from 1965–72 is given in the first column of Table A.8. To calculate the median tax rate on capital gains there is a problem in that the final answer depends upon whether we believe in Method I or Method II for calculating the tax rate on persons. In the former case the median rate is one-half the standard rate of income tax, and in the latter it is 30%. These two values differ quite substantially. Under Method I the percentile corresponding to a 30% tax rate is always near 50%, and so we shall take the median tax rate to be 30%. This is also the modal tax rate on capital gains. Unlike the distribution of tax rates on dividends, the distribution of capital gains tax rates displays a median value greater than the mean.

These nominal rates of capital gains tax can be converted into effective rates using the method discussed in Chapter 3.

Appendix B

UNITED KINGDOM STATISTICS ON COMPANIES

There are two basic sources of data on the operations of companies in in the U.K. The national income accounts contain statistics for the company sector as a whole based on tax returns to the Inland Revenue. The second source of statistics is the official analysis of the annual accounts of quoted companies published by the Department of Industry. These two sources can be used to supplement each other, and for purposes of comparison. One source includes the entire company sector, and the other covers large quoted corporations. In this appendix is described the construction of income and appropriation accounts for five different groups of companies based on the two official sources. Three of the samples are derived from the national income statistics, and two from the analysis of quoted companies' accounts. Section 3 contains a comparison of the two sources as regards their coverage and treatment of certain accounting items. The remaining sections discuss particular problems such as the statistics on investment grants, depreciation provisions, and stock appreciation.

Companies in the national accounts The data for companies shown in the national income accounts cover the entire company sector, that is, all privately controlled corporate enterprises resident in the U.K. The company sector comprises nearly 11 000 registered public companies, 400 000 private companies (many of which are subsidiaries of public or other private companies), 900 co-operative societies engaged in production, wholesaling and retailing, and about 600 building societies. Company data are derived from tax returns processed by the Inland Revenue. This is possible because companies are taxed in a separate manner from individuals and partnerships, the former being liable to a separate corporation tax.

The published national income statistics provided the basis for constructing series for company income for the period 1950–71. It was not possible to obtain figures for 1948 and 1949 on a basis consistent with the later figures, because of a change in the treatment of income earned abroad. (See *National Income and Expenditure* 1961; p. 72.) To ensure consistency of the figures, and for greater detail of the appropriation of income, use was also made of official working sheets kindly made available by the Central Statistical Office. Figures were derived for three groups of companies. The first series is for 'all companies', that is, the whole company sector as described above. There is, however, a problem in using this source for time-series analysis, since the area covered by the company sector changes over time because of nationalization and denationalization, the transfer of the residence of companies between the U.K. and overseas, and the incorporation of unincorporated businesses. Thus a change in, say, the profits of the company sector may represent an underlying change or simply a change in the sample of companies. It is particularly important to be able to distinguish between these two causes when attempting to make econometric estimates of relationships involving lags. For, whereas a change in an exogenous variable brought about by a genuine change in circumstances will evoke a lagged response, changes due to differences in population sample will not involve a lag. The major changes in the coverage of the company sector in the U.K. since the war result from the nationalization, and denationalization, at various times of the steel and road haulage industries. To overcome this problem another series has been constructed for 'non-nationalized industries'. This covers all companies which remained in private hands throughout the period 1938–71.

The third series for company income is for industrial and commercial companies. The series for 'all companies' and for 'non-nationalized companies' both include substantial numbers of financial companies. Financial companies are banks, accepting and discount houses, building societies, hire purchase finance companies, unit and investment trusts, and insurance companies. These enterprises might be expected to behave in a different way from industrial concerns, and to test this hypothesis separate series are required. Unfortunately detailed income and appropriation accounts for industrial and commercial companies are available only for the period 1956–71.

The income and appropriation accounts for these three groups of companies are shown in Tables B.1–B.3. Row 1 in these tables shows gross trading profits which are defined to be the trading profits of U.K. resident companies before providing for stock appreciation or depreciation. A company is resident if the central management and control of the business is exercised in the U.K. Therefore the profits of U.K. branches and subsidiaries of overseas parent companies are included, and the profits of overseas branches and subsidiaries of U.K. parent companies are excluded. Payments and refunds of selective employment tax have been treated on a cash payments basis. In all these accounts transactions between companies, such as payments of dividends by one company to another, are excluded. Row 2 shows the other income of the companies. This comprises rent and non-trading income arising in the U.K., most of which is received by financial companies, and income from abroad. The latter item is defined as the profits of U.K. companies operating abroad and of foreign subsidiaries of United Kingdom companies (after deducting depreciation allowances, but before deducting taxes on income paid to overseas governments and before providing for stock appreciation), plus non-trading income from abroad. Total gross income, row 3, is the sum of rows 1 and 2.

The appropriation of gross income is shown in rows 4–13. In the national income statistics all interest payments are treated as appropriations of income, whereas, as will be explained in the next section, company accounts regard short-term interest payments as operating expenses to be deducted in arriving at profits. In Tables B.1–B.3, however, long-term interest payments are shown in row 4 and short-term interest payments are shown in row 7. Dividends on preference shares and ordinary dividends are in rows 5 and 6, respectively. These are shown gross of the income tax liability on dividends. The figures for dividends are for accruals which are equal to actual payments plus additions to dividend reserves. The assumption made in the official estimates of dividend accruals is that the interim dividend is paid at the end of the company's accounting period, and the final dividend some six months later. Row 8 shows profits and taxes due abroad. These are the profits earned in the U.K. by foreign-owned branches and subsidiaries, and taxes paid to overseas governments by U.K. resident companies operating abroad.

United Kingdom tax accruals are shown in row 9. This refers not to tax payments but to taxes accruing on the profits earned in that period. We have assumed that company behaviour is influenced by the ultimate tax liability and not its cash flow, and so in the income and appropriation accounts all payments are on an accruals basis. There is one important modification which must be made to the published accounts. In 1966 tax allowances for investment expenditure were replaced by cash investment grants. Receipts of grants are shown in the capital account, although it is reasonable to assume that companies behaved as though the grants replaced the tax allowances, and thus offset the higher tax bill resulting from the withdrawal of some of the allowances. An estimate has been made, therefore, of the investment grants accruing to companies on the expenditure made in the period, and this has then been deducted from tax accruals to arrive at a series for 'net tax accruals', which is shown in row 11. The calculation of the series for investment grant accruals is described in more detail in Section B.4 below. Total payments out of income are given by the sum of rows 4–8, and 11. If these are subtracted from total income the result is a series for undistributed profits before providing for depreciation, row 13.

Quoted companies The requirements of the 1948 Companies Act substantially improved the standard of accounts published by public companies, and the analysis of company accounts has subsequently proved a fruitful source of new statistical data. The first detailed study of these accounts covering 3025 companies in the years 1949–53 was published by the National Institute of Economic and Social Research in 1956. (NIESR, 1956.) Since then regular analyses of company accounts have been published, in varying degrees of detail, by the Board of Trade, and its successor the Department of Industry (DI). While some information on the behaviour of non-quoted companies is available for the period after 1960, continuous series from 1949 onwards exist only for quoted companies, and it is the quoted company sector for which data deriving from company accounts have been used.

The 'quoted company sector' for which statistics are published includes companies engaged mainly in the U.K. in manufacturing, distribution, construction, transport, property and certain other services. Companies whose main interests are in agriculture, mining, shipping, insurance, banking and finance, and those operating wholly or mainly overseas are not included. Wherever possible the accounts analysed are the consolidated accounts of groups of companies, including the balance sheets and profit and loss accounts of subsidiary companies within each group. The statistics are not, therefore, confined to activities in the U.K., but in some cases include the activities of subsidiaries operating overseas. Where a company is excluded because it operates mainly overseas, the exclusion also applies to its subsidiaries irrespective of the location of the subsidiaries' activities.

Until 1960 the published series covered all companies with share capital quoted on a U.K. stock exchange, plus a few unquoted companies included because of their size. (These were often U.K. subsidiaries of foreign-owned companies.) In 1960 the series were revised and between 1960 and 1964 the figures refer to companies with net assets of £0.5 million or more, or gross income of £50 000 or more in 1960. The sample population of companies was again revised in 1964, when companies which had fallen below the size criteria were excluded and quoted companies which had grown in size, or which had been granted a quotation, since 1960 and satisfied the size criteria in 1964 were included. At the same time the sample of non-quoted companies was revised and enlarged. The figures used in this study for 1970 and 1971 relate to companies with net assets of £2.0 million or more, or gross income of £200 000 or more in 1968. This change in sample for the last two years, while reducing the number of companies covered by over 400, reduced the coverage in terms of net assets by only about 1%.

There are, therefore, breaks in the series for all variables in 1960, 1964 and 1970. To obtain the consistent series of income accounts for companies shown in Tables B.4 and B.5 it was necessary to link the series using a simple proportional adjustment. Fortunately, for each year when the sample changed statistics were published on both the new and the old basis. The changes in sample population progressively omitted the smaller companies. Although the behaviour of the smaller quoted companies may have differed from that of the larger companies, the bias induced by the changes of sample population is likely to be small since the coverage in terms of net assets and profits changed little. The number of companies included in the sample population each year are shown overleaf.

The impact of the changes in population sample on the number of companies included can be clearly seen. The introduction of a size criterion for inclusion after 1960 reduced the coverage by about 400 companies. The revision of the sample in 1964 actually increased the number included, and the extension of the size criterion in 1970 again led to a fall in sample size of about 400 companies.

Number of companies analysed

Year	1949	1950	1951	1952	1953	1954	1955	1956
Number	2704	2766	2865	2909	2879	2892	2913	2931
Year	1957	1958	1959	1960	1961	1962	1963	1964
Number	2879	2815	2714	2618	2173	2095	2004	1916
Year	1965	1966	1967	1968	1969	1970	1971	
Number	2198	2109	1993	1829	1701	1308	1237	

It can be seen that the number of companies included falls steadily, especially towards the end of the period, because the number of takeovers and mergers within the company sector exceeded the number of new companies obtaining quotations. The companies included account for over one-half of all company income, and for between three-fifths and two-thirds of the net assets of all industrial and commercial companies.

Income and appropriation accounts for the quoted company sector are shown in Tables B.4 and B.5. These refer to companies in manufacturing, distribution, construction and certain other industries (termed 'manufacturing and distribution etc'), and in manufacturing only, respectively. The figures shown for a particular calendar year relate to profits earned in companies' accounting years between 6 April in that year and 5 April of the following year. The evidence reviewed in Appendix A suggests that the average accounting year ends in December and so it is reasonable to assume that figures relating to accounting periods ending in the fiscal year 1970/1, for example, approximate the figures for the calendar year 1970. It is important to note, however, that the data for both company income and dividends etc., and for tax rates refer to the same accounting period. It is simply for convenience that in all the tables the period is shown as the calendar year.

The income and appropriation accounts for quoted companies shown in Tables B.4 and B.5 differ from those for the company sector as a whole in a number of respects. Firstly, the figure for gross trading profits excludes a number of interest payments on short-term loans (such as bank loans) which are included in profits in the national accounts. Secondly, data are available on companies' own depreciation provisions which can be used to construct a series on company retentions net of depreciation. This problem is discussed in more detail below. Thirdly, dividends are shown net of the standard rate of income tax, and tax accruals are correspondingly inflated. Net dividends can be converted to gross dividends using the series for the rate of income tax relevant to dividend payments given in Appendix A. As in the case of national accounts statistics the data for accruals of investment grants were calculated separately, and their calculation is described below.

Row 1 of the income and appropriation accounts represents gross trading profits which are shown before providing for depreciation and stock appreciation, but after deduction of interest on short-term loans. Total income is obtained by adding other income. Rows 4–13 show how this income was appropriated. Total payments (row 10) comprise long-term interest payments, dividend payments, and tax accruals. The latter are defined as tax payments plus additions to tax reserves, minus investment grants accruing. The difference between total income and total payments is the level of undistributed profits (row 11), and this comprises depreciation provisions (row 12) and net retentions, (row 13).

A comparison of the two sources The two sources of statistics on companies differ in a number of important respects:

(1) the source of the data. The national accounts statistics are based on information supplied by the Inland Revenue, whereas the data for quoted companies are derived directly from company accounts. The samples are, therefore, independently constructed and this is a useful feature of the data.

(2) the extent of the sample. Statistics in the national accounts are for the company sector as a whole, comprising public companies, both quoted and unquoted, and private companies. The sample is based on tax returns for over 300 000 companies. The average number of companies whose accounts were used to compose the series for quoted companies was about 2000. This enormous disparity between the numbers of companies in each sample is not reflected in the figures for profits. The quoted company sector accounts for around one-half of the profits of the whole company sector.

(3) the industrial coverage. The data for quoted companies refer

Table B.1 Company income and appropriation – all companies 1950–71 (£m).

	1950	1951	1952	1953	1954	1955	1956	1957	1958
1. Gross trading profits	2126	2483	2180	2313	2578	2886	2928	3075	2983
2. Other income[1]	966	1000	1061	1063	1110	1263	1457	1582	1704
3. Total gross income, equals 1 + 2	3092	3483	3241	3376	3688	4149	4385	4657	4687
4. Debenture and loan interest	31	36	41	46	50	55	64	75	85
5. Preference dividends[2]	104	104	102	102	104	109	110	109	108
6. Ordinary dividends[2,3]	432	440	467	486	597	596	632	672	762
7. Other dividends and interest[4]	90	95	121	132	133	174	224	253	279
8. Taxes and profits due abroad	257	314	391	335	324	402	435	490	511
9. U.K. tax accruals	849	1142	941	963	1001	948	1000	1000	870
10. Investment grant accruals									
11. Net U.K. tax accruals, equals row 9 – row 10	849	1142	941	963	1001	948	1000	1000	870
12. Total payments, equals rows 4 + 5 + 6 + 7 + 8 + 11	1763	2131	2063	2064	2209	2284	2465	2599	2615
13. Undistributed profits, equals row 3 – row 12	1329	1352	1178	1312	1479	1865	1920	2058	2072

Source: 1950–54, *National Income and Expenditure 1961* : Table 26.
1955–71, *National Income and Expenditure 1972* : Table 26, and CSO working sheets.
Row 10, own calculations.

Table B.2 Company income and appropriation – non-nationalized companies 1950–71 (£m).

	1950	1951	1952	1953	1954	1955	1956	1957	1958
1. Gross trading profits	2077	2476	2180	2311	2547	2819	2823	2938	2847
2. Other income[1]	965	1000	1061	1063	1109	1143	1453	1577	1699
3. Total gross income, equals rows 1 + 2	3042	3476	3241	3374	3656	3962	4276	4515	4546
4. Debenture and loan interest	31	36	41	46	50	54	62	66	77
5. Preference dividends[2]	102	103	102	102	103	107	108	107	106
6. Ordinary dividends[2,3]	423	440	467	485	592	586	617	657	739
7. Other dividends and interest[4]	90	95	121	132	133	174	224	253	279
8. Taxes and profits due abroad	257	314	391	335	324	402	435	490	511
9. U.K. tax accruals	831	1139	941	963	992	923	969	963	843
10. Investment grant accruals[5]									
11. Net U.K. tax accruals, equals row 9 – row 10	831	1139	941	963	992	923	969	963	843
12. Total payments, equals rows 4 + 5 + 6 + 7 + 8 + 11	1734	2127	2063	2063	2194	2246	2415	2536	2555
13. Undistributed profits, equals row 3 – row 12	1308	1349	1178	1311	1462	1716	1861	1979	1991

Source: 1950–55, *National Income & Expenditure 1961* : Table 27.
1956–60, CSO working sheets.
1961–71, *National Income & Expenditure 1972* : Table 30.
Row 10, own calculations.

1959	1960	1961	1962	1963	1964	1965	1966	1967	1968	1969	1970	1971
3317	3736	3643	3595	4103	4544	4741	4446	4718	5061	4967	5161	5769
1713	1791	1888	1983	2071	2340	2655	2606	2910	3500	4030	4395	4972
5030	5527	5531	5578	6174	6884	7396	7152	7628	8561	8997	9556	10741
96	107	120	157	172	185	212	346	384	425	495	542	555
108	112	117	119	119	124	121	117	112	98	94	81	86
948	1103	1240	1255	1481	1565	1745	1637	1606	1691	1695	1683	1717
254	324	362	366	364	445	578	682	754	920	1097	1195	1272
595	548	537	581	610	739	799	724	791	1089	1137	1334	1717
770	1020	905	823	831	1010	678	1174	1266	1629	1724	1503	1164
							319	426	605	449	433	0
770	1020	905	823	831	1010	678	855	840	1024	1275	1070	1164
2771	3214	3281	3301	3577	4068	4133	4361	4487	5247	5793	5905	6511
2259	2313	2250	2277	2597	2816	3263	2791	3141	3314	3204	3651	4230

1959	1960	1961	1962	1963	1964	1965	1966	1967	1968	1969	1970	1971
3164	3561	3510	3485	3977	4394	4592	4333	4661	5051	4957	5151	5749
1708	1786	1882	1977	2065	2333	2647	2698	2901	3498	4030	4395	4972
4872	5347	5392	5462	6042	6727	7239	7031	7562	8549	8987	9546	10721
89	100	113	149	164	177	205	338	375	425	495	542	555
106	110	115	117	117	122	119	115	111	98	94	81	86
924	1075	1210	1229	1449	1527	1701	1613	1597	1690	1694	1682	1716
254	324	362	366	364	445	578	682	754	920	1097	1195	1272
595	548	537	581	610	739	799	724	791	1089	1137	1334	1717
743	985	894	827	828	1002	642	1145	1246	1626	1724	1503	1164
							319	426	605	449	433	0
743	985	894	827	828	1002	642	826	820	1021	1275	1070	1164
2711	3142	3231	3269	3532	4012	4044	4298	4446	5243	5792	5904	6510
2161	2205	2161	2193	2510	2715	3195	2733	3116	3306	3195	3642	4211

Table B.3 Company Income and Appropriation – industrial and commercial companies 1956–71 (£ m)

	1956	1957	1958
1. Gross trading profits	3071	3243	3150
2. Other income[1]	946	1003	1110
3. Total gross income, equals rows 1 + 2	4017	4246	4260
4. Debenture and loan interest	60	70	80
5. Preference dividends[6,7]	106	105	104
6. Ordinary dividends[7]	607	651	742
7. Other dividends and interest[8]	154	165	169
8. Taxes and profits due abroad	402	456	478
9. U.K. tax accruals	893	879	744
10. Investment grant accruals			
11. Net U.K. tax accruals, equals row 9 – row 10	893	879	744
12. Total payments, equals rows 4 + 5 + 6 + 7 + 8 + 11	2222	2326	2317
13. Undistributed profits, equals row 3 – row 12	1795	1920	1943

Source: 1956–60, CSO working sheets.
1961–70, *National Income & Expenditure 1972*: Table 28.
Row 10, own calculations.

Table B.4 Company income and appropriation – quoted companies, manufacturing and distribution etc. 1949–71 (£ m).

	1949	1950	1951	1952	1953	1954	1955	1956	1957	1958
1. Gross trading profits	1045	1254	1487	1330	1477	1667	1809	1869	1952	1983
2. Other income[9]	52	61	57	56	52	60	67	76	82	93
3. Total gross income, equals row 1 + 2	1097	1315	1544	1386	1529	1727	1876	1945	2034	2076
4. Interest on long-term loans	16	18	22	25	27	32	37	44	53	61
5. Net preference dividends [2,10]	28	29	28	27	28	29	30	31	31	31
6. Net ordinary dividends[2,10]	124	137	141	149	176	215	237	244	271	281
7. Tax accruals[11]	479	584	737	666	695	722	737	775	795	734
8. Investment grant accruals										
9. Net tax accruals, equals row 7 – row 8	479	584	737	666	695	722	737	775	795	734
10. Total payments, equals rows 4 + 5 + 6 + 9	647	768	928	867	926	998	1041	1094	1150	1107
11. Undistributed profits	450	547	616	519	603	729	835	851	884	969
12. Depreciation provisions[12]	167	191	212	220	253	281	322	367	415	463
13. Net retentions, equals row 11 – row 12	283	356	404	299	350	448	513	484	469	506

Source: 1949–60, *Economic Trends*, April 1962: Table 1 A.
1960–68, *Business Monitor M3*, Second issue: Table 5.
1969–71, *Business Monitor M3*, Fourth Issue: Tables 2 & 13.
Row 8, on calculations.

1959	1960	1961	1962	1963	1964	1965	1966	1967	1968	1969	1970	1971
3498	3941	3835	3788	4304	4836	5065	4826	5076	5473	5470	5662	6327
1145	1121	1127	1206	1267	1419	1583	1499	1588	1932	2251	2430	2782
4643	5062	4962	4994	5571	6255	6648	6325	6664	7405	7721	8092	9109
91	101	114	151	165	177	202	323	357	395	463	505	510
104	108	120	122	123	128	126	123	116	102	98	84	88
923	1071	1203	1210	1435	1508	1707	1598	1570	1633	1648	1608	1626
176	231	260	249	244	310	414	453	440	541	627	697	659
559	513	490	531	561	682	739	663	726	998	1018	1219	1591
656	860	712	642	643	838	473	973	1035	1392	1448	1193	878
							313	418	593	440	425	0
656	860	712	642	643	838	473	660	617	799	1008	768	878
2509	2884	2899	2905	3171	3643	3661	3820	3826	4468	4862	4876	5352
2134	2178	2063	2089	2400	2612	2987	2505	2838	2937	2859	3216	3757

1959	1960	1961	1962	1963	1964	1965	1966	1967	1968	1969	1970	1971
2258	2491	2418	2421	2738	3101	3211	3146	3193	3693	3750	3733	4316
101	121	134	138	140	136	162	140	151	188	227	265	267
2359	2612	2552	2559	2878	3237	3373	3286	3344	3881	3977	3998	4583
67	70	77	91	108	121	141	175	205	247	280	302	351
34	36	36	36	37	39	37	34	31	28	23	22	24
384	422	436	453	502	564	576	544	513	535	545	566	643
761	895	855	829	929	1091	872	1163	1286	1511	1554	1413	1547
							186	248	353	262	252	0
761	895	855	829	929	1091	872	977	1038	1158	1292	1161	1547
1246	1423	1404	1409	1576	1815	1626	1730	1787	1968	2140	2051	2565
1113	1189	1148	1150	1302	1422	1747	1556	1557	1913	1837	1947	2018
513	560	621	682	749	816	913	988	1003	1116	1193	1289	1410
600	629	527	468	553	606	834	568	554	797	644	658	608

Table B.5 Company income and appropriation – quoted companies, manufacturing only 1949–71 (£ m).

	1949	1950	1951	1952	1953	1954	1955	1956	1957	1958
1. Gross trading profits	865	1056	1259	1111	1236	1403	1524	1551	1630	1654
2. Other income[9]	42	52	48	46	41	48	54	63	69	76
3. Total gorss income, equals rows 1 + 2	907	1108	1307	1157	1277	1451	1578	1614	1699	1730
4. Interest on long-term loans	12	14	18	20	23	28	32	38	47	55
5. Net preference dividends[2,10]	22	22	22	21	22	22	24	24	24	25
6. Net ordinary dividends[2,10]	100	112	115	122	144	173	191	196	217	225
7. Tax accruals[11]	398	493	626	554	579	603	614	634	653	603
8. Investment grant accruals										
9. Net tax accruals, equals row 7 – row 8	398	493	626	554	579	603	614	634	653	603
10. Total payments, equals rows 4+5+6+9	532	641	781	717	768	826	861	892	941	908
11. Undistributed profits	375	467	526	440	509	625	717	722	758	822
12. Depreciation provisions[12]	138	159	175	184	210	237	274	310	353	392
13. Net retentions, equals row 11 – row 12	237	308	351	256	299	388	443	412	405	430

Source: 1949–60, *Economic Trends*, April 1962: Table 2A.
1960–69, *Business Monitor M3*, Second Issue: Tables 2 & 14.
1970–71, *Business Monitor M3*, Fourth Issue: Table 2.
Row 8, own calculations.

Notes on tables B.1–B.5

[1]Rent and other non-trading income, and income from abroad.

[2]In Tables B.1–B.3 dividends are shown gross, that is before deduction of income tax. In Tables B.4 and B.5 dividends are shown net of the standard rate of income tax.

[3]It was assumed that 'additions to dividend reserves', which must be added to dividend payments to arrive at accrued dividends, consisted entirely of ordinary dividends.

[4]This comprises co-operative society dividends, interest on building society deposits, and other interest payments on deposits such as bank deposits.

[5]It was assumed that all investment grants paid to companies were paid to 'non-nationalized companies'. The difference in coverage between this sector and 'all companies' was very small in the period when investment grants were paid.

[6]Additions to dividend reserves were estimated by assuming that all such additions were in industrial and commercial companies. The additions to reserves for all companies were added to the payments of dividends by industrial and commercial companies to arrive at an estimate of the latter group's accruals of dividends.

[7]Figures are available for total dividends only. The breakdown into ordinary and preference dividends was made by applying the ratio of ordinary to preference dividends for all companies, to the figure for total dividends of industrial and commercial companies.

[8]This largely comprises payments to financial companies by way of interest payments on bank loans and commercial bills. This item also includes a small amount of co-operative society dividends.

1959	1960	1961	1962	1963	1964	1965	1966	1967	1968	1969	1970	1971
1888	2079	1984	1962	2219	2522	2606	2537	2547	2989	3047	3021	3447
83	101	112	114	117	109	135	115	125	159	192	205	216
1971	2180	2096	2076	2336	2631	2741	2652	2672	3148	3239	3226	3663
60	62	68	81	95	105	120	149	173	213	236	259	300
27	29	29	29	29	30	28	26	22	21	17	16	20
311	340	349	358	397	450	459	430	402	423	433	443	497
628	743	690	656	736	872	694	927	1015	1202	1236	1118	1196
							168	225	319	237	223	0
628	743	690	656	736	872	694	759	790	883	999	890	1196
1026	1174	1136	1124	1257	1457	1301	1364	1387	1540	1685	1608	2013
945	1006	960	952	1079	1174	1440	1288	1285	1608	1554	1618	1650
434	471	521	571	627	677	754	817	814	917	975	1067	1160
511	535	439	381	452	497	686	471	471	691	579	551	490

[9]Income from trade and other investments, plus prior year adjustments other than tax.

[10]The published data for dividends of quoted companies are gross of income tax for the years 1967–71. To make the series compatible with those for earlier years the data have been converted to net dividends using the series on the standard rate of income tax relevant to dividend distributions given in Appendix A.

[11]In Tables B.4 to B.5 tax accruals include income tax on dividends deducted at source at the standard rate.

[12]For 1949–63 this item comprises 'depreciation and other provisions'; for 1964–71 it comprises 'depreciation provisions and amounts written off'. The magnitude of the component 'other provisions' was always small.

to manufacturing, distribution, and certain other industries. They do not cover financial companies, nor shipping companies, both of which appear in the statistics for all companies.

(4) the treatment of overseas income. The sample of quoted companies excludes those operating mainly overseas. The total income of companies as shown in the national accounts, however, includes both the profits of U.K. companies operating overseas, and the profits of subsidiaries of foreign-owned companies operating in the U.K. The latter item is then distinguished separately in the accounts of appropriation of total income.

(5) the treatment of interest payments. Long-term interest payments are treated in the same way in both sets of accounts. Short-term interest payments, however, which have been growing in magnitude in recent years, are regarded as an appropriation of income in the national accounts but as an operating expense in the accounts of quoted companies. Thus the trading profits of quoted companies are shown net of short-term interest payments.

It cannot be said that one source is more reliable than the other. They are independent samples and should be used as complementary sources of information, while always bearing in mind the differences mentioned above when evaluating the results obtained using the two sets of data.

Investment grants Between 1966 and 1970 a substantial number of the tax allowances for investment expenditure were withdrawn, and replaced by cash investment grants. During this period the apparent tax burden on companies rose, and the published statistics on retained profits fell. This is a direct consequence of the substitution of cash grants for a system of tax allowances. Whereas the latter increase retentions by reducing the tax burden, investment grants are shown as a receipt on capital account. There is no reason, however, to expect firms to view the receipt of investment grants in a completely different light from the benefits flowing from a reduced tax burden. Both systems increase the amount available to the firm for distribution or retention. In this section we describe the methods used to estimate, for each of the five groups of companies described above, the level of investment grants accruing on expenditure made in a given year. This concept of accruals of investment grants, as opposed to actual receipts of grants, corresponds to the treatment of tax payments adopted in the accounts constructed above.

Investment grants were made for expenditure incurred between 17 January 1966 and 26 October 1970. (The main exception to this was that grants could be paid on expenditure incurred after 26 October 1970 which consisted of a sum or sums falling due under a contract made on or before that date.) The grants were made to manufacturing, construction and extractive industries, the rate of grant varying both regionally and, to a limited extent, according to the type of asset. The basic rates of grant were 20% of the cost of the asset in most of the country and 40% in the Development Areas, although in 1967 and 1968 the rates were 25% and 45% respectively.

Following the principle we adopted for taxation, the figures required are for accruals of investment grants not receipts of such grants. The basic sources of data on companies which were used above give no information on accruals, but relate to receipts. To convert the figures for receipts into a series for accruals, some information is needed on the time lag between when the expenditure on the asset was made, and when the investment grant arising from that expenditure was received. On average it would appear that the lag involved was about one year. (Board of Trade '*Investment Grants – Annual Report*', HMSO London, 1968.) Making this assumption would give an approximate method of converting receipts into accruals. It would not be entirely satisfactory since the lag decreased during the duration of the investment grants scheme, and in the last year payments were substantially speeded up in a deliberate attempt to improve the cash flow of industry. ('*Investment Grants*', House of Commons Paper 580, HMSO, London, 1971.) A recent study, however, has provided much more detailed information on accruals of investment grants. ("Statistical analysis of investment grant payments made under the Industrial Development Act 1966", *Trade and Industry*, **10**, No. 4, January 1973.) This study covers grants payable on expenditure incurred between 1966 and 1969. It does not, unfortunately, include grants payable on expenditure made in 1970. The levels of total investment grants payable on expenditure incurred in each year between 1966 and 1969 is shown below.

Year	Accruals of investment grants (£m)
1966	342.0
1967	455.8
1968	648.1
1969	480.0

Source: *Trade and Industry*, **10**, No. 4, Table 4, p. 176.

Figures for total payments of investment grants are given in the analysis of public expenditure in the national income accounts. Payments did not begin until 1967 although expenditure in 1966 qualified for a grant. The figures for total payments are shown below.

Payments of investment grants Year	(£m)
1967	209
1968	460
1969	600
1970	521
1971	575

Source: *National Income and Expenditure* 1972, Table 38.

An estimate of the accruals of investment grants for 1970 can now be made by subtracting the total accruals for 1966 to 1969, from the total of payments made before the end of 1971. This gives an estimate for accruals in 1970 of £439 million. This refers to grants for 1970 which were paid before the end of 1971, and some grants were paid after this date. An estimate of £25 m has been made for the grants on expenditure made in 1970 which were paid after 1971. This gives a revised estimate for accruals in 1970 of £464 million. Thus we now have estimates of both total accruals and total payments of investment grants for each year of the scheme's operation. These cover payments of grants to companies and public corporations. The income and appropriation accounts constructed above are for different samples of companies, and for each sample information is available only for payments of grants. To construct series for accruals we shall assume that the relationship between accruals and payments of grants in the aggregate holds good also for each sample of companies. This relationship will be expressed by the proportion of total payments received which accrued in each year between 1966 and 1970. The fractions of total payments accruing in each year are as follows

Year	1966	1967	1968	1969	1970
%	14.3	19.1	27.1	20.1	19.4

Although investment was higher at the end of the period than in the earlier years, a high proportion of grants accrued in 1967 and 1968 when the rates of grant were higher. This is particularly marked in the case of 1968 when some investment expenditure was brought forward in anticipation of the reduction in the rate of grant for 1969.

All that is now indeed to construct series for accruals of investment grants for each of the five samples of companies considered above, is the figure for total receipts of investment grants for each sample. The proportions of the grants accruing in each year, which are shown above, can then be applied to the total figure. In calculating the total receipts of grants two additional assumptions were made:

(1) the receipts of grants after the end of 1971 were assumed to be

		(£m)
(i)	all companies	23
(ii)	non-nationalized companies	23
(iii)	industrial and commercial companies	23
(iv)	quoted companies – manufacturing and distribution etc.	15
(v)	quoted companies – manufacturing only	12

The estimate of receipts of £23 m by the company sector is lower than the estimate of total payments after 1971, the difference being attributed to receipts by public corporations and the personal sector.

(2) The capital accounts for quoted companies show receipts of investment grants under the heading 'other receipts on capital account'. This item also includes items of funds which were previously distinguished separately, (for example, surplus on disposal of fixed assets), but before the introduction of investment grants the level of other capital receipts was small and fluctuated little. Thus we have assumed that the contribution of items other than investment grants was constant and equal to the average of its value for the three years preceding the introduction of investment grants. For manufacturing and distribution the average for 1964–66 was £46 million, and for manufacturing was £39 million.

The figures for total accruals, and total payments, of investment grants for each year between 1966 and 1971 are shown in Table B.6. Separate figures for non-nationalized companies are not given because in the period 1967–71 there was very little difference between the coverage of 'non-nationalized companies' and 'all companies'.

The advantage of using this method to calculate grant accruals, as opposed to assuming a simple lag between expenditure and grant payments of one year, can be seen by looking at the figures for quoted companies. It would appear from the table that the receipts of grants by quoted companies in 1967 exceeded the receipts of all companies. This, of course, is impossible. But the figures for quoted companies refer to receipts in company accounting years ending in the fiscal

Table B.6 Accruals and payments of investment grants (£ m).

	1966	1967	1968	1969	1970	1971
All companies						
Payments	0	201	420	564	484	540
Accruals	319	426	605	449	433	0
Industrial and commercial						
Payments	0	198	414	556	473	526
Accruals	313	418	593	440	425	0
Quoted – Manufacturing and Distribution						
Payments	0	271	246	230	261	278
Accruals	186	248	353	262	252	0
Quoted – Manufacturing only						
Payments	0	251	223	204	230	257
Accruals	168	225	319	237	228	0

Source: Own calculations
National Income and Expenditure 1972: Tables 27 and 28
Business Monitor M3, Second Issue: Tables 2 and 5
Business Monitor M3, Fourth Issue: Table 2.

year 1967/8, and so will include some payments received in the early part of 1968. The level of grants paid out at this time was high. Using the information in the Department of Trade and Industry study enables a much more accurate estimate to be made of accruals of investment grants. This is important because accruals is the relevant concept, and, as can be seen in Table B.6, there was a substantial difference in most years between accruals and payments of grants.

Depreciation and capital consumption To examine the true profitability of companies we need estimates of the value of that part of the capital stock which wears out during the relevant time period. In the national accounts this item is termed 'capital consumption', and in company accounts is called 'depreciation provisions'. It is quite distinct from the value of tax allowances which companies may claim for the decline in value of depreciating assets (see below).

Tables B.4 and B.5 contain (in row 12) the estimates for depreciation shown in the accounts of quoted companies. The utility of these figures will depend upon the purpose for which they are being used. If company behaviour is determined by companies' own estimates of depreciation, as, for example, in deciding on dividend payments, then the figures may be perfectly adequate. If, however, we are trying to measure profitability then these estimates of depreciation may be unsatisfactory.

There are several reasons for not accepting companies' own estimates of depreciation at face value. Firstly, many companies calculate depreciation on historic cost, and take no account of changes in the price of assets since the date of purchase. A survey of 300 major British companies found that 210 of these companies carried out no significant revaluation of their fixed assets other than property (Institute of Chartered Accounts (1972; Table 22)). Most companies, however, did revalue assets held in the form of property. Thus only a minority of companies allowed for inflation and calculated depreciation at replacement cost. The figures shown in company accounts are therefore likely to understate the value of true depreciation.

Secondly, since the estimates of depreciation depend on accounting conventions, changes in depreciation provisions may reflect changes in these conventions. This is particularly likely in periods, such as the present, when companies are becoming increasingly aware of the need for 'accounting for inflation'. For these reasons companies' own provisions for depreciation are not thought suitable for use in the national income accounts, and the Central Statistical Office makes estimates of depreciation at current replacement cost.

To do this it is necessary to make assumptions about the lives of fixed assets, and the pattern of depreciation over the asset life. The official method is to assume that assets are consumed in equal amounts in each year of their life – the so-called 'straight-line' method of depreciation. Whether or not this is a realistic assumption, it seems to be the practice followed by most companies in constructing their accounts. The same survey of 300 large companies found that in 1970–71 the basis adopted for depreciating most assets was:

Basis	Number of companies
Straight line	96
Reducing balance	1
Mixture	17
Not disclosed	186
	300

Source: Institute of Chartered Accountants (1972; Table 9).

The estimates of capital consumption in the national accounts are based on the perpetual inventory method of Redfern and Dean (described in Maurice (1968; p. 384)). The errors involved are large, and the estimates are at best a rough approximation. In particular, even if the assumptions of the straight-line method are correct, the figures for capital consumption are the cost of replacing existing assets with identical assets, not the cost of replacing them with an equivalent amount of new capacity. Thus the capital consumption estimates do not allow for technical progress, and so will overestimate true depreciation. The only published statistics for capital consumption of corporate assets are for the company sector as a whole, corresponding to Table B.1. These are shown in the first column of Table B.7. (Both columns in Table B.7 refer to assets in the U.K. The estimates of income from abroad included in 'other income' in the income and appropriation tables are after depreciation allowances.) The second column contains the value of depreciation allowances which com-

Table B. 7 Capital consumption and depreciation all companies (£m).

Year	Capital consumption (1)	Tax allowances (2)	Ratio of column 2 to column 1
1950	323	474	1.47
1951	360	592	1.64
1952	407	398	0.98
1953	439	407	0.93
1954	476	521	1.09
1955	534	625	1.17
1956	598	727	1.22
1957	665	838	1.26
1958	729	956	1.31
1959	762	1013	1.33
1960	812	1082	1.33
1961	878	1352	1.54
1962	938	1451	1.55
1963	989	1752	1.77
1964	1062	2040	1.92
1965	1161	2161	1.86
1966	1262	1832	1.45
1967	1315	1687	1.28
1968	1411	1828	1.30
1969	1546	2033	1.32
1970	1757	2465	1.40
1971	2002	3591	1.79

Source: 1950–60, *National Income and Expenditure 1961*: Table 61 and p. 80. 1961–71, *National Income and Expenditure 1972*: Table 57 and p. 111.

panies were allowed to offset against tax. The ratio of these tax allowances to the estimates of capital consumption is given in the third column. It shows that tax allowances for depreciation have almost always been in excess of the value of capital consumption. However, there have been pronounced fluctuations in this ratio. In the 1950s and early 1960s the ratio increased reflecting the generous initial and investment allowances, and the peak was reached in 1964 and 1965. Then investment grants replaced tax allowances and the ratio fell sharply until 1970 when allowances were again restored.

The estimates of capital consumption shown in Table B.7 may be used to derive a series for profits net of depreciation for the company sector.

Stock appreciation Stock appreciation is that part of the increase in value of stocks held by a company which arises solely from a rise in the price of the commodities which comprise the stocks. Stocks are a heterogeneous quantity. They include raw materials awaiting use in the productive process, work in progress, and finished goods awaiting delivery or sale.

The measurement and treatment of stock appreciation is a vexed question. The trading profits of a company are its receipts from sales less its operating costs. Since the materials used are usually valued at original purchase cost, and not at replacement cost, recorded profits will include a monetary capital gain (loss) in times when raw material prices are rising (falling). The income and appropriation accounts of quoted companies, therefore, show profits inclusive of stock appreciation, and no information is available for these companies on the levels of stock appreciation. There are, however, estimates of stock appreciation in the company sector as a whole published in the national accounts. The methods used to make these estimates of stock appreciation are described in *Economic Trends* August 1960, and Maurice (1968: Chapter XIII). They are based on the assumption that commercial accounting practice deems materials to be used in the order of their acquisition, the 'first in, first out', or FIFO, convention.

Table B.8 shows stock appreciation for the company sector as a whole for the period 1950–71 (no breakdown for non-nationalized or industrial and commercial companies is available, although it is not unreasonable to suppose that almost all stock appreciation arises with industrial and commercial companies).

Table B.8 Stock appreciation 1950–71 all companies (£m).

Year	Stock Appreciation	Year	Stock Appreciation
1950	440	1961	123
1951	465	1962	105
1952	– 22	1963	163
1953	– 44	1964	242
1954	53	1965	268
1955	119	1966	259
1956	131	1967	145
1957	79	1968	536
1958	– 34	1969	688
1959	93	1970	746
1960	84	1971	724

Source: 1950–60, *National Income and Expenditure 1961*: Table 63.
1961–71, *National Income and Expenditure 1972*: Table 69.

Table B.9 Sources of funds, UK industrial and commercial companies 1954–71 (£m).

Year	Ordinary share issues	Issues of debt	Bank borrowing	Retentions
1954	60	83	225	1391
1955	117	105	164	1567
1956	125	57	109	1590
1957	127	155	178	1730
1958	73	118	315	1957
1959	139	109	538	2131
1960	238	77	488	2159
1961	321	109	314	2011
1962	152	161	461	2068
1963	123	202	639	2308
1964	158	247	999	2546
1965	63	359	856	2840
1966	123	427	614	2120
1967	65	353	686	2294
1968	299	194	739	2292
1969	177	336	1000	2030
1970	39	142	1267	2354
1971	149	203	935	2936

Source: Columns 1 and 2; HMSO (1975; Table 29).
Column 3; *Financial Statistics* and Bank of England (1972)
Column 4; Undistributed profits less stock appreciation, *National Income and Expenditure*, various issues.

Sources of funds of industrial and commercial companies Chapter 5 examined the sources of funds of both quoted companies and industrial and commercial companies. The data for the former sample were presented in Chapter 5 and the data for industrial and commercial companies are shown in Table B.9. A comparison of the two samples of companies is contained in the section beginning on page 279.

A LIST OF WORKS CITED

Adelman, M.A. (1964). Evidcnce reprinted in U.S., Congress, Senate, Committee on the Judiciary, Subcommittee on Antitrust and Monopoly. *Economic Concentration.* Hearings, July and September 1964 pt. 1, Washington 1964.

Akerlof, G.A. (1970). The Market for 'Lemons': Qualitative Uncertainty and the Market Mechanisms. *Quarterly Journal of Economics*, **84**, 488–500.

Alexander, S.S. (1961). Price Movements in Speculative Markets: Trends or Random Walks, *Industrial Management Review*, **2**, 7–26.

Arrow, K.J. (1951). *Social Choice and Individual Values*, Wiley, New York.

Arrow, K.J. (1964). The Role of Securities in the Optimal Allocation of Risk-Bearing. *Review of Economic Studies*, **31**, 91–96.

Arrow, K.J. (1974). General Economic Equilibrium: Purpose, Analytic Techniques, Collective Choice. *American Economic Review*, **64**, 253–272.

Atkinson, A.B. (1971). The Distribution of Wealth and the Individual Life-Cycle. *Oxford Economic Papers*, **23**, 239–254.

Bailey, M.J. (1969). Capital Gains and Income Taxation in Harberger, A.C. and Bailey, M.J. (ed.), *The Taxation of Income from Capital*, Brookings Institution, Washington DC.

Bain, J.S. (1970). Changes in Concentration in Manufacturing Industries in the United States, 1947–66: Trends and Relationships to the Levels of 1954 Concentration. *Review of Economics and Statistics*, **LII**, 411–416.

Bain, J.S. (1972). *Essays on Price Theory and Industrial Organization*, Little, Brown & Co., Boston.

Baron, D.P. (1976). Default Risk and the Modigliani-Miller Theorem: A Synthesis. *American Economic Review*, **66**, 204–212.

Batra, R.N. (1975). A General Equilibrium Model of the Incidence of Corporation Income Tax Under Uncertainty. *Journal of Public Economics*, **4**, 343–360.

Baumol, W.J. (1959). *Business Behaviour, Value and Growth.* Harcourt, Brace & World, New York.

Benston, G.J. (1969). The Effectiveness and Effects of the SEC's Accounting Disclosure Requirements in Manne, H.G. (ed.), *Economic Policy and the Regulation of Corporate Securities*, American Enterprise Institute, Washington.

Berle, A.A. and Means, G.C. (1932). *The Modern Corporation and Private Property*, Harcourt, Brace & World, Revised Edition 1967.

Bhatia, K.B. (1970). Accrued Capital Gains, Personal Income and Saving in the United States, 1948–64, *Review of Income and Wealth*, series **16**, 363–378.

Bossons, J. (1971). An Economic Overview of the Tax Reform Legislation. *1971 Conference Report*, Canadian Tax Foundation, Ottawa.

Bossons, J. (1973). The Distribution of Assets Among Individuals of Different Age and Wealth, Appendix V in Goldsmith, R.W. (ed.), *Institutional Investors and Corporate Stock*, National Bureau of Economic Research, New York.

Brealey, R.A. (1969). *An Introduction to Risk and Return from Common Stocks*, M.I.T. Press, Cambridge, Massachusetts.

Brechling, F. (1975). *Investment and Employment Decisions*. Manchester University Press.

Brittain, J.A. (1964). The Tax Structure and Corporate Dividend Policy. *American Economic Review*, **54**, Papers and Proceedings, 272–287.

Brittain, J.A. (1966). *Corporate Dividend Policy*, Brookings Institution, Washington D.C.

Cain, T.E. (1972). *Company Law*. Stevens and Sons, London.

Chamberlin, E.H. (1933). *The Theory of Monopolistic Competition*. Harvard University Press.

Chateau, J-P. (1975). An Empirical Contribution to the Aggregation Problem: The Corporate Divident Policy Case. Paper presented at the 50th Conference of the Western Economic Association, San Diego.

Christenson, L.R., Jorgenson, D.W., and Lau, L.J. (1973). *Transcendental Logarithmic Utility Functions*. Harvard Institute for Economic Research Discussion Paper No. 285.

Cootner, P.H. (1964). *The Random Character of Stock Market Prices*, M.I.T. Press, Cambridge, Massachusetts.

Davis, E.W. and Yeomans, K.A. (1974). *Company Finance and the Capital Market*. University of Cambridge Department of Applied Economics Occasional Paper 39.

Debreu, G. (1959). *Theory of Value*, Wiley, New York.

Denny, M. (1974). The Relationship between Functional Forms for the Production System. *Canadian Journal of Economics*, **VII**, 21–31.

Diamond, P.A. (1967). The Role of a Stock Market in a General Equilibrium Model with Technological Uncertainty. *American Economic Review*, **57**, 759–776.

Diamond, P.A. (1970). Incidence of an Interest Income Tax. *Journal of Economic Theory*, **2**, 211–224.

Diamond, P.A. (1975). Inflation and the Comprehensive Tax Base. *Journal of Public Economics*, **4**, 227–244.

Diewert, W.E. (1971). An Application of the Shephard Duality Theorem: a Generalised Leontief Production Function. *Journal of Political Economy*, **79**, 481–507.

Diewert, W.E. (1974). Applications of Duality Theory, in Intriligator, M.D., and Kendrick, D.A. (eds.), *Frontiers of Quantitative Economics*, North-Holland, Amsterdam.

Dobrovolsky, S.P. (1951). *Corporate Income Retention 1915–43*, National Bureau of Economic Research, New York.

Drèze, J. (1974). Investment under Private Ownership: Optimality, Equilibrium and Stability, in Drèze, J. (ed.) *Allocation under Uncertainty: Equilibrium and Optimality*, Macmillan, London.

EEC (1975). Proposal for a Council Directive Concerning the Harmonization of Systems of Company Taxation and of Withholding Taxes on Dividends. *Bulletin of the Commission of the European Communities*, Supplement 10/75, Brussels.

Eis, C. (1969). The 1919–30 Merger Movement in American Industry. *Journal of Law and Economics*, **12**, 267–96.

Ekern, S. (1973). *On the Theory of the Firm in Incomplete Markets*, Ph.D. dissertation, Stanford University.

Ekern, S. and Wilson, R. (1974). On the Theory of the Firm in an Economy with Incomplete Markets. *Bell Journal of Economics and Management Science*, **5**, 171–180.

Elton, E.J. and Gruber, M.J. (1970). Marginal Stockholder Tax Rates and the Clientele Effect. *Review of Economics and Statistics*, **LII**, 68–74.

Fama, E.F. (1970). Efficient Capital Markets: A Review of Theory and Empirical Work. *Journal of Finance*, **25**, 383–417.

Fama, E.F. and Babiak, H. (1968). Dividend Policy: An Empirical Analysis. *Journal of the American Statistical Association*, **63**, 1132–1161.

Fama, E.F. and Blume, M.E. (1966). Filter Rules and Stock Market Trading. *Journal of Business, Security Prices: A Supplement*, **39**, 226–241.

Fama, E. and Miller, M. (1972). *The Theory of Finance*, Holt, Rinehart and Winston, New York.

Fane, G. (1975). The Determination of Quarterly Dividend Payments in the United Kingdom, in Renton, G.A. (ed.), *Modelling the Economy*, Heinemann, London.

Feldstein, M.S. (1970). Corporate Taxation and Dividend Behaviour. *Review of Economic Studies*, **37**, 57–72.

Feldstein, M.S. (1973). *Incidence of a Capital Income Tax in a Growing Economy with Variable Savings Rates*. Harvard Discussion Paper 300, mimeo.

Feldstein, M.S. (1974). *Personal Taxation and Portfolio Composition:*

An Econometric Analysis. Harvard Institute of Economic Research Discussion Paper 349.

Feldstein, M.S. and M. Rothschild (1974). Towards an Economic Theory of Replacement Investment. *Econometrica*, **42**, 393–423.

Fisher, G.R. (1970). Quarterly Dividend Behaviour, in Hilton, K. and Heathfield, D.F. (eds.), *The Econometric Study of the United Kingdom*, Macmillan, London.

Fisher, M.R. (1957). L'Epargne et les Profits des Enterprises dans l'Hypothèse du 'Revenu Permanent'. *Economie Applique*, **X**, No. 4, 539–562.

Flemming, J.S. (1976). A Reappraisal of the Corporation Income Tax. *Journal of Public Economics*, **6**, 163–169.

Florence, P. Sargant (1961). *Ownership, Control and Success of Large Companies*, Sweet and Maxwell, London.

Galbraith, J.K. (1973). Power and the Useful Economist. *American Economic Review*, **63**, 1–11.

Goldsmith, R.W. (ed.) (1973). *Institutional Investors and Corporate Stock* National Bureau of Economic Research, New York.

Gower, L.C.B. (1957). *The Principles of Modern Company Law*, 2nd Edition, Stevens & Sons Ltd., London.

Grandmont, J-M. (1974). On the Short-Run Equilibrium in a Monetary Economy. Chapter 12 of Drèze, J.H. (ed.), *Allocation Under Uncertainty: Equilibrium and Optimality*, Macmillan, London.

Grunfeld, Y. and Griliches, Z. (1960). Is Aggregation Necessarily Bad?. *Review of Economics and Statistics*, **42**, 1–13.

Hadden, T. (1972). *Company Law and Capitalism*, Weidenfeld and Nicolson, London.

Hagen, K.P. (1976). Default Risk, Homemade Leverage, and the Modigliani-Miller Theorem. *American Economic Review*, **66**, 199–203.

Hahn, F.H. (1973). *On the Notion of Equilibrium in Economics*. Inaugural lecture, Cambridge University Press.

Hammond, P.J. (1976). Changing Tastes and Coherent Dynamic Choice. *Review of Economic Studies*, **XLIII**, 159–173.

Hannah, L. (1976a). *The Rise of the Corporate Economy*, Methuen, London.

Hannah, L. (1976b). Business Development and Economic Structure in Britain since 1880, in Hannah, L. (ed.), *Management Strategy and Business Development*, Macmillan, London.

Hannah, L. and Kay, J.A. (1977). *Concentration in Modern Industry: Theory, Measurement and the UK Experience*, Macmillan, London.

Harberger, A.C. (1974). *Taxation and Welfare*, Little, Brown, and Co., Boston.

Hart, O.D. (1976). *Take-Over Bids and Stock Market Equilibrium*, mimeo., Churchill College, Cambridge.

Helliwell, J.F., (1976). Aggregate Investment Equations: A Survey of

Issues, in Helliwell, J.F. (ed.), *Aggregate Investment*, Penguin, London.

Hendry, D.F. and Trivedi, P.K. (1972). Maximum Likelihood Estimation of Difference Equations with Moving Average Errors: A Simulation Study. *Review of Economic Studies*, **39**, 117–145.

Hirshleifer, J. (1966). Investment Decisions under Uncertainty: Applications of the State-Preference Approach. *Quarterly Journal of Economics*, **80**, 237–77.

H.M.S.O. (1975). Royal Commission on the Distribution of Income and Wealth, Report No. 2, *Income from Companies and its Distribution*, Cmnd. 6172.

Hughes, A. (1976). Company Concentration, Size of Plant, and Merger Activity in the Manufacturing Industries of the United Kingdom and West Germany, 1954–72, in Panić, M. (ed.), *Studies in the Industrial Structure of West Germany and the United Kingdom 1954–72*, National Economic Development office, London.

Institute of Chartered Accountants (1972). *Survey of Published Accounts 1970–71*, General Educational Trust of the Institute of Chartered Accountants, London.

Kaldor, N. (1971). The Economic Effects of Alternative Systems of Corporation Tax, Appendix 15 of the *Report of the Select Committee on Corporation Tax*, House of Commons Paper 622, HMSO.

Keynes, J.M. (1933). *Essays in Biography*, Royal Economic Society Edition, *The Collected Writings of John Maynard Keynes:* **X**, 1972, Macmillan, London.

Keynes, J.M. (1936). *The General Theory of Employment Interest and Money*, Macmillan, London.

King, M.A. (1971). Corporate Taxation and Dividend Behaviour – A Comment. *Review of Economic Studies*, **38**, 377–80.

King, M.A. (1972). Taxation and Investment Incentives in a Vintage Investment Model. *Journal of Public Economics*, **1**, 121–147.

King, M.A. (1974). Taxation and the Cost of Capital. *Review of Economic Studies*, **41**, 21–35.

King, M.A. (1975a). The UK Profits Crisis: Myth or Reality?. *Economic Journal*, **85**, 33–54.

King, M.A. (1975b). *Equilibrium Concepts in Stock Market Economies.* Paper presented to the Third World Congress of the Econometric Society, Toronto.

King, M.A. (1975c). Taxation, Corporate Financial Policy, and the Cost of Capital – A Comment. *Journal of Public Economics*, **4**, 271–279.

Lampman, R. (1959). Changes in the Share of Wealth Held by Top Wealth-Holders 1922–56. *Review of Economics and Statistics*, **41**, 379–392.

Larner, R.J. (1966). Ownership and Control in the 200 Largest Nonfinancial Corporations, 1929 and 1963. *American Economic Review*, **56**, 777–787.

Lau, L.J. and Mitchell, B.M. (1970). *A Linear Logarithmic Expenditure*

System: An Application to US Data. Paper presented to the Second World Congress of the Econometric Society at Cambridge.

Leland, H. (1972). Theory of the Firm Facing Random Demand. *American Economic Review*, **62**, 278–291.

Leland, H. (1974). Production Theory and the Stock Market. *Bell Journal of Economics and Management Science*, **5**, 3–15.

Linter, J. (1953). The Determinants of Corporate Savings, in Heller, W.W. (ed.), *Savings in the Modern Economy*, University of Minnesota Press, Minneapolis.

Linter, J. (1956). Distribution of Incomes of Corporations Among Dividends, Retained Earnings, and Taxes. *American Economic Review*, **46**, Papers and Proceedings, 97–113.

Lintner, J. (1959). The Financing of Corporations, in Mason, E.S. (ed.), *The Corporation in Modern Society*, Harvard University Press.

Lorie, J.H. and Hamilton, M.T. (1973). *The Stock Market, Theories and Evidence*, Richard D. Irwin, Illinois.

Lorie, J.H. and Niederhoffer, V. (1968). Predictive and Statistical Properties of Insider Trading. *Journal of Law and Economics*, **11**, 35–53.

Lund, P.J. (1976). The Econometric Assessment of the Impact of Investment Incentives, in Whiting, A. (ed.), *The Economics of Industrial Subsidies*, HMSO, London.

Lydall, H.F. and Tipping, D.G. (1961). The Distribution of Personal Wealth in Britain. *Bulletin of the Oxford Institute of Economics and Statistics*, **23**.

Malinvaud, E. (1972a). *Lectures on Microeconomic Theory*, North-Holland, Amsterdam.

Malinvaud, E. (1972b). The Allocation of Individual Risks in Large Markets. *Journal of Economic Theory*, **4**, 312–328.

Marris, R. (1964). *The Economic Theory of 'Managerial' Capitalism*. Macmillan, London.

Marshall, A. (1890). *Principles of Economics*, Macmillan, London (8th Edition, 1949).

Matthews, R.C.O., and King, M.A. (1977). The British Economy: Problems and Policies in the late 1970's. *Midland Bank Review*, February.

Maurice, R. (ed.) (1968). *National Accounts Statistics: Sources and Methods*, HMSO, London.

Meeks, G. and Whittington, G. (1976). *The Financing of Quoted Companies in the United Kingdom*. Royal Commission on the Distribution of Income and Wealth, Background Paper No. 1, HMSO, London.

Melliss, C.L. and Richardson, P.W. (1976). Value of Investment Incentives for Manufacturing Industry 1946 to 1974, in Whiting, A. (ed.), *The Economics of Industrial Subsidies*, HMSO, London.

Milne, F. (1975). Choice Over Asset Economies: Default Risk and Corporate Leverage. *Journal of Financial Economics*, **2**, 165–186.

Modigliani, F. (1949). Fluctuations in the Savings Income Ratio: A problem

in Economic Forecasting. *Studies of Income and Wealth*, Part V, Vol. II, National Bureau of Economic and Social Research, New York.
Modigliani, F. and Miller, M.H. (1958). The Cost of Capital, Corporation Finance, and the Theory of Investment. *American Economic Review*, **48**, 261–297.
Moyle, J. (1971). *The Pattern of Ordinary Share Ownership 1957–1970.* University of Cambridge Department of Applied Economics Occasional Paper 31.
Nader, R. (ed.) (1973). *The Consumer and Corporate Accountability*, Harcourt Brace Jovanovich, New York.
Nelson, R.L. (1968). Mergers, *International Encyclopedia of the Social Sciences*, Crowell Collier and Macmillan.
Nickell, S.J. (1977). *The Investment Decision of Firms*, James Nisbet and Co.
Niederhoffer, V. and Osborne, M.F.M. (1966). Market Making and Reversal on the Stock Exchange. *Journal of the American Statistical Association*, **61**, 897–916.
NIESR (1956). *Company Income and Finance 1949–53*, National Institute of Economic and Social Research, London.
Nordhaus, W.D. (1972). Recent Developments in Price Dynamics, in Eckstein, O. (ed.), *The Econometrics of Price Determination*, Federal Reserve System, Washington, D.C.
OECD (1972). *Expenditure Trends in OECD Countries 1960–80*. Paris.
OECD (1976). *Revenue Statistics of OECD Member Countries 1965–74.* Paris.
Orhnial, A.J.H. and Foldes, L.P. (1975). Estimates of Marginal Tax Rates for Dividends and Bond Interest in the United Kingdom, 1919–70. *Economica*, **42**, 79–91.
Prais, S.J. (1976). *The Evolution of Giant Firms in Britain: A Study of the Growth of Concentration in Manufacturing Industry in Britain 1909–70*, Cambridge University Press.
Radice, H.K. (1971). Control Type, Profitability and Growth in Large Firms: An Empirical Study. *Economic Journal*, **81**, 547–562.
Radner, R. (1972). Existence of Equilibrium of Plans, Prices, and Price Expectations in a Sequence of Markets. *Econometrica*, **40**, 289–303.
Robichek, A.A. and S.C. Myers (1966). Problems in the Theory of Optimal Capital Structure. *Journal of Financial and Quantitative Analysis*, **1**, 1–35.
Robinson, J. (1933). *The Economics of Imperfect Competition*, Macmillan, London.
Sandmo, A. (1971). On the Theory of the Competitive Firm under Price Uncertainty. *American Economic Review*, **61**, 65–73.
Samuelson, P.A. (1964). Tax Deductibility of Economic Depreciation to Insure Invariant Valuations. *Journal of Political Economy*, **72**, 604–606.
Singh, A. (1971). *Take-overs: Their Relevance to the Stock Market and the Theory of the Firm*, Cambridge University Press.

Smith, A. (1776). *An Inquiry into the Nature and Causes of the Wealth of Nations*, 1904 edition, Cannan, E. (ed.), 2 Vols, Methuen, London.

Smith, J.D. and Franklin, S.D. (1974). The Concentration of Personal Wealth 1922–69. *American Economic Review*, **64**, Papers and Proceedings, 162–167.

Smith, K.R. (1969). The Effect of Uncertainty on Monopoly Price, Capital Stock, and Utilization of Capital. *Journal of Economic Theory*, **1**, 48–59.

Smith, V.L. (1970). Corporate Financial Theory Under Uncertainty. *Quarterly Journal of Economics*, **LXXXIV**, 451–471.

Smith, V.L. (1972). Default Risk, Scale, and the Home-Made Leverage Theorem. *American Economic Review*, **62**, 66–76.

Solow, R.M. (1971). Some Implications of Alternative Criteria for the Firm, in Marris, R. and Wood, A. (eds.), *The Corporate Economy*, Macmillan, London.

Stiglitz, J.E. (1969). A Re-examination of the Modigliani–Miller Theorem. *American Economic Review*, **LIX**, 784–793.

Stiglitz, J.E. (1972). Some Aspects of the Pure Theory of Corporate Finance: Bankruptcies and Take-Overs. *Bell Journal of Economics and Management Science*, **3**, 458–82.

Stiglitz, J.E. (1974). On the Irrelevance of Corporate Financial Policy. *American Economic Review*, **64**, 851–866.

Stiglitz, J.E. (1976). The Corporation Tax. *Journal of Public Economics*, **5**, 303–311.

Stone, R., Revell, J., and Moyle, J. (1966). *A Programme For Growth 7: The Owners of Quoted Ordinary Shares; A Survey for 1963*, Chapman and Hall, London.

Strotz, R.H. (1956). Myopia and Inconsistency in Dynamic Utility Maximisation. *Review of Economic Studies*, **23**, 165–80.

Sumner, M.T. (1975). Neutrality of Corporate Taxation, or On Not Accounting for Inflation. *Manchester School*, **43**, 353–361.

Tawney, R.H. (1926). *Religion and the Rise of Capitalism*, John Murray, London.

Tawney, R.H., and Power, E. (1924). *Tudor Economic Documents*, 3 vols., Longmans, London.

Tinbergen, J. (1939). *Statistical Testing of Business Cycle Theories*, Vol. 2, League of Nations.

Thorp, W.L. (1931). The Persistence of the Merger Movement. *American Economic Review*, **21**, Papers and Proceedings, 77–89.

Vernon, R.A., Middleton, M., and Harper, D.G. (1973). *Who Owns the Blue Chips?—A Study of Shareholding in a Leading Company*, Gower Press, London.

Whittington, G. (1972). Changes in the Top 100 Quoted Manufacturing Companies in the United Kingdom 1948–68. *Journal of Industrial Economics*, **XXI**, 17–34.

Williamson, O.E. (1964). *The Economics of Discretionary Behaviour: Managerial Objectives in a Theory of the Firm*, Englewood Cliffs, New Jersey.

Worswick, G.D.N. and Tipping, D.G. (1964). *Profits in the British Economy, 1909–1938*, Blackwells, 1964; Kelley, 1967. Oxford University, Institute of Economics and Statistics, Monograph 8.

Yarrow, G.K. (1974). *Shareholding Concentration and Company Performance in the UK*. Paper presented to the European Meeting of the Econometric Society, Grenoble, mimeo.

Zabel, E. (1967). A Dynamic Model of the Competitive Firm. *International Economic Review*, **8**, 194–208.

INDEX

AUTHORS

SUBJECTS